Praise for

How to Read Literature

by Thomas C. Foster

"I know of no other book that so vividly conveys what it's like to study with a great literature professor. In a work that is both down-to-earth and rich in insight, Thomas Foster goes far toward breaking down the wall that has long divided the academic and the common reader."   —James Shapiro, author of
A Year in the Life of William Shakespeare

"By bringing his eminent scholarship to bear in doses measured for the common reader or occasional student, Professor Foster has done us all a generous turn. The trained eye, the tuned ear, the intellect possessed of simple ciphers bring the literary arts alive. For those who've ever wondered what Dr. Williams saw in a 'red wheel barrow glazed with rain water'—here is an essential text."
—Thomas Lynch, author of *The Undertaking*

"A smart, accessible, and thoroughly satisfying examination of what it means to *read* a work of literature. Guess what? It isn't all that hard when you have a knowledgeable guide to show you the way. Dante had his Virgil; for everyone else, there is Thomas Foster."
—Nicholas A. Basbanes, author of *Patience & Fortitude*

"Tom Foster's casual, unpretentious, yet brilliant *How to Read Literature Like a Professor* is a painless introduction to crucial—and sophisticated—skills of reading. What a knowledge of modern literature! What good stories!"   —Linda Wagner-Martin,
author of *Sylvia Plath: A Biography*

About the Author

THOMAS C. FOSTER is a professor of English at the University of Michigan-Flint, where he teaches classic and contemporary fiction, drama, and poetry, as well as creative writing and composition. He is the author of the *New York Times* bestselling *How to Read Literature Like a Professor*, *How to Read Novels Like a Professor*, and several books on twentieth-century British and Irish fiction and poetry. He lives in East Lansing, Michigan.

TWENTY-FIVE
BOOKS THAT
SHAPED AMERICA

ALSO BY THOMAS C. FOSTER

How to Read Novels Like a Professor
How to Read Literature Like a Professor

TWENTY-FIVE BOOKS THAT SHAPED AMERICA

HOW WHITE WHALES, GREEN LIGHTS,
AND RESTLESS SPIRITS
FORGED OUR NATIONAL IDENTITY

Thomas C. Foster

HARPER

NEW YORK • LONDON • TORONTO • SYDNEY

HARPER

TWENTY-FIVE BOOKS THAT SHAPED AMERICA. Copyright © 2011
by Thomas C. Foster. All rights reserved. Printed in the United States of
America. No part of this book may be used or reproduced in any manner
whatsoever without written permission except in the case of brief quota-
tions embodied in critical articles and reviews. For information address
HarperCollins Publishers, 10 East 53rd Street, New York, NY 10022.

HarperCollins books may be purchased for educational, business, or sales
promotional use. For information please write: Special Markets Department, HarperCollins Publishers, 10 East 53rd Street, New York, NY
10022.

FIRST EDITION

Designed by Justin Dodd

Library of Congress Cataloging-in-Publication Data is available upon
request.

ISBN 978-0-06-183440-0

11 12 13 14 15   OV/RRD   10 9 8 7 6 5 4 3 2 1

For Brenda,
with love and gratitude

ACKNOWLEDGMENTS

It is self-evident that books do not write themselves, perhaps less so that authors do not write them alone. A book is the end point of the efforts of a great many people, only one of whom typically gets a name on the title page. I have been blessed to study under and work with some great Americanists. I had the very good fortune to learn from outstanding scholars and teachers: Professors James M. Cox and A. G. Medlicott (on loan from the University of Connecticut) at Dartmouth College and Linda W. Wagner-Martin, Victor Howard, and R. K. Meiners at Michigan State University. My colleagues at the University of Michigan–Flint have been invaluable. For years Professor Fredric Svoboda and I have solved the world's problems and discussed every conceivable topic on American modernism during our commutes up and down the interstate. Professor Alicia Kent has been ever so helpful on matters of multicultural literature. And since I rarely leave the friendly confines of the twentieth century, this book could not have happened without the insights and wisdom of Professor Jan Furman, a specialist in earlier periods of American writing who doubles as one of the world's best critics on Toni Morrison. When I grow up, I hope to write one book almost as good as hers.

I also have benefitted from the wisdom of students, who push me to greater clarity and offer wonderful observations of their own. Both my university classes and the many students I have met in high schools have been extremely helpful. More than one chapter of this book has been shaped, and even determined, by interactions with very bright seventeen- and eighteen-year-olds. Anyone who thinks kids don't read anymore should meet the students I have.

As ever, this book could not have happened without the publishing team at HarperCollins, including Rakesh Satyal, Cal Morgan, and Diane Burrowes, who were instrumental in shaping the project. I am especially grateful to my editor, Michael Signorelli, for all his guidance and friendship. Editors do so much more than edit. And to my agent, Faith Hamlin, and her associate, Courtney Miller-Callahan, profound thanks for doing their best to keep me on the straight and narrow. Sometimes, they even succeed. Finally, words cannot express my debt to my wife, Brenda, who puts up with my many moods, listens to my whining when I'm stuck, and keeps my writing mess from taking over the universe.

CONTENTS

IN THE FOUR CORNERS

Okay, here's what was actually written: "In the four corners of the globe, who reads an American book?" The question came in an essay in the *Edinburgh Review* in 1820 from the writer and clergyman Sydney Smith. There's more, of course, in the same vein, "or goes to an American play? or sees an American picture or statue?" But our concern here is books, so we'll pull the focus tight.

Talk about sore losers! How snotty. How British. Clearly Sydney Smith was deeply stung by a couple of ringing losses to the former colonists, one in the American Revolution and the other in the War of 1812. He probably would have smarted still more had he lived to hear Jimmy Driftwood's paean to Andrew Jackson, "The Battle of New Orleans." Still, he was sufficiently annoyed to take refuge in literature, where the upstarts across the pond were in fact only beginning to write books. Virtually everything we think of as American literature still lay in the future. There was a smattering of poems and narratives, mostly personal or historical, dating back to the earliest years of colonization, but little to compare to William Wordsworth or Thomas Gray or Samuel Coleridge in verse or to Henry Fielding or Laurence Sterne in fiction.

Smith's larger point was that America had, in the thirty or so years of independence, added nothing to the sum of human understanding or, more particularly, English culture. To a great extent, he was right. He was certainly right that no civilized country was built on a system where "every sixth man is a slave," but that's an argument for a bit later. And he was substantially correct that very little was being produced in the way of arts and culture, although perhaps mistaken in suggesting that such a shortcoming meant we had squandered all the advantages we had been given by being subjects, "and by no means the most valued subjects" of His Majesty, King George. His point obtains: by 1820, books, plays, and paintings, to say nothing of musical compositions, scientific discoveries, and works of moral philosophy, were not exactly thick on Yankee ground. To which, one must counter with a mature and reasoned response.

So what?

Hey, we had more pressing issues to attend to, such as not starving to death, clearing forests, subduing natives, carving a republic out of bits of contemporary philosophy and very mixed feelings about human nature, building cities and villages out of thin air, embracing the concept of liberty while enslaving fellow humans.

Not all pressing issues, clearly, are created equal.

Creating literature is a leisure activity, rarely undertaken by those for whom food and shelter are at issue. What Americans lacked in the period 1783–1819 in leisure, however, they made up for in energy, enthusiasm, rudimentary learning, and vivid experience. How many miles of road, for instance, was England required to build during those decades? What the snobbish Smith couldn't know was that this populace he denigrated was on the verge of cutting loose.

Besides, what he probably couldn't recognize, despite his training in moral philosophy and theology, was that America had already contributed the two most important documents of political philosophy in the history of the world. All of the writers and thinkers Smith adduces in support of his claim of America's insufficiency, combined, changed the world less than the Declaration of Independence and the Constitution. We have sometimes had trouble living up to our two holy documents, and heaven knows, it's still a struggle. But they're ours, and they're amazing in their influence and reach. Much of the rest of the world has looked to them for guidance in seeking liberty, in establishing new governments, in hoping for a better day.

A people who can produce them in their first fifteen years of existence is one to reckon with.

We'll not, however, dwell on the literary or cultural achievement of the Declaration and Constitution. Rather, we'll look at books, mostly from later, that helped shape the process they set in motion. Shaped the nation, you might say. I'm one who believes every piece of writing changes something, shapes someone or something beyond itself. Occasionally, that change isn't positive; there are plenty of scurrilous, vicious, bigoted books and pamphlets, poems and essays, plays and articles in every culture. Most will, like water, seek their own level. I'm much more interested in those that leave a positive trace. You can call it a "Great Books" list if you like, but they may not all be all that great. Some of the artistically finest may not make the cut, having shaped the republic, or the discussion about the republic, somewhat less than some lesser works.

From the beginning of the nation, indeed, even before it, America has been shaped by writing. From Thomas Harriot's *Brief and True Account of the New Found Land of Virginia* in 1588 and William Bradford's history *Of Plymouth Colony* in 1647, authors have been directing our thoughts about America before any such place even existed. What, then, can we say about those seminal texts of the American Experience. What would a list of those books look like? How could we even compile such a creature?

A list of three hundred books that changed America is easy to compile; one of twenty-five, nearly impossible. The difficulty lies in selection: What criteria does one apply? How is change measured? How significant must the shaping be? If we allow that every book changes something or someone—and it might be a stretch in some instances—then we're confronted with a continuum of impact. That scarcely helps, since there are no standards of measurement to be applied (change must be *this* tall to be recognized). What I settled on is the idea of change as something that helps develop the national character, that defines but also in some way directs *who* and, possibly more importantly, *what* we are. There are as many ways to construe significance as there are persons judging it. Or more—I have changed my mind numerous times on this subject. For now, though, I want to focus attention on the national story.

Which is to say, the myth of America.

Oh, calm down. By "myth" we do not mean something patently untrue, although parts of it may be. Rather, what is meant here is the body of story that has been constructed over the course of the last two and a half centuries. I have elsewhere defined myth as a body of story that matters; this one matters to the national psyche. What's in that body of story? Not much. Just everything we think about ourselves, our history, our capabilities, our values, our interests, our most basic principles.

How about an example? I'll give you two.

What the Reverend Mr. Smith could not foresee—okay, there were mountains he couldn't foresee, but that's beside the point—was that those yokels he belittled were about to get busy. And what they would write about was themselves. Almost everyone knows, or thinks they know, a cute little story about a henpecked husband named Rip Van Winkle. To get away from his shrewish wife, he takes to the woods with his dog and his squirrel rifle for a bit of sport. There, he runs into some strange characters who look like early Dutch explorers in archaic dress even for Rip's day. Some games and a wee bit of drinking take place, and under the influence, our hero takes a little lie-down. When he awakes, twenty years have passed, his gun has rotted and rusted apart, his dog is gone, and he has a beard grown into next week. Things aren't all bad, though. Despite things in town being strange and slightly suspicious, he's a free man: Dame Van Winkle has popped a vessel and died during his absence. That's the part everyone remembers.

Here's the part they mostly don't. During that interval, things have changed. There's been a revolution, *the* Revolution. The portrait at the inn of George III has been repainted (the accoutrements altered, the face itself untouched) to become George Washington. The flagpole has become a liberty pole, complete with Phrygian cap atop it. Things are a little more disheveled and seedy, but the people are freer to express themselves, more disputatious, more open. Rather than looking far away to solve their problems, they take them in hand, electing their own leaders based on merit, not class. Things are different and not all better, but on the whole, people are happier, more driven to succeed, more character- istically American. The story of Rip Van Winkle was written in 1819, while its author, Washington Irving, was living in *England*. Go figure.

So, class, what do you think that story is about?

For the other example, you should see the whole thing:

THE VILLAGE BLACKSMITH
Under a spreading chestnut-tree
The village smithy stands;

The smith, a mighty man is he,
With large and sinewy hands;
And the muscles of his brawny arms
Are strong as iron bands.

His hair is crisp, and black, and long,
His face is like the tan;
His brow is wet with honest sweat,
He earns whate'er he can,
And looks the whole world in the face,
For he owes not any man.

Week in, week out, from morn till night,
You can hear his bellows blow;
You can hear him swing his heavy sledge,
With measured beat and slow,
Like a sexton ringing the village bell,
When the evening sun is low.

And children coming home from school
Look in at the open door;
They love to see the flaming forge,
And hear the bellows roar,
And catch the burning sparks that fly
Like chaff from a threshing-floor.

He goes on Sunday to the church,
And sits among his boys;
He hears the parson pray and preach,
He hears his daughter's voice,

Singing in the village choir,
And it makes his heart rejoice.

It sounds to him like her mother's voice,
Singing in Paradise!
He needs must think of her once more,
How in the grave she lies;
And with his hard, rough hand he wipes
A tear out of his eyes.

Toiling,– rejoicing,– sorrowing,
Onward through life he goes;
Each morning sees some task begin,
Each evening sees it close;
Something attempted, something done,
Has earned a night's repose.

Thanks, thanks to thee, my worthy friend,
For the lesson thou hast taught!
Thus at the flaming forge of life
Our fortunes must be wrought;
Thus on its sounding anvil shaped
Each burning deed and thought.

I have a soft spot for this poem, which is the first and almost only I was ever required to memorize in school. It's by Henry Wadsworth Longfellow, our first great poet, the man who gave us "Paul Revere's Ride" and *The Song of Hiawatha* and a whole body of work that we think of, properly, as national treasures. It was written a bit later than "Rip," in 1841. His blacksmith is an idealized figure, with arms like "iron bands." He is strength and power personified, with his long black hair, his sinewy hands, his tanned face, his mighty hammer blows. He's also a man completely integrated into the life of his community, right down to the daughter singing in the choir. My favorite part, however, is the autonomy of the smith. Everything he earns is due to his own efforts, so he "looks the whole world in the face, / For he owes not any man." This is the most perfect expression of the American hope that has ever been written. Beholden to no one but oneself, the individual succeeds or fails on his own merits. No lord of the manor to answer to, no king with absolute power, each man his own king. But it takes effort and hard labor, as he tells us in the closing stanza, where the smithy becomes representative of our collective experience. We hammer out "each burning deed and thought" at the "flaming forge of life," which is where "our fortunes must be wrought." It's your life, Bub, so make something of it. Okay, Longfellow didn't use "Bub," but the message is clear enough. Destiny is in front of you. Grab it. Work for it. Forge it for yourself.

Do you suppose Sydney Smith could see all this coming?

To select, from among the thousands of writers and the tens of thousands of books a group of twenty-five is obviously insane. What follows is nobody's list but my own. It falls to a compiler of such a group to articulate a rationale and probably an apology. I'll start with the apology, or at least an excuse. One thing I have resisted from the outset is any attempt to make the list definitive. Wallace Stevens has a poem, not widely known, called "The Man on the Dump," which asks the question, "Where was it we first heard of the truth?" and responds with the answer, "The the." Besides being hard to say, that reply says something very profound, considering that it contains no words of substance. The difference between "truth," which is a condition, and "the truth," which is an absolute, is the presence of the definite article. From the first, I have worked against the notion of a definite article in my title or in my process. These are not *the* twenty-five books that shaped America, as if they and only they could do the job. Rather, they are simply twenty-five books, out of the multitude that also performed that task, that shaped America. They are illustrative, not definitive.

They also happen to be very, very good books, but not inevitably the best. It may well be that your candidate for the greatest American book is absent. It may even be that mine is. Or even by a given author. I have mostly picked the best books by the writers represented here, but not in all cases. Why? The book I chose offers something that the "greater" book does not.

Back to that rationale. It has several steps to it. For one thing, I elected to focus on works of imaginative literature. That means no self-help, no histories, no memoirs or kiss-and-tells or autobiographies, with two exceptions. Even there, the two I chose have, if not exactly a fictive quality about them, a good deal of imaginative purpose and invention. We do not read Franklin's *Autobiography* for its unswerving commitment to the truth, although it contains plenty of truth. Another principle of selection was that I avoided "message" books; that is, those whose overt purpose was to effect social change. There is no doubt that *Uncle Tom's Cabin* had a profound effect on American attitudes toward slavery, or that Upton Sinclair's *The Jungle* drew important attention to the handling of food in this country. Rather, I have been concerned with a different sort of shaping—that business of myth. And the myth of America is an ongoing conversation where every book brings some addition, some refutation, some contribution to the dialogue. For me, and I hope for you, too, the nature of that dialogue is a source of continuing fascination. Writer A exerts a strong influence on Writer B, who is nevertheless her own strong force and whose work changes what we think about Writer A—and what we think about ourselves. The books

I included in this study all make what seem to me important contributions to that story-in-progress that has been going on from the first writings on this new land and will continue as long as we do.

What are the criteria for a book's eligibility? First, it needs to have been written during the time of our existence, so the Bible and the works of Shakespeare are out. It needs to be a secular, not sacred book. Some arguments are not worth having, some value judgments not worth offering. The author needs to be an American or an extended visitor to these shores, the book's subject in some way about us. No Tolkien, therefore; no Orwell, and no Solzhenitsyn who, although resident here for a number of years, never really turned his authorial eye on the United States. For that, we should probably be thankful. The book in question can be fiction or nonfiction, prose or poetry. I'm excluding plays as something not *read* in the first instance. A book has impact by being read. And it has to be something we can care deeply about. I believe the works represented here all have that in common.

Not every excellent book is here, but the books here are excellent. I regret that I only had time and energy for twenty-five. Forty or two hundred would have been about right. Books got left out for all sorts of reasons and sometimes for no reason in particular. My only justification is that the books included are all there for a reason, chiefly that they refused to be left behind.

Perhaps the final irony in all this hubbub that Sydney Smith began lies in the venue in which he published his remarks. He had cofounded the *Edinburgh Review* some years earlier and had hung around town long enough to edit its first number before taking a church assignment elsewhere. He continued to contribute essays and reviews for many years, including this piece excoriating a former colonial subject in a journal published in Scotland, whose own rebellions against the crown had failed but whose inhabitants chafed against London's benevolent protection as those ungrateful Americans once had. Scotland has spent much of the same time period since Smith engaged in a similar literary project: what does it mean to be Scottish, to write for Scotland, to shape the idea of Scotland in writing?

For that's what we're talking about here: the idea of America. It's an idea that just might catch on. So who, in the four corners of the earth, reads an American book? *Tout le monde,* as our French friends would say. All the world. But most importantly, we do. Americans. We're the most important who, in answer to the good reverend. Our literature travels well and widely. Mark Twain behind the old Iron Curtain. Robert Frost in the British Isles. Hemingway and Steinbeck pretty much everywhere. It also continues to talk to us at home. It has something to offer the world, even more to offer its primary audience. Let's see what that is.

ONE

MAYBE JUST A LITTLE MADE-UP
The Autobiography of Benjamin Franklin

A Field Guide to the American Character (from the inside):

- We Americans are an earnest bunch. Forthright. Honest. Fair. Decent. Truthful. Above all, truthful. Gary Cooper could be our national bird.

- We Americans are a duplicitous lot. Sneaky. Low-down. Willing to say anything. Completely untrustworthy. Untruthful, especially in writing. We should take the presidents off our money and replace them with Truman Capote.

Both statements are true. Except maybe for the bird thing.

What we know for sure is that we can't trust one another when it comes to nonfiction in general, autobiographies and memoirs in particular. Periodically we get reminders of this. Someone's Pulitzer Prize–winning series of newspaper articles is revealed as a fraud, the homeless child living on his own or the eighty-seven-year-old granny cooking meth a total fabrication. Or Clifford Irving comes along with a bogus autobiography of Howard Hughes. Or James Frey sets the gold standard with his "memoir" of addiction, *A Million Little Pieces*, whose chief crime was fooling Oprah Winfrey into believing it. Or Forrest Carter's *The Education of Little Tree*, ostensibly a Native American first-person tale, is actually written by Asa Carter, a former Klansman and thoroughgoing racist. Hey, nobody's perfect.

Okay, then, we get the idea that sometimes factual accounts may be fictive. But what about autobiographies and memoirs that are considered legitimate? Surely they're true, aren't they? Depends on what we mean by true. Norman Mailer's *Armies of the Night* is somewhat less fictive than *The Naked and the Dead*, which is a novel, but *Armies* is very artfully shaped and only loosely attached to fact. Lillian Hellman's *Pentimento*, which was the basis of the movie *Julia*, is quite freely adapted from life. Twain's nonfiction, from *Life on the Mississippi* to *A Tramp Abroad*, would have been seriously inconvenienced by a fact-checker. Same with Hemingway's *A Moveable Feast*. And none of them would have been improved by the endeavors of that personage. The problem with the truth is that it's often not very interesting. We're far better being guided in our nonfiction by the pronouncement of Twain's most famous creation, who said of his master that "he told the truth, mainly." A certain amount of verisimilitude is nice in an autobiography, but not so much as to get in the way of a good story.

You probably think I'm kidding.

Naturally, we're conflicted. We want a good story, a certain amount of dash and thrill, entertainment with our instruction. The pulp vats are full of books that were too dutiful to the truth, that subscribed too much to Sgt. Joe Friday's just-the-facts-ma'am school of reporting. At the same time, we're outraged by transgressions of the Word. How dare he make things up? How dare she take liberties? I think it's a Protestant thing. No, it doesn't just afflict Protestants, but that's where this particular mind-set originates. The energies of the Reformation, from the moment Martin Luther nailed his ninety-nine theses to the door of the cathedral, moved us toward a direct, personal encounter with Holy Writ, which in turn led us to seek to embrace all writing with a determined adherence to the literal truth of the written word. This may explain why so many Americans call themselves "strict constructionists," even when they can't remember which parts of their Constitution are actually in the Declaration of Independence. Whatever the Framers said, by golly, is an immutable truth for all people in all ages. When they went from being farmers and planters and shopkeepers and nasty in-fighters and slave-owners and petty squabblers and slavery opponents and tavern habitués to Framers of the Sacred Document, they became infallible. Nice work if you can get it. And we want to treat all writing as some subspecies of the Word, even when it's written by a lowlife pretending he was an even lower life in a genre where one has to limbo all the way down to get attention.

Clearly, however, people who have inherited this set of values will have some difficulties with autobiography or even with general nonfiction. Because almost everyone is going to pretty things up—or maybe ugly them up, if that's what the market demands—from time to time. At least, almost everyone has so far. Our earliest documents are highly suspect. Did the colony at Roanoke really look as good as Thomas Harriot portrayed it in 1588 in *A Briefe and True Report of the New Found Land of Virginia*? Were the natives really as beautiful, as virtuous, as kindly as he portrayed them? Did they really become that much more warlike by the time Captain John Smith arrived? That much less attractive and civilized? Somebody here is not telling the truth, the whole truth, et cetera. Probably two somebodies. We know that it took Smith nine years to get around to thinking the Pocahontas story was important enough to publish, and that each time he returned to it, the tale got more colorful. So how can we explain this? Harriot was writing a travelogue, an enticement to others to come to this newfoundland. Smith was doing the same, but with a difference; his economic model included moving the natives out to make way for new colonists and larger profits. The process of dehumanizing the locals was under way, and it had very little to do with veracity. The Puritan narratives would continue that process and bring the devil into the mix. At least John Smith didn't think Satan was involved.

All of this is by way of saying that we shouldn't expect too much reality in our autobiographies. Not even in our most famous. Especially not in our most famous. I should start by admitting that there was, indeed, a Benjamin Franklin. You can look it up. And that Franklin makes an appearance in *The Autobiography*. We just can't tell how much of him is there, which parts are made up, or how to tell the difference. The star of this show is a character by the name of "Benjamin Franklin," an invention, a literary device, a mechanism for imparting moral instruction. He shares with the historical personage many experiences and acquaintances, a positive outlook and can-do spirit, and a general good humor. He diverges in having the rough edges knocked off, the inconvenient portions ignored.

Actually, there are two creations named Benjamin Franklin at work here. One, as we have discussed, is the character. The other is the narrative presence. He, too, is a fiction, and a most handy one at that. Like every author, Franklin must decide what sort of presence will narrate his tale, and the fact that this particular tale is his own life matters not a whit. Throughout his writing life, Franklin adopted personae, characters who could speak for their author in the tone and manner appropriate to the piece. Of these numerous creations, his favorite was what the late University of Delaware English professor J. A. Leo Lemay called the "*ingénu* narrator": less worldly than Franklin really was, slightly surprised at his own actions, perhaps not quite up to speed. This stance, literally speaking, is patent nonsense. No one was speedier than Franklin. Besides, by the time he writes *The Autobiography*, he is past sixty-five and very worldly, having traveled widely and become what Professor Lemay calls "the most famous and the most politically powerful American in the world." Yet that bit of nonsense works splendidly for his purposes. It allows him to share in the surprise of his character's discoveries. It helps him avoid bombast and sentimentality, the bedeviling elements in old men's memoirs. And it makes him companionable to readers. See, he says, we're all in this together. Most importantly, it allows him to undertake the central mission of the work, the creation of the myth of Franklin, without seeming to become "mythic." That strategy is aided by the device of the letter to his son, with which he frames the first sections.

How does this narrative miracle occur? Here's the beginning. Having just reminded his son that he, Franklin *père*, has taken pleasure in knowing his own ancestors' activities, he declares:

> *Imagining it may be equally agreeable to you to know the circumstances of my life, many of which you are yet unacquainted with, and expecting the enjoyment of a week's uninterrupted leisure in my present country retirement, I sit down to write them for you. To which I have besides some other inducements. Having emerged from the poverty and obscurity in which I was born and bred, to a state of affluence and some degree of reputation in the world, and having gone so far through life with a considerable share of felicity, the conducing means I made use of, which with the blessing of God so well succeeded, my posterity may like to know, as they may find some of them suitable to their own situations, and therefore fit to be imitated.*

It's all at work here. The elements of the myth—obscure birth, rise to prominence, success and happiness, blessings of heaven (used here as elsewhere chiefly as a means of deflecting charges of boasting or egotism), possibility of instructive lessons to be drawn—are all present and accounted for. There's the indirect approach to instruction as he comes sidling up, almost indecisive: "my posterity *may* like to know," "it *may* be equally agreeable to you." *I don't want to force anything on you young people, but if you think it would be worth your while to hear, I'll say a few words. Would that be okay?* Franklin wouldn't say "okay," having died about the time of the first recorded use, but you get the idea. But the real beauty of this passage, and of the book as a whole, is the tone. He is familiar, digressive, self-deprecating, avuncular rather than paternal, slightly doting or even foolish, a sort of Polonius minus the insistence. It is an artful performance. There is nothing meandering or doddering about the old man here; he knows exactly where he's going and how he wants to get there. And it works. We take the companionable old man's hand as he leads us through the life—or selected highlights, since any modern "life" would come in at six or seven times the length—and take in the lessons he offers.

Including one lesson he hadn't counted on. I firmly believe Franklin intends us to live as he lived, or at least as he said he lived—frugally, simply, honestly, seizing advantages where they arise but treating others equitably. I'm less sure he foresees us writing as he writes. Does he know that he will become not merely the model for American lives but for American autobiography? Doubtful. But he is. For at least the next century, and perhaps right up to today, no public figure could write his life without the Philadelphia Everyman looking over his shoulder. A hundred years later Henry Adams, in *The Education of Henry Adams*, employs the ironic, self-deprecating tone, even if he does so in a third-person narrative. He's less optimistic, more concerned with how he didn't take up the family business of being president, but in a couple of ways he's still following the same template.

And what is this story Franklin is telling in such a genial manner? Oh, on some level it's his story. He's there in all the scenes. But it's not "Ben Franklin, individual," or even "Ben Franklin, future public servant and all-around man." Rather, it's "Ben Franklin, representative American." Or perhaps, "exemplary American." What Old Ben is really interested in is shaping a version of the American master-story, what we can call the "American myth" if we don't get hung up on the idea that "myth" means "untruth." It doesn't. A myth is simply a body of story that matters. He hoped that this particular story would matter to his future countrymen, that they would organize their lives around the lessons found in it.

Those lessons would have to come from the first two-thirds of his life, since the four parts he managed to complete take him only to 1758 and his failed attempt to petition English authorities for redress of colonial grievances. Their refusal would come back to haunt them, but not in this book. He had outlined a fifth section taking him up to the Treaty of Paris, but death intervened. Strangely, that loss may have strengthened the book thematically. True, we are poorer for not having his account of the momentous events surrounding the Revolution, for not hearing his version of drafting the Declaration of Independence. At the same time, though, that larger political narrative might have swamped the personal tale he does relate. In any event, this one works fine for his purposes and ours. It's our favorite, the story of an individual's rise from poverty to affluence and from obscurity to prominence by means of what Saul Bellow will have Augie March call "luck and pluck," mostly the latter, although he invokes the blessings of Providence often enough for balance. See, he says, you can make a go of it if you try. It's easy. Be like me.

Perhaps the greatest strategy of *The Autobiography* is the use of his craft as the conceit or controlling metaphor. The mistakes he wishes us to note particularly he calls his "errata." Now an erratum is a mistake in editing or printing a document, historically amended by an errata sheet, which, depending on the number of such gaffes, was a single slip of paper with a correction on it or an entire sheet of corrections, added loose-leaf to the book. The practice, alas, has largely vanished from modern publishing. Do not take that as a sign that modern books are inevitably better edited. His errata are a cute device, very tied into his life's work and interests, from printing to lending libraries to vast reading. They are so much better, however, when considered etymologically. "Erratum" comes from the Latin *errare*, "to stray." His follies, then, take the form of straying from his set path. Another writer of the day, I dare say almost any other writer of the day, would emphasize the Latin root. But Franklin is not any other writer. Instead, he goes with the homey, the familiar term of trade to stress his drifting from the marked trail. And he gets it both ways, a word that is both slightly alien and entirely personal. His errata, too, often cut two ways, reflecting poorly on him but not being completely his fault. The first of them occurs when he lends part of Mr. Vernon's money, which had been entrusted to him for safekeeping, to his friend Collins, who decamped without repayment and was never heard from again. Franklin learns a valuable lesson about borrowing and lending (recalling the advice of Polonius), yet any criminality resides with another; the most he can accuse himself of, or is willing to, would be poor judgment in the matter of friends. And learn he does.

The early portions of the book especially are taken up with lessons in practical morality and right conduct. Franklin, though at the time of writing he had been an intimate of David Hume and other notable philosophers of the day, does not concern himself with the abstract issues of ethics. Instead, rising burgher that he fashions his earlier self to be, he focuses on the sensible and immediate aspects of morality. More than one commentator has noted that he is a pragmatist nearly a century ahead of William James, and he shows that tendency in his famous thirteen virtues:

1. Temperance. Eat not to dullness; drink not to elevation.

2. Silence. Speak not but what may benefit others or yourself; avoid trifling conversation.

3. Order. Let all your things have their places; let each part of your business have its time.

4. Resolution. Resolve to perform what you ought; perform without fail what you resolve.

5. Frugality. Make no expense but to do good to others or yourself; i.e., waste nothing.

6. Industry. Lose no time; be always employ'd in something useful; cut off all unnecessary actions.

7. Sincerity. Use no hurtful deceit; think innocently and justly, and, if you speak, speak accordingly.

8. Justice. Wrong none by doing injuries, or omitting the benefits that are your duty.

9. Moderation. Avoid extreams; forbear resenting injuries so much as you think they deserve.

10. Cleanliness. Tolerate no uncleanliness in body, cloaths, or habitation.

11. Tranquility. Be not disturbed at trifles, or at accidents common or unavoidable.

12. Chastity. Rarely use venery but for health or offspring, never to dulness, weakness, or the injury of your own or another's peace or reputation.

13. Humility. Imitate Jesus and Socrates.

This may be the funniest list anyone ever composed. And he knows it. "Imitate Jesus and Socrates." Really? Under "Humility"? How arrogant is that? My favorite, however, is "Chastity": *rarely* use venery but for health or offspring. Define "health," please. Is mental health included? Which elements of physical well-being are implicated? And that "rarely" is the perfect out: okay, you can cut loose for no reason every once in a while, just so long as you can apply the word "rare" to the occasion. Nearly every item has an out built into it: mostly do this, try not to do that too often, except for these reasons or unless the moon is new. But the best part is the implementation phase. Franklin knows that he can't achieve goodness all at once, and the effort would be counterproductive, so he will undertake one at a time, beginning at the top, because temperance will make the others easier to achieve. Notice the placement of "Chastity" and "Humility." That's just like a man, isn't it?

At the same time, it really is a great list. If one can master items one through twelve, number thirteen will have pretty well taken care of itself. What it really says is, I wish to become better in terms of all of these virtues that will make me a more productive worker and a better citizen. The list is notably short on church virtues—nothing on faith, hope, or charity. Jesus exists with Socrates as a social exemplar rather than a figure of worship. In some quarters, equating them would be sacrilege, but they share the billing in the Franklin pantheon, and together with the other enumerated virtues, they point to his real belief system. One suspects he would agree with Marx that religion is the opiate of the masses, except that he would append, "and that's just fine." But his worship is of something far more modern. We could call it "humanism," even allowing for the heat the term sometimes generates, but even that doesn't quite reach the truth. What he really venerates is a society that allows for the maximum development of the individual, where men (and women, to an extent) can rise or fall on their own merits, without the limitations of inheritance or privilege, where men of reason can govern themselves without the interference of monarch or aristocracy, where creativity and the advance of knowledge can flourish without the imposition of Church or untested belief—a society, in other words, that will allow the boy he was to become the Renaissance man he grew into. The society, in fact, he wished us to become.

That desire is the most notable element of *The Autobiography* and gets at Franklin's real purpose. We can profitably think of every memoir as serving multiple masters. They typically seek to tell a story, first of all—the story of a life. There's more than a little self-justification built into the act; it may be defensive or self-aggrandizing or revisionist or purely fictive. They will select the elements for inclusion in order to make the subject look better or worse than or merely different from the original. They may wish to shed light on a social or historical period or movement: this is what people were like at that time, in this place, among the Beat writers, New York Yankees in their heyday, disillusioned communists of the 1950s, or what have you. They may wish to espouse a social or political cause: see what you can accomplish if you only believe *X*? They may wish to explore the philosophical or theological implications of their existence, or use that existence to demonstrate the superiority of a philosophical or religious position. Or they may wish to change the course of history. In the case of Henry Adams, he wants both to explore the mystery of how he failed to get into the family business of being president and more generally to explore the ways in which the demands of modern life, with its frantic pace (circa 1895), its constant technological innovation, and its social complexity, render the classical education he received at Harvard obsolete. Or in one or two cases, they seek to shape an entire nation, even though that nation does not yet exist at the time of the initial writing. Okay, one. We might stretch the definition to include, just barely, J. Hector St. John de Crèvecoeur's *Letters from an American Farmer* (1782), but I don't think we will. That leaves us with *The Autobiography*.

Franklin's writing is uniquely placed to attempt such a conjuring act. When he begins compiling his life in 1771, there are already stirrings of discontent and have been for a number of years, but no one could seriously contemplate a single entity stemming from thirteen fractious colonies, each with its own agenda, its own history with the Crown, and its own suspicions of the other twelve. A visionary, however, would see the possibilities for a common interest and a common future, if only these disparate beings could be made to see the things that unite them. And Franklin is nothing if not visionary. On one level, certainly, we could argue that he attempts to tie us together by creating a template for American success, a sort of composite of *How to Win Friends and Influence People* and *How to Succeed in Business by Really, Really Trying*. That emphasis, however, is only part of his program. What he really sets out to do for the first time is to establish an American character, to use the myth of himself as a template for the myth of all of us. We could do worse; he's not Cotton Mather or Davy Crockett. The goal of his exercise, it seems to me, is unity. Recognizing the virtual impossibility of knitting the colonies together into a cohesive political whole, he goes at the project from the other direction: if we see the elements common to our character (and if he can give that seeing a nudge in the right direction), then maybe we could be made to pursue a common interest or better still, an interest that grows out of that common character.

And what are those qualities of the American character, per Ben? I have extrapolated the following not merely from his list but from the whole of his text and not just from his catalog of cardinal virtues. They are, I think, rather more telling.

1. Independence
2. Enterprise, hustle
3. Honesty, or the appearance thereof
4. Shrewdness, slyness
5. Inquisitiveness, reason
6. Self-reliance, DIY
7. Resentment of authority
8. Skepticism
9. Pragmatism
10. Sociability, equanimity
11. Good humor
12. Generosity of spirit
13. Superiority

Do you suppose it's an accident that there are thirteen items in that list? Not mine, which is obviously in thrall to the original. His. And how many colonies would there have been? The chief feature of this list of qualities—and feel free to make up your own based on what you see in *The Autobiography*—is the way it reflects distance from a center. When one lives several weeks away by sea from the seat of authority, of economic stability, of established learning, one must make do with the materials at hand. In this case, the main material at hand was Benjamin Franklin. The more he must rely on his own abilities, the less enthusiasm he has for centralized power, whether it be his father or brother, the great universities, or the British government. If you need it, you design it yourself, which goes for governance as well as tools and mores. Even without a fancy education, he has advantages over most. As a product of the Enlightenment, he believes that reason can be applied to most problems and that questions are made to be answered. The source of stock answers lies thousands of miles away, so intellectual self-reliance was not merely desirable but essential.

He's scientific, but rarely in an abstract way. Even his experiments with lightning are performed with an eye toward useful applications, or at least a better understanding in order to prevent calamities. In general, however, his interests in scientific matters could better be expressed as interest in technological advancement. His is the country, after all, where the development of fighter jets that can land and take off vertically are hailed as great innovations but explorations of the history of the universe are largely regarded as boondoggles.

More important than his scientific interests, in the long run, are his views on the individual in society. On the one hand, he's fiercely independent, taking marching orders from no authority. On the other, he is a determined communalist. He's constantly setting up schemes for collective personal improvement. There is the Junto, which may well have been America's first reading group, in which tradesmen get together to discuss significant works of contemporary thought. There's the lending library, and while it is by subscription rather than truly public, the concept underwrites every public library in the country. These developments are absolutely typical of Franklin: improve society by improving the individual, increase the individual's chances by making society run more smoothly. Which is what it's all about. Prosperity. Opportunity. Advancement. Order is more conducive to prosperity than chaos, amicability than enmity. Is it selfish? Perhaps.

And what is most conducive to prosperity? Pragmatism. Principle with an out clause, of which Franklin is the master:

> I believe I have omitted mentioning that, in my first voyage from
> Boston, being becalm'd off Block Island, our people set about catch-
> ing cod, and hauled up a great many. Hitherto I had stuck to my res-

olution of not eating animal food, and on this occasion consider'd,
with my master Tryon, the taking every fish as a kind of unprovoked
murder, since none of them had, or ever could do us any injury that
might justify the slaughter. All this seemed very reasonable. But I
had formerly been a great lover of fish, and, when this came hot out
of the frying-pan, it smelt admirably well. I balanc'd some time be-
tween principle and inclination, till I recollected that, when the fish
were opened, I saw smaller fish taken out of their stomachs; then
thought I, "If you eat one another, I don't see why we mayn't eat
you." So I din'd upon cod very heartily, and continued to eat with
other people, returning only now and then occasionally to a veg-
etable diet. So convenient a thing it is to be a reasonable creature,
since it enables one to find or make a reason for everything one has
a mind to do.

It's a lofty precept. Not a bad inclination. And a wonderful justification. If the fish eat one another, what business have I to be better
than they are? "So convenient a thing it is to be a reasonable creature,"
indeed. Convenient is hardly the word. Reason, evidently, is much
aided by cornmeal and hot fat. And a pinch of salt. If that's not an
American position, there has never been one. Morality, like all things,
is best in moderation.

TWO

A MAN, A PLAN, A FLINTLOCK
The Last of the Mohicans

Okay, we might as well get this out of the way right off the top: Mark Twain is absolutely right. James Fenimore Cooper's offenses against literature, taste, and the English language, Yankee subsection, are many and serious. But here's his most serious crime: he won't go away, won't allow himself to be forgotten or ignored. There are a hundred reasons he ought to absent himself from the public sphere, only one or two why he stays. Those one or two will always win.

Reasons against? Ponderousness. Stilted language. A certain creakiness in the joints. Pretty much everything Twain said, plus a couple. Here's a classic of undermining the thrill of a fight scene, Cooperstyle. Remember if you can that this is a deadly battle between armed experts:

> The battle was now entirely terminated with the exception of the protracted struggle between "Le Renard Subtil" and "Le Gros Serpent." Well did these barbarous warriors prove that they deserved those significant names which had been bestowed for deeds in for-

mer wars. When they engaged, some little time was lost in eluding the quick and vigorous thrusts which had been aimed at their lives. Suddenly darting on each other, they closed, and came to the earth, twisted together like twining serpents, in pliant and subtle folds. At the moment when the victors found themselves unoccupied, the spot where these experienced and desperate combatants lay could only be distinguished by a cloud of dust and leaves, which moved from the center of the little plain toward its boundary, as if raised by the passage of a whirlwind.

What's that? You think maybe the secret lies in dialogue rather than narrative? Okay, but remember, you asked for it:

"I tell you, Uncas," said the former, as Heyward joined them, "you are wasteful of your powder, and the kick of the rifle disconcerts your aim! Little powder, light lead, and a long arm, seldom fail of bringing the death screech from a Mingo! At least, such has been my experience with the creatur's. Come, friends: let us to our covers, for no man can tell when or where a Maqua will strike his blow."

There. Satisfied? Mingo and Maqua are alternative names, from the Delawares and the Dutch, for the Iroquois. And they may be the most natural thing in Natty's speech. "Seldom fail of bringing the death screech"? Really? There's a stiffness in every speech in the novel, which is full of unnatural, convoluted, and "written" locutions. Even allowing for the passage of time, no human ever spoke the language of a Leatherstocking character. This failing, of course, is one of Twain's chief complaints against Cooper, but then, what would you expect one of the great champions of dialogue to think of one of the also-rans?

Here's what Twain, who occasionally committed something like art, actually says about *The Deerslayer*, although the criticisms are largely applicable to *The Last of the Mohicans*, too:

> A work of art? It has no invention; it has no order, system, sequence, or result; it has no lifelikeness, no thrill, no stir, no seeming of reality; its characters are confusedly drawn, and by their acts and words they prove that they are not the sort of people the author claims that they are; its humor is pathetic; its pathos is funny; its conversations are—oh! indescribable; its love-scenes odious; its English a crime against the language.

Twain is absolutely right about everything he finds appalling in Cooper, with the exception of Natty's sidekick's name, which is not really "Chicago." He's also hilarious. This has been one of my favorite pieces of writing since I was eighteen years old and is the chief reason why I come with so much resistance to reading Cooper. If you love language, love narrative grace, love prose style, Cooper offends every part of your literary sensibility.

So why can't we live without him? How did his most famous creation come to define us? Why, when the doughboys disembarked on French soil to help win the Great War, were they met with cries of "It is the spirit of Natty Bumppo"?

The answer is remarkably simple: because Cooper works. For all his stylistic infelicities, all the things that make it hard to get to the bottom of the page, he keeps us turning that page to get to the next.

His characterization may be clunky, but he takes those wooden figures and sets them in motion in ways that compel our attention. When the novel's villain, Magua, fails to convince the Delawares to hand over all the whites to his keeping, he at least succeeds in retaining the one captive he personally brought to their custody, the doomed Cora. We watch for pages as he works rhetorical magic on a tribe who normally are his rivals, winning them over with crafty slogans and gifts of stolen trinkets, taken during a recent massacre. It's a meta-performance, really: we watch him not merely giving the speech but watching himself give it, satisfied both with the effects and with his cleverness at bringing the effects about. Soon enough, we watch him, lacking railroad tracks to tie her to, raise the knife above poor Cora again and again, teasing out the suspense to the last moment, when an attack by the heroic, if equally doomed, Uncas drives him off, leaving it to an assistant to deliver the coup de grâce. The fight scene between Magua and Uncas, from the latter's heroic leap in attempting to save Cora to his death under Magua's knife, from Magua's desperate effort to escape Hawkeye's wrath to his fall to destruction, reads like a screenplay fight scene. It is at such moments that Cooper is most like modern action writers; allowing for insertions of stilted phrasings, it could appear in any thriller of the last twenty years. Indeed, the narrative of action has changed perhaps least of all narrative conventions since Homer. A look at fight sequences in *The Iliad*, *The Last of the Mohicans*, *For Whom the Bell Tolls*, *Goldfinger*, and *The Da Vinci Code* will establish how very little conventions have shifted in three thousand years. In Cooper's case, these sequences are when the books come most alive. The thirty pages or so from the war dance of Uncas to the death of Magua, in sharp contrast to so much of the book, are masterful.

Those deaths point to another, less savory aspect of Cooper: the treatment of race. It's not that he is particularly bigoted; indeed, rather the opposite. By his lights, or those of his time, he's pretty open-minded. His research for his novels included reading the best studies of Native cultures he could find, and that research typically shows up in the novels as serious and even appreciative depictions of their customs. In this book, both the rituals of preparation for battle and the burials of Cora and Uncas are treated intelligently and sensitively. We *feel* the seriousness of the rites not only for the participants but also for the author. And in Chingachgook and Uncas we have the originals of the "noble savage" archetype that so bedevils us to this time in print and on film. We see Uncas's nobility repeatedly, particularly when he gives himself up in his failed attempt to save Cora. Even so, half of that appellation is troubling: they *are* savages. They are the Other writ large; however useful they may prove to be, they remain beyond the pale, figures of the wilderness who cannot be tamed. The "bad" Indians are, of course, much worse. Magua is simply a figure of pure evil. There is no nasty trick or wickedness of which he is not capable. The slaughter of the innocents that he oversees and likely instigates outside Fort William Henry is brutal in the extreme, wantonly bloodthirsty, and, well, savage. He thinks nothing of kicking his opponent when he's down, stabbing Uncas, not yet recovered from a fall, in a situation that is clearly unfair. You would never see Natty Bumppo do that.

The message is clear: they are not like us. They don't have our values. Our honor. Our respect for human life. Stop me if you've heard this before. Your version will substitute maybe the North Vietnamese, the Japanese, the Soviets, the Chinese and North Koreans, or whatever group can fill in the blank at the moment. I am in possession of postcards from a great-uncle who served in the Canadian Expeditionary Force in World War I and who uses those phrases exactly to describe the iniquities of the Germans. He was a sniper. Somewhere in Germany a Thomas Mueller no doubt has in his closet postcards saying nearly identical things about the Canadians.

But we can't blame poor old Cooper. Or not too much. His chief literary offense is writing BW—Before Walt. American letters divides very neatly at 1855, with the publication of a book almost no one noticed. Oh, there were a few. Ralph Waldo Emerson up in Cambridge headed a few nice words toward Trenton. And there was this impossibly tall, lanky, obscure lawyer out in Springfield, Illinois, who sometimes summoned his clerks to his office to hear a choice passage. The rough-hewn, unschooled but widely read Lincoln must have been attracted to the earthy populism of Whitman, but he was one of the few who caught on. Even despite its limited initial appeal, *Leaves of Grass* changed everything, separating the things American literature *might have become* from the thing it did. It made possible Twain with his caustic appraisal of Cooper. Hemingway and Faulkner. Kerouac and Ginsberg and Ferlinghetti. Langston Hughes and Louise Erdrich. Edna St. Vincent Millay and Dorothy Parker. Heck, probably even Mickey Spillane, although he's a lot to blame on the patron saint of American writing. And one of the things Whitman makes impossible, as you will have guessed, is Cooper. AW, After Walt, there can be no Leatherstocking tales, or at least not with this cautious, clunky, quasi-British prose.

Our book, however, is not A, but decidedly B, W. The year is 1826, and there is no hint in the air that a Whitman could exist. It's a mere six years after the egregious Sydney Smith offered his snotty assessment of American writing. *The Last of the Mohicans* constitutes a major part of the first return salvo.

The other saving grace of Cooper and answer to our earlier questions: he's mythic. One unstated objection of Twain's is that Cooper is not a realist. Of course he's not. He's a romantic at bottom, and the heart of romance is myth. The late, great Northrop Frye would have us understand that all literature is descended from the source in what he calls "displacement of myth." The first level of displacement—that is, the mode of literature that is closest to the original—is romance, which includes the great epics and stories, from *The Iliad* to *Batman*, ghost tales, horror tales, vampire tales, and, well, you get the idea. What you'll notice about this group is that verisimilitude—fidelity to everyday life—is not high on the punch list: characters stylized, action a little over the top, heroes better and villains slightly worse than persons we might actually know (or be), and meaning heavily symbolic or metaphorical. Romance is perhaps the dominant mode in classic American literature, what with the quest narratives, monomaniacs chasing white whales, lunatics shunning sin by moving to caves or donning black veils. If we're going to persist in talking about American books, I have but one thing to say:

Get used to it.

And romance is just the place for creating mythic figures doing mythic things. Like carving "civilization" out of the wilderness. Like showing us what a hero looks like, a real, American, sprung-from-the-soil, lethal-weapon-with-leggings, bona fide hero. And for a guy who never marries, he has a lot of offspring. Shane. The Virginian. The Ringo Kid. The Man with No Name. Just think how many actors would have had no careers without Natty Bumppo. Gary Cooper. John Wayne. Alan Ladd. Tom Mix. Clint Eastwood. Silent. Laconic. More committed to their horse or buddy than to a lady. Professional. Deadly. In his *Studies in Classic American Literature*, D. H. Lawrence waxes prolix on Natty's most salient feature: he's a killer. And so are his offspring. This hero can talk, stiltedly to be sure, but prefers silence. He appreciates female beauty but is way more committed to his canoe or his business partner (his business being death and war) or, most disturbingly, his long rifle, Killdeer. Dr. Freud, your three-o'clock is here. Like those later avatars, he is a wilderness god, part backwoods sage, part cold-blooded killer, part unwilling Prince Charming, part jack-of-all-trades, but all man. Here's how his creator describes him: "a philosopher of the wilderness, simple-minded, faithful, utterly without fear, yet prudent." A great character, no doubt, but hardly a person. A paragon. An archetype. A miracle. But a potentially real person—not so much.

I use the word "god" advisedly here, for that's what he is: a mythic creature of the woods who can only exist there, who commands our awe, even our reverence, but not our fellow feeling. He's not one of us. He's all sinew (Cooper's favorite term), endurance, woodscraft, warcraft, instinct, and power. Yet what does he feel? More importantly, what do we feel for him? He's distant and detached, like a god. His coolness under fire translates into a coldness about other humans in general. As he transports and protects the daughters of the garrison in *The Last of the Mohicans*, he speaks kindly of them as "the delicate ones," among other quaint locutions, and he admires the pluck and savvy of Cora, the elder girl, toward whom we sense he should have some romantic inclination. Yet any tender or sexual impulses are felt not by Natty but by Uncas, the doomed son of his business associate and scion of the firm Chingachgook and Bumppo, PLC. Indeed, the death of Cora inspires less pathos than we might expect and far less than that a short time later of Uncas, who leaves his father as the dubious being of the title.

Before I turn Natty and Chingachgook loose, there's another matter for which their creator deserves some credit. As nearly as I can tell, these two are the first mixed-race couple in American fiction. Stop that! This isn't one of those come-back-to-the-raft-Huck-honey revisionist essays. I can write that one if you want, but for now, we're talking buddy stories, especially the sort where the buddies represent different, sometimes warring tribes. American fiction and film are full of them. Huck and Jim. The Lone Ranger and Tonto. Spenser and Hawk. Han and Chewbacca. That's a big deal; for all our faults, we do sometimes aspire to be more open, more accepting, better. What's most remarkable is that such pairs got their start during a thoroughly racist period in our history, although there have been more of those eras than the other sort, so maybe it's not so surprising.

And here's another gift the book gives to the country. It, along with its companion titles, made Cooper the first professional author in our history. He sold a lot of books and, copyright being what it was(n't) in those days, had a lot more pirated. Hawkeye, Deerslayer, Natty—call him what you will, since his creator gives you so many options—made the boss rich and famous. That's not enough to make a great national work, but it matters to the history of the country. Call it the business history, literary division. Not that the dollars and cents are the point. Someone had to go first, show that there was a life to be recorded here, that this place, this new set of possibilities, could inspire a new literature. Cooper set the signpost on the road, and hearty travelers have been following it ever since.

THREE

THE ALLEGORY MAN COMETH
The Scarlet Letter

Believe me, if there were any way to avoid this next discussion, I certainly would. It's not that I don't have respect for the novel in question or that I don't recognize its importance. Aye, there's the rub: one can't pretend it isn't important, even perhaps central, to the American experience. And it isn't that I don't like the author and his work. Were it up to me, we'd be having this discussion about his short stories or perhaps a different novel of his. Some decisions, however, are out of my hands. What's that you say? I'm the writer and get to decide who's in and who's out of my book? Negative on that one, friends. Some decisions are bigger than an individual—the vote was taken before I ever came along, and it keeps getting taken, and it keeps coming out the same way. Maybe I first read the book at the wrong time of my life. Maybe its rhythms aren't mine. Maybe I just don't like Puritans. I haven't known any bona fide Puritans, but based on encounters with some of their latter-day versions, it's doubtful we would have been fast friends. Sadly, there's no getting around the facts of the case: as much as it pains me to say so, and as unhappy as the declaration will make my English-teaching friends, I just do not care for *The Scarlet Letter*. I'm sorry.

Don't get me wrong. I like Nathaniel Hawthorne. Love the short stories. Would have chosen to write about any of them in a heartbeat. Would have preferred to discuss *The House of the Seven Gables*, which, by the way, still stands in Salem, Massachusetts. It's altogether more subtle and interesting, at least to me. Plus, it has a character named Hepzibah, and how often does one of those come along? It's just that when Hawthorne gets started on the Puritans, he ought to have a length limit. I'm thinking about twelve pages. "Young Goodman Brown" is as far as he should be permitted to go. One can take the goofiness of a bad pun like "My Faith is gone," Faith being both Goodman Brown's belief and the name of his wife, in good humor if one knows it will all be over in a few pages. Beyond that, the heavy-handed symbolism and tormented souls just become strange and overbearing. The scarlet *A* pinned to Hester Prynne's dress, okay. That one makes sense and tells us something about the people who surround her in early Boston. The *A* seared into Arthur Dimmesdale's chest and the meteor that flares across the sky in a red *A*—really? I'm as susceptible to the magical in fiction as the next guy, but this just strikes me as ham-handed. Or perhaps it's the vehemence with which Hawthorne, descended from some notable Puritans himself, rejects them. Seems a little unnecessary a hundred and fifty or so years after the fact.

But what do I know? All the world thinks otherwise, and I have only D. H. Lawrence as an ally, which does not incline one toward confidence. He thought it the most perfect expression of America in fiction, but the America it expresses is corrupt in spirit, hypocritical in practice, debased in ethics. That seems to be more or less what Hawthorne had in mind, too. As for the rest, I'm on my own. In fact, a short while ago I was in a group of Advanced Placement English students, two classes worth, for a talk. At the end of my little presentation I told them about my new project and asked which books they thought merited inclusion in a list of twenty-five titles. They gave me an earful about Hemingway and Fitzgerald and Ayn Rand (two different titles) and Toni Morrison and Chuck Palahniuk and the *Twilight* virginity-and-vampires series and a few dozen others. The big winner, by a landslide, was Hawthorne's somber tale of adultery among the Puritans. Who would have guessed? And who's going to buck a roomful of very bright, impassioned eighteen-year-olds? Certainly not me.

The Scarlet Letter is the first major novel Hawthorne published. By the time it appeared, in 1850, he had already brought out almost all the great short stories and tales for which he is known—"My Kinsman, Major Molineux," "Young Goodman Brown," "The Minister's Black Veil," "The Maypole of Merry Mount," "The Man of Adamant," "The Birth-Mark"—and was fairly famous as a writer of short fiction. He followed up with *The House of the Seven Gables* a year later, *The Blithedale Romance* a year after that, and *The Marble Faun* in 1860. It's fair to say that few writers in history have had a better baker's decade than that. Because he had written so many stories already, his mastery of fictional form is already on display in what we might fairly call his "first novel" (he published *Fanshawe* anonymously in 1828, thereby saving his reputation). He had planned this book as a novella or novelette, probably the more likely term, but his publishers, Ticknor and Fields, wanted a full-length novel, so he obliged. It was an instant success. The first edition, in February 1850, sold out in ten days; another edition of twenty-five hundred was published in late March, and it, too, was soon gone. He never made huge money on it, something like $1,500 in a decade and a half, but it cemented his reputation, and in any case, more books followed.

What separates Hawthorne from much of American literature is the direction of his gaze. The great bulk of writing in our tradition, and here Whitman is the great exemplar, looks forward. We are a people who are going someplace, and that place is not behind us. We are self-invented, detached from our European past, driving, striving, contentious, litigious, and sometimes just plain ornery, but we're always moving ahead. There may be little else to connect Ralph Waldo Emerson's "Self-Reliance" or his "Harvard Divinity School Address" with Henry James's "Daisy Miller," Henry Miller's *Tropic of Capricorn*, and Erica Jong's *Fear of Flying*, but they are united in pointing a way—several ways in these cases—forward. Hawthorne turns around and faces the other way. His interest is not so much in where we're going as in how we got to where we are. Or perhaps it would be equally valid to say that he's as interested in our future as everyone else but takes a different approach to getting there. In any case, he routinely looks back to the colonial days, especially those days inhabited or informed by the dark cloud of Puritanism.

The Boston of the narrative is a place of punishment and death. The first chapter stakes out that territory, suggesting that the two primary accomplishments of the settlers was constructing a jailhouse and marking out a graveyard. The true center of gravity in the novel, however, is the structure that feeds both, the gallows. When we first meet Hester Prynne, she has been hauled up onto that platform to receive her sentence for adultery. She had been sent ahead by a much older husband, who never arrived, leading to the general conclusion that he has been lost at sea. Although she refuses to name her partner, she cannot deny the crime, since she holds the evidence, her infant daughter, Pearl, in her arms. She undergoes public shaming and a sentence to wear henceforth a scarlet letter A, for adulteress, on her breast. One of the participants in this event is her pastor, Arthur Dimmesdale, a brilliant orator but faulty moralist; he fails, as we later discover, to admit that he is the father of the child. Also present is a new arrival, an elderly man calling himself Roger Chillingworth and passing for a physician, who is in fact Hester's long-lost husband. He plots revenge not upon Hester but upon her unnamed accomplice, and in the way of these things, he soon settles on Dimmesdale as the likely culprit. From the shaming to the final revelation of Dimmesdale as Hester's lover and Pearl's father, a biblical seven years elapse. During that time several changes occur. Hester becomes a paradoxical figure in the community, valued for her needlework for the living and the dead but nevertheless ostracized for her earlier conduct. Chillingworth insinuates his way into Dimmesdale's life and house, burrowing his malice into his victim while posing as a healer. The pastor grows increasingly frail and deathly, but the venomous intentions also rebound on the physician; unlike the typical vampire tale, where the villain grows stronger as the victim weakens, Chillingworth grows more twisted and ghastly as he wreaks his vengeance.

Young Pearl, meanwhile, grows healthy and wild, wholly unconstrained by social conventions or even parental expectations. This is hardly surprising, given their living circumstances. Hester's "crime" puts her beyond the pale, literally. She is forced to live outside the town, finding quarters in an abandoned cottage "on the outskirts of the town, within the verge of the peninsula, but not in close vicinity to any other habitation." She is on the edge of everything—town, sea, life—and always beyond respectability. Both the living arrangement and every social encounter remind her of her outcast status. No one ever addresses her without adverting to her past, and even those who seek favors do so while letting her know her place. Their children do not play with her child, so Pearl grows without the pernicious influence of Puritan society. She is uncontrollable but loving, and wholly independent, as if she is a manifestation of her mother's spirit, for Hester grows to be entirely self-reliant in spiritual as well as financial matters.

Chillingworth, back from the dead and calling himself by a different name, reveals himself to Hester while she is still in prison but swears her to secrecy. She keeps her word for seven years, breaking it only when she sees Dimmesdale on the point of death from his enemy's attentions. She and Pearl meet the minister one night on the town scaffold, where he has been seeking punishment or revelation or *something* in his madness. Hester sees that she must do something to save him, but Chillingworth refuses to stop his torment of Dimmesdale. The two former lovers meet in the woods, where Hester reveals her husband's secret and they plan an escape by sea. Somehow, Chillingworth discovers the plan and books passage on the same ship, planning to thwart their happiness. The day before the departure is a celebration of the election of a new governor to replace the deceased Winthrop. A less festive occasion is hardly to be imagined, yet even here the spirit of carnivalesque works its magic. Parties, feasts, and carnivals exist in literary works largely to loosen ordinary constraints so that the expected order can be upended, and that is emphatically the case here. Dimmesdale mounts the scaffold with Hester and Pearl, revealing that he, the trusted religious leader and brilliant orator, is Hester's lover and the father of her little girl. Only moments before, he has given the election-day sermon in the meetinghouse, so the movement from sanctuary to scaffold is telling: the minister can find his redemption not in the place of worship but in the place of punishment. He announces his criminality, tears back his garments to reveal, presumably—we never see it ourselves and must rely on contradictory testimony—a companion *A* to Hester's etched into his own flesh, and collapses toward death. Before he goes, however, he confronts the frustrated, demonic Chillingworth, asking that God forgive even the evil physician, and receives a kiss from

Pearl, who has twice refused to kiss him when he has declined to acknowledge paternity (it's all quite symbolic, since paternity is a concept that is beyond her). The kiss breaks his final tie to life, and after a brief word (at least for a Puritan minister as envisioned by Hawthorne), he expires.

It remains only to pick up the pieces. The effort to destroy Dimmesdale also consumes Chillingworth, who dies within the year, leaving his considerable wealth to Pearl. Her mother takes her to England, where they live for a number of years without anyone in Boston hearing from or of them. Eventually, Hester returns, still in uniform, to continue performing good works, and she becomes a sort of unacknowledged saint of the place. When she dies, she is buried next to Dimmesdale under a single letter A. Pearl is said to have married into nobility, although no one is sure of what country, and to have lived very well, although the contents of her occasional letters to her mother are never revealed. A more characteristic nineteenth-century tidy ending Dickens never wrote.

That ending sells out Hester, as a friend of mine complains, becoming as it does a vehicle for Dimmesdale's redemption, and it does so for the worst of artistic reasons: popularity. Had the novel been written seventy-five or more years later, we would accuse it of going Hollywood, seeking the big, dramatic effect that will sell with audiences. As it is he probably went stagey, not that he saw adaptations so much as that he was as susceptible to big, theatrical moments as anyone else. On one level he's probably right; that splashy finale probably makes the book more palatable for more readers, and writers do want to be read. Artistically, though, or perhaps we should say philosophically, it feels like a failure. One isn't asking for the proto-feminist text that might have been had Marilyn French or Kate Millett only lived a century earlier. They probably wouldn't have written *that* novel, either. It's just that, having suffered through Hester's banishment and struggles for a couple hundred pages, readers might fairly expect that the resolution, when it comes, might have something to do with her. Instead, Dimmesdale mounts the scaffold, reveals his sin, acknowledges his daughter, gets his kiss, professes his undying love, and promptly dies. Except that he doesn't profess undying or any other sort of love. Rather, he admonishes her that their crime will keep them apart in the next world as it has in this, that it can never be forgiven. She believes they have "ransomed" one another with their suffering and contrition; he says not. His confession is not about her, just as his secrecy has never been about her. His "triumph" is escaping persecution by the demonic Chillingworth. It does absolutely nothing for her, which will pretty much describe the entirety of their relationship.

Somehow, though, having achieved its big set-piece ending, the narrative decides that it is satisfied. It seems not to notice that her love has been focused on an unworthy object, that his final act has no bearing on her life for good or ill, that Dimmesdale has in no measure earned his reward, either from heaven or from readers. Having written an adventurous novel of ideas for its duration, at the end Hawthorne punts, allowing *The Scarlet Letter* to become conventional. What happens to those hard-won lessons on individualism, on rising above herd thinking, on self-sufficiency? Vanished. Traded away for a parlor trick. E. M. Forster says in *Aspects of the Novel* that, roughly, at the end, every novel sacrifices character to plot to achieve its final form, that they always do battle and plot always wins. This is in part, I believe, because character is more subtle and less ostentatious. In the case of this novel, the Dimmesdale-Chillingworth revenge plot is a showy and rather simpleminded good-versus-evil struggle, and we all know that at the end of such a tussle, the villain must be defeated. So, pastor-gallows-revelation-shock-farewell-death. Inadequate? Yes. Unfair to the heroine? Certainly. Another in a vast line of great books with unsuitable endings. Did I mention that they are the one thing I dislike in Dickens, too?

Here's the thing. Dimmesdale dies. Good. Serves him right. But Hester doesn't. And that's what should command our attention. She not only lives but lives with the lessons she has learned over the previous seven-plus years. Instead, those lessons, from a narrative standpoint, die with her lover. In order to understand what the novel is really about, we must swim upstream against the current until we arrive at the moment before his revelation, the moment when the novel is still about her, before he hijacks it and tries to make it about him. And *that* novel is important. It's about the individual and the community, about private conscience and public morality, about where God resides in the human condition, about the ideas that were floating around New England, or at least around Concord and environs, that generally go by the name of transcendentalism, and significantly, about the place of female experience in human society. It is as great a novel as any written by a man in that last regard, until Hawthorne loses his nerve and sacrifices human insight to symbolic gesture. Those are things we ought not lose sight of but that threaten to vanish in the novel's last moments.

In other places, perhaps most notably *The Blithedale Romance*, his satire of the utopian Brook Farm, Hawthorne could be scathing about the shortcomings of American transcendentalism, that movement centered around Concord, Massachusetts, and based almost wholly on the essays of Emerson. Yet our novel may be the purest expression of Emersonian thought ever written by someone not named Ralph. The novelist's doubts about organized religion as the wellspring of truth are couched in terms of a long-ago sect, yet there should be no doubt that he means to include current religions as well. Hester goes her own way, entering into freethinking of a sort not because it is natural for her but because of her forcible estrangement from the center of orthodoxy. She must become her own spiritual and moral authority whether she wants to or not, just as she must become self-reliant in the material realm. The lights she follows are intuitive rather than intellectual; indeed, we repeatedly see her rational self take a much more conventional position than her intuitive or subconscious self does, not thinking herself through to conclusions so much as arriving there by feeling. This position is one of transcendentalism's debts to William Wordsworth and the English romantics, who argue that man most natural—the child, the rustic, the untutored person—is closest to his or her true self. Emerson insists on the importance of the individual and, by extension, the American experience as the center of meaning. Truth, he suggests, will be revealed neither by intellection nor by divine revelation but intuitively through direct contact with nature. And just as the individual must not be beholden to the collective, so also must the new republic cease to be beholden to European traditions. American culture for Americans! Hawthorne, of course, needs no such injunction; he is already busily forging native art from native materials, specifically from the inheritance of New England's first English settlers. Like Cooper and Irving before him and his Bowdoin College classmate Henry Wadsworth Longfellow, Hawthorne knows from the first that his stories must grow from our stories. They concern themselves with peculiarly American problems and, sometimes, solutions: faith and doubt, generosity and suspicion, public pronouncements and private actions, and identity in a new land.

I've said "novel" several times here, but the book is in fact a romance. This term gives pause to contemporary readers, for whom "romance" should follow another word, such as "Gothic" or "Harlequin" and for whom it means invariably tales of love and desire, often of dubious probability. In fact, that meaning is but one of several attached to an older narrative tradition that had nothing to do with covers bearing the image of Fabio. We could take this discussion all the way back to medieval times, when the adjective of choice was typically "courtly," but let's limit ourselves to the era of book-length prose. The novel usually was taken to be a prose fiction that sought, so far as possible, to emulate real life. My students would say, "Oh, you mean it's realistic," but that gets us into another definitional nightmare, so let's not go there. Instead, as I discussed in the case of Cooper, let's say that the novel typically involves a high degree of verisimilitude and presents a world very like our own. Characters tend to behave very much like ordinary people and find themselves involved in surprising but ordinary crises, usually of their own making. The romance, by contrast, involves heightened realities, stylized characters, exaggerated actions, improbable events and outcomes. Heroes are heroic, villains dastardly. Hemingway wrote novels; Tolkien wrote romances. At shorter lengths, we can make a similar distinction between the short story and the tale. So is Hawthorne closer to Hemingway or Tolkien? Exactly. With perhaps one or two exceptions, he wrote tales and romances. In fact, as noted above, one of his books was called *The Blithedale Romance*. So we shouldn't be too disappointed when, in this book, the only bodice ripped is Reverend Dimmesdale's, and he promptly dies.

What distinguishes Hawthorne's sort of romance from, say, Mary Shelley's or Barbara Cartland's is the psychological depths he explores in his characters. His people are tormented not merely in mind or heart but in their souls, which for him is a richer place altogether. We may not know them as minutely as Faulkner's characters since they rarely get to speak for themselves, but we see as much complexity in their motivation and guilt, elation and suffering. Hester is not merely a victim, nor is she merely good in the way some later Dickens heroines are "young, beautiful, and good"—and dull. She has issues beyond those visited upon her by the Puritan authorities. Dimmesdale is not merely a careerist who lets her take the fall alone for their indiscretion; other factors are at work on him as well. Okay, Roger Chillingworth is uniformly villainous, but the romance form really does demand that. If Darth Vader has doubts, at least before the very end of the trilogy, then George Lucas is up the cosmic creek. But the main characters are more subtly drawn than the stock figures of much romance. Here's the narrator's version of Hester's rationale for not fleeing to the mother country:

> What she compelled herself to believe,—what, finally, she reasoned upon, as her motive for continuing a resident of New England,— was half a truth, and half a self-delusion. Here, she said to herself, had been the scene of her guilt, and here should be the scene of her earthly punishment; and so, perchance, the torture of her daily shame would at length purge her soul, and work out another purity than that which she had lost; more saint-like, because the result of martyrdom.

Hester has no doubt that the judgment visited upon her is correct. Indeed, she colludes in that punishment by remaining in the place where her shame will be maximized, where she will meet with the greatest possible reproach. Where she exceeds the views of her contemporaries, however, is in the outcome of that punishment. For them, with their crudely Calvinist notions of election and depravity, she is lost in this world and the next. For her, this punishment is "earthly" and not eternal. She is working, moreover, toward a personal, rather than a social or spiritual, redemption. If she becomes "a kind of saint," it is only of a kind, and that by her own definition.

Pearl is often referred to as an elf-child, an imp, a spirit of misrule in some form or other, as when Roger Chillingworth declares that there is no law natural or divine that holds her or to which she will conform. The narrator, however, has other ideas:

> *So she drew her mother away, skipping, dancing, and frisking fan-*
> *tastically among the hillocks of the dead people, like a creature that*
> *had nothing in common with a bygone and buried generation, nor*
> *owned herself akin to it. It was as if she had been made afresh, out*
> *of new elements, and must perforce be permitted to live her own life,*
> *and be a law unto herself, without her eccentricities being reckoned*
> *to her for a crime.*

This is not the description of a child of demons, despite what the community and even her mother may believe. Or if she is, it's a demon we can embrace. True, she is constantly in motion in ways not authorized by Puritan orthodoxy. Hawthorne launches her into ceaseless participial frenzy, forever skipping, running, laughing, jumping, crying, smirking, and, most dangerously, dancing. She is separated from the mass of Bostonian children not merely by her mother's criminality but by her own irrepressible nature. They are the past; she is the future. An American future. In other words, she is us, or who we may be if we have the luck and the courage. It can be no one else in the novel. Both Hester and her oppressors, however much they may see themselves as starting out anew, are products of an old way of thinking, an old set of preoccupations, an Old World. Pearl owes nothing to the past: she is "made afresh, out of new elements," following no rules but her own, "a law unto herself," her "eccentricities" to be judged by no one but herself. Those qualities ought to ring a bell with anyone who has ever studied Americans—or been one. She is the very embodiment of the "life, liberty, and the pursuit of happiness" that would make their appearance in our first sacred document a century or so later. She refuses to assent to being governed from without, insisting on living by her own standards, her own governance. If that governance is at times unruly, even alarming, it remains hers, and she remains true to her own lights.

Yet there is inevitably a war in the narrative between young Pearl and the older, sour, judgmental conventionality that would revile her. With the promise she figures, Hawthorne issues a warning: it may be true that we "are, and by Right ought to be, Free and Independent States"—or individuals—but it is equally true that the forces of despotism, whether of social institutions or public opinion, always await their chance to thwart that freedom. We may even collude, in the manner of Hester, in the destruction of our own freedom.

So who cares about Hawthorne these days? Specifically, who cares about *The Scarlet Letter*? Aside from English teachers, that is. Based on the evidence, I'd say just about everybody. Or maybe just American everybodies. Throughout the last century there have been innumerable reworkings of the story as film, drama, and even opera and ballet. There were multiple silent-film versions as both shorts and features, several talkies, and even one in German by the typically off-kilter Wim Wenders. There was a 1994 rock musical, written by Mark Governor. Hey, I'm sure we've all had the experience of reading the book and thinking, "Why didn't The Who do this instead of *Tommy*?" The 1994 Roland Joffé film starring Demi Moore and Gary Oldman may have been so "freely adapted" that it seemed to have little to do with the original but the title and some names, but adapted it was. The novel has been cited by David Lynch (in *Twin Peaks*), Marilyn Manson, Tool, Mudvayne, the Christian rock band Casting Crowns, and the metal-punk band As Blood Runs Black. Clearly, Hawthorne's dark romanticism appeals more to the fringe sectors. Indeed, a musical version was performed at Edinburgh's Fringe Festival in 2001. Not to mention novels. It's pretty much impossible to write a tale about adultery and its aftermath and *not* in some way be in the master's debt. John Updike would have had no later career at all without the salutary influence of Hawthorne. Both *The Witches of Eastwick* (1984) and *The Widows of Eastwick* (2008) display a heavy obligation, although not as much as the so-called Scarlet Trilogy of *A Month of Sundays* (1975), *Roger's Version* (1986), and *S.* (1988), all of which are direct descendants of *The Scarlet Letter*. And then there are all those readers. Even adjusted for inflation, the book makes much more money a year than it ever made for its author—and no, those are not all compulsory purchases by captive audiences in AP English.

One measure of literary influence is what I would call the "provocation index": did that writer create an itch that keeps us scratching? And just who's doing that scratching all these years later? This novel has a high PI. It's not just about popularity or how much fun the book is to read. I suspect you could walk a lot of beaches for a lot of summers and never see a copy of *The Scarlet Letter*; that doesn't mean it's not out there. It has never attracted cult followings in the way of *On the Road* or *Tropic of Capricorn*; that doesn't mean it's not influential. It may not be written to contemporary taste. As I said at the outset, it's certainly not written to mine. That doesn't matter greatly, since it's largely a product of the changes wrought by time. It was very well written for its day and a significant stylistic advance over much nineteenth-century fiction. Besides, novels survive for what they can give us and what we can find in them, and those things vary from book to book. This book is a winter's tale, a story for dark times when we're alone with our thoughts and wanting to puzzle out what it means to be human, a fallen being in a flawed world. There will always be a place for that, for work in which the reader is, in British poet Philip Larkin's phrase, "surprising / a hunger in himself to be more serious."

Lawrence said of the novel that it was "the most perfect expression" of the American imagination. He did not mean it as a compliment. He was right, though, and I do mean it as a compliment. This study is about what I call the American myth. As Karl Marx noted, however, every movement carries within it the seeds of its own destruction. So, too, does every myth contain the seeds of its own countermyth. Before we're done, we may hear as much from the countermyth as from the straight-ahead version. We might as well begin here. Make no mistake, Hawthorne knows and believes in the American myth. He embodies it in young Pearl and does so largely without irony. But she's merely one branch on a much larger tree, whose name is not optimism and progress. He has a discerning eye for folly, hypocrisy, suspicion, redemption, stubbornness, and our capacity for error. As long as those remain part of our experience, as long as defenders of the public morals will continue having private scandals, as long as we persist in condemning Hester Prynne and embracing Arthur Dimmesdale, whatever their outward guises, as long as we're tempted by the corrosive attraction of vengeance, he will continue to speak to us.

CHAPTER FOUR

GOTTA GET BACK TO THE POND AND SET MY SOUL FREE
Walden

You want influence? How about this: think of the book that has done more damage to more lives than any other. Led more people to make really bad choices. Created more mayhem. Underwritten more communes. That's right. The most dangerous book in the history of the republic is . . . *Walden*? Henry David Thoreau is all earnestness in his classic memoir, first published in 1854, but that can't save it, or us. Never, I dare say, has a work so good, so honest, so forthright exerted such pernicious influence. And the reason is quite simple.

Americans can't read.

Here's what *Walden* does not enjoin its readers to do:

a. Withdraw permanently from society
b. Go charging out to the frontier with no support system and no plan
c. Attempt to survive the Alaskan winter in a school bus, tent, or lean-to

d.   Try to master the wilderness with zero practical skills

e.   Form hare-brained enclaves based on shared irresponsibility

And here's what Americans—and to be fair, certain Canadians and others—have done based on the book: all of the above. It's all more than a little mystifying, but especially that last one. How did it happen that a book that says, "I never found a companion more companionable than solitude" and that extols chastity and sobriety becomes a bible for those who would live in groups while getting high and raising promiscuity to an art form? No, of course not all communes were that way; at least, I heard there were a couple of the other sort. They may not have been urban legends. Still, the main point obtains: group living based on a work of a radical individualist is a distinctly odd outcome. And I don't think I ever had a conversation with someone who had spent time in a commune where Thoreau didn't come up in, say, the first fifteen minutes as part of the rationale for the experiment.

Henry David Thoreau was one of the great cranks of Western civilization. He was the sort of person who, where I come from, they call an "aginner"—show him an idea not his own, and he's against it. More than that, if he was against it, there was no possible argument in its favor, so being for it was prima facie evidence of your shortcomings. Among the things he was against: material acquisition, rail travel, any travel not on foot, the Mexican-American War, expansionism, government, professors, people in groups, taxes used for any purpose not on his agenda, most taxes no matter the purpose, being what is generally called a productive member of society, received wisdom, owning things. One can hardly imagine what he would have made of Facebook or Twitter or the objects that make them possible. On the other hand, he was for quite a few things, too: solitude, fresh air, walking, sustainable living, help from friends and family, close observation of the world, irony, frugality, living by one's own values, sheer cussedness. Many of those positions are laudable, others debatable. Such a list makes for difficult friendships but interesting reading. That's okay; we're limiting our acquaintance to a book.

That book is unlike almost any other you'll meet in a day's walk. It is divided into eighteen sections, or chapters, with titles like "Economy," "Where I Lived, and What I Lived For," "Reading," "Solitude," "The Bean-Field," and "The Pond in Winter." While he does include a conclusion, there is no introduction as such. Rather, he simply launches right into what he wants to talk about. Even the famous quotation that seems so natural as a lead-in to the work is nowhere near the beginning. "I went to the woods because I wished to live deliberately, to front only the essential facts of life, and see if I could not learn what it had to teach, and not, when I came to die, discover that I had not lived." So he tells us, but not until the end of the second chapter. The abruptness of the opening should serve as fair warning to readers expecting a more conventional structure: there will be nothing conventional about this book. Thoreau picks up a topic, holds it up to the light—or rather *his* light, which is not always the same thing—examines it until he makes a point about it or something else or until he gets bored, and then drops it. The next point, picked up just as randomly, may or may not have anything to do with the one just dispensed with. The effect is less chaotic than one might suppose, largely because he is so amusing, so profound, so ornery, sometimes all at once. Moreover, the seeming randomness actually masks a fair degree of consistency, since Thoreau's free association typically moves from like to like, one practice or observation leading him to a related topic.

Besides, there is such pleasure in his pronouncements. Thoreau may not be much for narrative structure, but his aphorisms often rise to a kind of poetry:

The mass of men lead lives of quiet desperation.

There is no odor so bad as that which arises from goodness tainted. It is human, it is divine, carrion.

I never found a companion so companionable as solitude.

That last one typifies Thoreauvian cleverness. It relies on the repetition of a noun in its adjectival form (companion . . . companionable) yoked to its opposite (solitude). By the time readers have traveled seventy or eighty pages, they will know the pattern. Even so, his epigrams rarely fail to delight, largely because they contain both predictability and surprise. We may feel, simultaneously, that he has taken us to somewhere predictable and astonishing. There is something of the Zen koan to many of his pronouncements. And indeed, he is a mix of hardheaded Yankee pragmatist and Eastern mystic. Many of his sayings about simplicity, about being owned by the things we think we own, about the debilitating effects of pride or acquisitiveness or desire, would fit nicely into a Buddhist sermon, and a few of them sound suspiciously like they came from the Buddha's Fire Sermon itself. Taken together, they strongly resemble the Buddhist insistence on harmony between the soul and the universe.

He says things, moreover, that *feel* so true. Yes, humans do live lives of quiet desperation—why didn't I see that before. Of course—mere evil is less troubling than goodness tainted. Yes, yes—we do know the flavor of ambrosia:

And pray what more can a reasonable man desire, in peaceful times, in ordinary noons, than a sufficient number of ears of green sweet-corn, with the addition of salt? Even the little variety I used was yielding to the demands of appetite, and not of health. Yet men have come to such a pass that they frequently starve, not for want of nec-

*essaries, but for want of luxuries; and I know a good woman who
thinks that her son lost his life because he took to drinking water
only.*

What more indeed? That's such an American statement; it's our
crop, something we adapted to very quickly upon meeting it, so much
so that just a couple of centuries on, Thoreau can extol the virtues of
this native food to make his point. Would a European ever think of a
lunch of nothing more but sweet corn, boiled and salted? Very doubtful. But at least one American can, and others will readily assent, even
if they've never had such an exclusive menu. And, of course, in his
thrifty Yankee way, he's absolutely right. We *can* live simply, eat simply,
think simply, if we so choose. Our insistence on complexity and profusion is nothing more than vanity run amok.

Sometimes, then, Thoreau offers insight and wisdom. Other times,
he's just being spiky:

*Shams and delusions are esteemed for soundest truths, while real-
ity is fabulous. If men would steadily observe realities only, and not
allow themselves to be deluded, life, to compare it with such things
as we know, would be like a fairy tale and the Arabian Nights' En-
tertainments.*

We can excuse him in part by calling him a prophet, a visionary.
Still, there's something slightly obnoxious about a person who claims
to be alone in seeing the truth that eludes everyone else. On the other
hand, that jeremiad strain is partly responsible for our being here, our
being who we are, and our being so obstreperous. From the Puritans
forward, one group or another has always had a lock on Truth. They
came with complete confidence in their vision. When someone else's,

Roger Williams's, say, did not comport with theirs, out he went, both sides certain of the apostasy of the other.

But even his difficulty can have roses as well as thorns:

New England can hire all the wise men in the world to come and teach her, and board them round the while, and not be provincial at all. That is the uncommon school we want. Instead of noblemen, let us have noble villages of men. If it is necessary, omit one bridge over the river and go round a little there, and throw one arch at least over the darker gulf of ignorance which surrounds us.

In many ways, this is the crux of his argument. His experiment in solitary living is not owing to a sense of exceptionalism but rather the reverse. We are not a nation, he says—accepting that New English is a nationality—of nobility and royalty. To the contrary, we are a nation in which every man is a peer of the realm. A great deal of his rhetoric about his own situation certainly suggests that he is master of all he surveys despite not owning the land on which the cabin sits. His larger point, however, is that greatness comes not from the status of a few individuals but from the advancement of the mass of people. "Noble villages of men" is simply great phrasemaking. It is also an ideal toward which we can aspire. Why should we not have noble villages in which men—and women, since his language needs updating—are brought into contact with the best that has been thought? How can we not be better off when wisdom is brought to the entire community? You can make the argument that this passage argues for public universities and the Land Grant Act if you like, but I don't think Thoreau has anything so institutional in mind. He hardly ever has institutions in mind, at least in a positive way. But we can see in it the insistence that the individual is the key to society. Improve citizens and you improve the nation. He comes at things from a rather different standpoint from Franklin, but his belief in the perfectibility of humans is equally unshakable. We can be better; we should be better; we need to be better. This famous solitary, then, is really a social animal.

The nineteenth and early twentieth centuries were a great time for hermits generally. Many communities had one, some old fellow who only came into town once a year for provisions and confirmation that avoiding his fellows was the right path. Curiously, such men—and they were almost always men—became sources of something like civic pride. Near where my parents grew up in southern Ohio there had been a locally famous one, William Hewitt, known by one and all as Hewitt the Hermit, and although he had died almost a century before my father was born, we never passed by the hamlet of Alma on U.S. 23 without his remarking that "Hewitt's cave was right up there somewhere" and pointing vaguely up the hillside. I mention this because, based on *Walden*, Thoreau is often lumped in with the mountain men and cantankerous characters of American lore. Attractive, perhaps, but the suit won't fit. Thoreau was a perfectly sociable, gregarious soul. During his "wilderness" biennial, he made frequent, sometimes even daily, trips to town and entertained guests with equal regularity. The Emersons, who owned the land on which Henry built his cabin, came to see him often. His mother baked bread and goodies for him each Saturday. The simplicity of hoecakes is easier to appreciate without the prospect of their being one's only baked goods. Sometimes, a nice salt-rising loaf can be a great comfort.

The regularity of his contact with civilization points out one of the great errors in our thinking: Walden Woods was no wilderness. It was, by all accounts, a second-growth forest, meaning that earlier settlers had logged it over. It lay, moreover, a scant mile and a half from the village of Concord and was within sight of both road and this new innovation, rail. Getting to the pond, or away from it, was no great undertaking. I mention this not to demean the larger undertaking but to offer some perspective. One sometimes sees the project dismissed as some sort of kid's camping trip to the backyard, and while there may have been an element of that in Thoreau's adventure, such comments miss the mark. Any fool can hide himself away in a wilderness—or at least could have a century and a half ago. Now, doing so and getting the book done and getting safely back, that would have been a different story, but none of it is our story. What Thoreau accomplished in moving to the woods was to strip "modern" life of its accoutrements and frills and get back to first principles. He wants to see if he can live without the things town folk have come to regard as essential to the experience of existence, to leave behind the labor-saving appliances and the parlor pianos and anything else not absolutely essential. Put into today's terms, he wants to abjure the cell phones and laptops and plasma televisions and get by with just the necessities. If one of those necessities is a walk to town every day or two, so be it.

And that, it seems to me, is Thoreau's real contribution to the American dialogue. We of European descent fell out of a crowded and degraded space into something empty and fresh and new. Nothing but *nature* in every direction. And we were horrified. From the moment the first boot cleared the first gunwale and sank its heel into the wet sand, we had two reactions to all of this bounty: it is the enemy, and we must rip it apart for gain. Sometimes one or the other impulse prevailed, but on the whole, resourceful, clever souls that we were, we could manage both thoughts simultaneously. The Puritans were convinced that, not only was Satan out there in the wilderness cavorting with "savages," but in some sense the wilderness *was* Satan, or a very precise analog thereunto. Nothing untamed could ever be holy. And in some senses we have never recovered from that view. No forest that should not fall to the ax, no prairie that didn't yearn for the plow. We measure our success acreage tilled and board-feet milled, mirror divine order with row crops and plat maps. But always, a few other voices have offered a countering view, Thoreau's among the first. Wait a minute, they say, have you tried meeting nature on its own terms? Actually *looked* at it? Smelled it? Listened to its racket—and its silence?

This is the great contribution of *Walden*, the plea to be quiet just for a little bit, to step out of the pencil factory and observe the woods and the pond, to observe ourselves in that environment and contemplate the changes in us when removed, if only for a little while, from our accustomed haunts. It doesn't suggest that we should all move to the forests, doesn't even suggest that its author should or ever intended to. This is, after all, the guy who managed to burn down three hundred or so acres of the Concord forest just a year before he repaired to the shores of the pond, who never even felt much guilt about it, reckoning that he did little more damage than a well-placed lightning strike might have and that in any case woodlands grow back if left to their own devices. Unlike the lightning, he could have known that using a tree stump for a brazier during a dry spring is a bad idea, but that seems not to have troubled him. Clearly, he's not speaking as a strict preservationist.

Rather, his words lead us to other conclusions about the interaction of human and natural, and maybe about human nature itself:

Not even rats in the walls, for they were starved out, or rather were never baited in,—only squirrels on the roof and under the floor, a whippoorwill on the ridge pole, a blue-jay screaming beneath the window, a hare or woodchuck under the house, a screech-owl or a cat-owl behind it, a flock of wild geese or a laughing loon on the pond, and a fox to bark in the night. Not even a lark or oriole, those mild plantation birds, ever visited my clearing. No cockerels to crow

nor hens to cackle in the yard. No yard! but unfenced Nature reach-
ing up to the sills. A young forest growing up under your windows,
and wild sumachs and blackberry vines breaking through into your
cellar; sturdy pitch-pines rubbing and creaking against the shingles
for want of room, their roots reaching quite under the house.

This is great stuff. He divides the world into the wild and the tamed
and rather archly includes rats among the latter as requiring human
activity to generate any enthusiasm for a habitation. Anyone who has
ever kept a corncrib knows what he's talking about. We might object
that larks and orioles get short shrift from this dichotomy, but he's
really thinking about fields versus woodlands and the way the forest
is reclaiming its own in its assault on the clearing. He is also tacitly
identifying with the woods. The spirit, he suggests, is a forest, inclined
toward wildness and most at home, if we only pay attention, in its native environment. For Thoreau, we've allowed ourselves to become too
domesticated, too tamed, too removed from essential nature. And that
can't be good, can it?

Part of that is his resistance to the Industrial Revolution. He is very
hard on technological innovation that merely makes us greater slaves to
an economy external to ourselves, the chief emblem of which, for him,
is the railroad. Through some tortured math he works out that he can
walk somewhere not only cheaper but quicker than if he went by train,
since the train ticket causes him to have to work longer than the time
it would save over walking. A skeptic might ask if he doesn't cook the
books by lowballing the wages he could expect to earn, but we'll leave
that for now. His argument is not entirely against machinery, although
there is little enough evidence that he is in favor. If you seek a debate,
walk into a roomful of Thoreau readers and drop the word "Luddite."
Everyone has an opinion on whether he was a knee-jerk opponent of

technology, but those opinions rarely agree. I think his chief complaint has to do with noise. The newly industrialized world drowns out the silence needed for contemplation, which for him is the key to living. To do things mindfully—I'm not sure he actually employs the term, but the concept is everywhere—the individual requires space and silence, two commodities in notably short supply in a world determined to make more and more commodities. On this point he is pretty clear, even invoking Izaak Walton:

> I grew in those seasons like corn in the night, and they were so much better than any work of the hands would have been. They were not time subtracted from my life, but so much over and above my usual allowance.

Walton extols the hours spent fishing, which "the gods do not deduct from man's allotted span," precisely because the stillness they afford do not weigh on the spirit—or stress the heart, in modern parlance. Fishing for him is largely a contemplative activity. So too for Thoreau the seasons at the pond, where he emulates not lilies of the field but corn in the night. Not above wetting a line himself, he recognizes the value of contemplation, of meditation, of silence and slow time, all of which he finds at Walden.

His ideas are not original to him, but no one had expressed quite so many of them in a secular way before him. His sources are wide-ranging, from ancient Greeks to Eastern religion to contemporary social thinkers. And his followers are legion. Of them, some may not have met with his approval. His legacy has been more abused and misrepresented than almost any other public figure (again, secular), with the possible exceptions of Karl Marx and Che Guevara. One can only ask, again citing Yeats, "was there ever dog that praised his fleas?" At the same time, he has been enormously influential where it matters. Gandhi and Martin Luther King Jr. have drawn strength from his writings, chiefly "Essay on Civil Disobedience," but *Walden* as well. All sorts of people have taken his message of simple living to heart and sought to unclutter their lives. Those dubious about the benefits of modernity have found a champion; it is fair to say that *The Education of Henry Adams*, and particularly its famous chapter, "The Virgin and the Dynamo," with its sense of modern life spinning ever faster and hopelessly beyond our control, could not have taken the shape it did without Thoreau's sanctioning text. Misguided or otherwise, a thousand back-to-the-land movements got their start in the pages of *Walden*. I for one am not willing to blame him for Woodstock, but he was there, not that he would have liked the noise or anything else about it.

In the final analysis, however, none of that is what makes him important for us now as he was then. The message we really need is not about anything external but about finding that space around us and within to embrace silence, not to find but to be that still point in the turning world. He discovered a place where he could encounter the universe and his own existence without the interfering hands and prying eyes and loud voices of others, a place like prayer where the spirit can grow like corn in the night. So may we all.

FIVE

I'VE BEEN WORKIN' ON THE WHALE-ROAD
Moby-Dick

Three words. That's all it takes. A tiny sentence and already we know what we're in for. For these aren't just any triplets but the most famous opening statement in American literature. They've been the subject of innumerable parodies, perhaps most famously by the comic novelist Peter de Vries, who causes mayhem with the mere insertion of a comma, thereby changing everything. Other openings have accomplished as much with as little. One recalls "Marley was dead," but that clause then has a semicolon and three more words, and in any case has the disadvantage, from our point of view, of being English. So here's the problem with such a short burst at the start. With three words, it is difficult for most of us to accomplish anything beyond a simple statement. Hard to accomplish mystery or innuendo or nuance: It was hot; I was tired; oh, not now. See the problem. And this sentence is the more remarkable for beginning a book in which almost no other sentences of such brevity dare show their faces. A lesser artist might begin with the second three words, "Some years ago," followed by an insertion in dashes and a compound subordinate clause. But a real genius would—and did—start out like this: "Call me Ishmael."

And just like that, we have ourselves a mystery. And a theme. Good work if you can get it. Why "Call me"? Why not simply say, "I am Ishmael." A suspicious mind—and there are some of those in the vicinity—might wonder if this "Ishmael" is hiding something. Ishmael is the bastard son of Abraham by Hagar, ultimately cast into exile by his father at the instigation of Sarah, Abraham's wife. The possibilities of the naming strategy, never pursued in the novel, abound.

Aside from slaughtering bison (and natives) and cutting down forests, there is no activity more typically American for a nineteenth-century narrative to explore than whaling. Before the advent of petroleum derivatives for oiling machinery, whale oil lubricated the Industrial Revolution. Rivers may have driven the machinery, but whales kept it from breaking down. Whale oil and other products also figured in lighting lamps, setting perfume scents, waterproofing leather, making soaps and crayons and even margarine and almost everything that today we do with any sort of oil. That oil, by and large, was gathered by the American whaling fleet, which in the middle of the nineteenth century was the largest in the world, making the island of Nantucket the center of the whaling universe. Whaling is one of the most preposterous activities in which humans ever engaged. Consider: men attacking the vastness of the ocean in relatively small ships powered by wind, then lowering themselves into even smaller boats in an attempt to affix themselves by means of oversized darts to the largest creatures ever to inhabit land or sea, and expecting to get away with it. Mostly, they did. A few of them became very wealthy. Small wonder, then, that in 1851 a book would appear first in Britain with the nondescript title: *The Whale*, which would become the subtitle in America for a work much more widely known: *Moby-Dick*. Less prosaic, more enigmatic as titles go. Like its subject, this work is vast, overly ambitious, audacious, appalling. Unlike that subject, it is brilliant, satiric, sensitive, philosophical. That title is the name of the creature in question, a white sperm whale, the name adapted from a real-life whale of noted ferocity called Mocha Dick. There is only one *Moby-Dick*, though; accept no substitute.

Never, I daresay, has a longer and more complicated narrative had a simpler plot. The story line of *Moby-Dick* is simplicity itself: it's a revenge tragedy. On the previous voyage the monstrous albino sperm whale of the title took off the leg of Captain Ahab. Now, although he is ostensibly in charge of a three-year whaling voyage, there is only one whale that interests him. His monomania dooms him and the entire expedition. Everywhere he goes he seeks signs of Moby-Dick, and he is particularly interested in stories from anyone else who has encountered this demon of the deep. Of course, the novel climaxes with the fatal encounter, in which he throws the harpoon that latches onto the whale, only to be garroted by a loop in the rope and swept overboard. The whale destroys the whaler, the *Pequod*, and the chase boats, causing the death of all hands except Ishmael, providentially saved to tell the tale by his best friend's coffin. Simplicity itself.

Except that, as we all know, plots aren't novels. There is so much going on beyond the story line that one barely knows where to begin. In the first place, this is not Ahab's story and not the whale's. It is Ishmael's. Indeed, Ahab is only occasionally onstage, although he commands everyone's attention when he is. The story that Ishmael chooses to tell, moreover, concerns itself with almost everything about whaling, of which the story of Ahab is but one element. When we first meet Ahab, we deduce from his encounter with Stubb, the second mate, that not only may he be mad but that he may provoke madness in others. This encounter is followed by a lengthy chapter, "Cetology," on the natural history of the whale, or perhaps the failures of natural historians to invent an appropriate taxonomy of whales. Along with depictions of nearly every member of the crew, Ishmael gives us far more about all aspects of whaling than we ever hoped to know. Want instructions on throwing a harpoon or butchering a whale? No problem. Rendering out the oil? That's in the chapter called "The Try-Works." A rumination on whiteness, especially as it applies to this albino whale. Got that, too. And along with all this science and procedure, he tells us about loyalties and rivalries, friendships and resentments, and personal interactions of all kinds aboard ship. Many of those chapters do nothing to advance the plot, but they are invaluable in advancing the novel.

That split was most likely the source of the confusion among early reviewers of the book. In 1851 as now, reviewers often launch into a book with preconceived ideas. In this case, many had been fans of his simpler adventure stories, *Omoo* and *Typee*, and they were ready for more of the same. They did not, alas, get it, and disappointed reviewers can be ruthless. Many were simply flummoxed by a book that was considerably bigger than they were, and the reviews often reflected their confusion rather than his. The *London Morning Chronicle* called it "sheerest moonstruck lunacy," which seems a trifle redundant, but they didn't want to be misunderstood. The *London Literary Gazette* used the words "purposeless" and "rambling," evidently unaware that one can ramble to a purpose. Charges of madness also came the author's way from South Carolina and Tennessee. To be sure, a number of perceptive reviewers on both sides of the Atlantic understood what he had achieved, among them the newspaperman Horace Greeley and George Ripley in *Harper's Magazine* and William A. Butler in the *Washington National Intelligencer*, who caught the genius of the piece. To be fair to the English, some of their reviewers also noticed, as with the *Illustrated*

London News: "Herman Melville's last and best and most wildly imaginative story, *The Whale* . . . will worthily support his reputation for singularly vivid and reckless imaginative power—great aptitude for quaint and original philosophical speculation, degenerating, however, too often into rhapsody and purposeless extravagance—an almost unparalleled power over the capabilities of the language." Still, the positive reviews were lost in the mass of negatives, and in any case, nothing could save the book from word of mouth. Although *Moby-Dick* sold fifteen hundred copies in just two weeks, it failed to manage five hundred more in the next ten; the great hope was a flop. The problem with being ahead of your time, we see, is that your time will not reward you.

No one seems to be able to categorize *Moby-Dick* without qualifications and hedges: well, it's this, you see, but some of that, not quite A, but certainly not B, and so on. And there's a perfectly good reason: it refuses to hold still. There are long books, short books, difficult books, easy books, but most books fit comfortably into their category. This novel falls into that rare class of fiction that is, as the cycling world calls some mountains, HC—*hors catégorie*, or beyond classification. In cycling, it means that the numbers by which climbs are ranked, 1 through 5, simply can't account for inclines beyond a certain point. They're not straight vertical; they just feel like it if you're on two wheels. In novels, it would suggest that the book doesn't play by the expected rules, that it doesn't follow the conventions of its type. *Ulysses* would be perhaps the premier example of the sort, and we could throw in Laurence Sterne's *Tristram Shandy* and a few by John Fowles and Italo Calvino and Vladimir Nabokov. They're often called "experimental," which on some level they are, but more than anything such books merely follow their own lights. A conventional book, for instance, gives readers a consistent flow of plot data: chapter two builds on chapter one, three on two, four on three, and so on, until such time as everything is revealed.

Moby-Dick, on the other hand, throws us around from one chapter to the next. Things don't come quite when we're expecting them, and one chapter may, as in the case of "Cetology," in no discernible way build on the one previous.

For an illustration of the problem, we have only to look at the appearance of the star attraction. No, not the whale. Ahab. Rarely has a character been the cause of so much speculation, discussion, strong emotion, and tale-telling for so long without making an entrance than Captain Ahab. He comes clumping onto the quarterdeck in Chapter 28 (of 135!). By page count, that's about a quarter to a fifth of the way into the book. By event, Ishmael has managed to get to New Bedford and thence to Nantucket, find a boarding house, begin his friendship with Queequeg, sign on with the *Pequod*, ship out, and settle into the shipboard routine. The ship has sailed for several days before Ahab steps out of his cabin and into the narrative.

Later, in Chapter 36, Ahab summons the entire crew for a bizarre occasion that is often called his Black Mass. It's part medieval knight ritual, part communion of blood as the harpooners drink wine from the "cups" of their harpoon blades that normally receive the shafts of the implements, and part insane pep talk as he nails a doubloon to the mast as a reward for spotting Moby-Dick and whips the crew into a frenzy—his frenzy—to abandon the hunt for the most whales and the greatest profits in favor of hunting down one very particular whale. It is one of the most astonishingly primal scenes you will ever read, and it is followed by three very short chapters in which first Ahab and then Starbuck and Stubb, the first and second mates, produce monologues that sometimes echo Shakespearean soliloquys and in other ways anticipate Faulknerian stream of consciousness. These performances are followed by a sort of expressionist Chapter 40, "Midnight, Forecastle," which appears less like fiction from the nineteenth century than a late Strindberg play or a lost passage from the Circe episode of Joyce's *Ulysses*. Then we get the chapter describing Moby-Dick himself, although no sighting of him takes place. The doubloon, which Ahab values at sixteen dollars, gets its own chapter, but not for another sixty-three. Loose, yes. Experimental, yes. Erratic, borderline. Yet that wild careering from narrative to background to psychological projection to dramatic form to interior monologue is precisely, if anything about this novel can be called precise, where its appeal lies. And its threat, of course. Generations of students have wished, wish, and will wish that it were shorter, easier, more direct. Certainly it is not a book that reads pleasurably on a short deadline. But it is a book full of reading pleasures, not merely an adventure to be read, but a *reading* adventure. It is big, sprawling, brilliant, occasionally chaotic, impassioned, violent, generous, tragic, mirthful, so various that it cannot be pinned down. Sound like anyplace you know?

The novel is sometimes called an epic, which appellation is almost always quickly withdrawn or qualified into nonexistence: it isn't really an epic, or it lacks the military scale, or it is more nuanced than an epic. I would contend, however, that it *is* an epic, that there is one model it resembles more than any other, and finally that its model has no armies, or at least none that were ever commanded by generals. *Moby-Dick* is *Paradise Lost* minus God. No writer born in America who was not actually a Puritan has a more Miltonian conception of existence than Herman Melville. In his world, good battles evil, but the existence of divine poles anchoring those forces is an unresolved issue. He asks the questions about conduct and being and meaning that will be taken up a century later by existentialism, but he does so in a particularly American romantic way, a sort of Emerson-meets-Camus nexus of thought and action. I'm pretty sure no one ever described Milton that way. Where he most resembles Milton, however, is in tackling the big questions of life and death, of good and evil, with an eye toward the spiritual component of humanity. And in his choice of fallen angel. The English romantics were very fond of claiming that Satan is the real hero of *Paradise Lost*; it's an extravagant claim but one not without merit. He is the most interesting figure, certainly, and very likely the one without whom the entire enterprise collapses. Adam and Eve and God and the archangels possess none of Satan's living qualities as a character. He's like many of Shakespeare's villains in that his evil imbues him with qualities that make him fascinating to the audience. He is Iago, Macbeth, Richard III, Claudius all rolled into one. So is Ahab. To call him, as Ishmael does at various points, mad, insane, monomaniacal, possessed of a single thought, hate-filled, vengeance-seeking, or obsessed is not to be incorrect but to miss much of the animating quality of the character. His particular evil is interesting because it is so very human, his failings, like Satan's, stemming from overreaching toward divinity.

At the heart of Ahab's struggle is the encounter with nothingness. When Moby Dick took off his leg on the previous voyage, he stole more than just a limb. As the whale was streaking away with the boat in tow, Ahab leapt toward him with a knife, not aiming to cut the line and save himself and his crew but to stab a creature completely beyond the reach of such a weapon. In the wake of the injury, Ahab withdrew into himself, forced to confront the reality of nonbeing. Now, his version of that encounter and what it stands for is a sort of cracked Platonism:

> "All visible objects, man, are but as pasteboard masks. But in each event—in the living act, the undoubted deed—there, some unknown but still reasoning thing puts forth the mouldings of its features from behind the unreasoning mask. If man will strike, strike through the mask! . . . To me, the white whale is the wall, shoved near to me. Sometimes I think there's naught beyond. But 'tis enough . . ."

Does he hope to destroy the great negation by striking through the whale? Does he think the universe—or possibly its maker, if any—mocks him? Does he merely invent a rationale for blind rage and desire for revenge? Perhaps some of each, perhaps other motives impinge. There can be no doubt, however, that for Ahab the encounter with the white whale is as much symbolic as literal: the whale *must* stand for something beyond itself, else the struggle is merely animalistic and meaningless. It takes some gall to see one's struggle being with God or the universe. Ahab has gall aplenty.

When dealing with Ahab, the issues of the text are highly theological; his struggles seem to have to do with finding either God (or his absence) or else with supplanting him, Satan's *non serviam* working as well for Ahab. In many other regards, however, the narrative is resolutely humanist. It is sometimes said these days of, say, a president's cabinet, that "it looks like America." We could say that of the *Pequod*, but it would be damning with faint praise. The crew of Ahab's ship looks like the world—if the world is more peculiar even than we think. The officers look greatly like coastal Massachusetts, which Ishmael acknowledges is the standard in an industry where American captains and mates rule over foreign crews. Ahab is Nantucket Quaker, although his bloodlust would be largely unrecognizable to the vast majority of the Society of Friends. First Mate Starbuck is also a Nantucketer, Second Mate Stubb from Cape Cod, and Third Mate Flask from Martha's Vineyard. Well, where else would one suppose whalers come from? Where else, indeed. The harpooners are from every nonwhite place Melville could think of. Ishmael's pal Queequeg is a South Sea Islander; that he is a cannibal ceases very early on to cause the narrator any concern. Tashtego is a Wampanoag native from Gay Head, on Martha's Vineyard. Daggoo is a giant from some unnamed African coast. And then there is Fedallah, Ahab's personal harpooner. He is Persian, possibly with considerable time spent living in China, and he dresses all in black, which contrasts with his gleaming white "turban" made of his own hair wound round and round his head. He yields to no man in strangeness. The rest of the crew of Ahab's boat are "tiger-yellow natives" of the Philippines. With them, Fedallah has been stowed out of view for many days until the first whales are sighted. When they do materialize, during the confusion of the first lowering of the boats, their appearance has roughly the same effect on the main crew as Tolkien's Ringwraiths. Nor does time make them more familiar. Fedallah is seen by various characters as a— or even *the*—devil in disguise; he seems something more like Ahab's shadow-self, his Dark Other; although in the case of our captain, his quotidian self is abundantly dark. Whale ships were noted in their time for being eclectic and surprisingly egalitarian places where men advanced on merit. Even so, the *Pequod* is a corker.

The colorful cast of characters is one of the chief pleasures of the novel. Another, often lost on the hapless seventeen- or twenty-one-year-old trying to finish the blasted thing by next Friday, is the language. Remember those three opening words? Melville is frequently happiest when using rather more, as in this passage from the chapter called "The Whiteness of the Whale":

> Though in many natural objects, whiteness refiningly enhances beauty, as if imparting some special virtue of its own, as in marbles, japonicas, and pearls; and though various nations have in some way recognised a certain royal pre-eminence in this hue; even the barbaric, grand old kings of Pegu placing the title "Lord of the White Elephants" above all their other magniloquent ascriptions of dominion; and the modern kings of Siam unfurling the same snow-white quadruped in the royal standard; and the Hanoverian flag bearing the one figure of a snow-white charger; and the great Austrian Empire,

Caesarian, heir to overlording Rome, having for the imperial color the same imperial hue; and though this pre-eminence in it applies to the human race itself, giving the white man ideal mastership over every dusky tribe; and though, besides all this, whiteness has been even made significant of gladness, for among the Romans a white stone marked a joyful day; and though in other mortal sympathies and symbolizings, this same hue is made the emblem of many touching, noble things—the innocence of brides, the benignity of age; though among the Red Men of America the giving of the white belt of wampum was the deepest pledge of honor; though in many climes, whiteness typifies the majesty of Justice in the ermine of the Judge, and contributes to the daily state of kings and queens drawn by milk-white steeds; though even in the higher mysteries of the most august religions it has been made the symbol of the divine spotlessness and power; by the Persian fire worshippers, the white forked flame being held the holiest on the altar; and in the Greek mythologies, Great Jove himself made incarnate in a snow-white bull; and though to the noble Iroquois, the midwinter sacrifice of the sacred White Dog was by far the holiest festival of their theology, that spotless, faithful creature being held the purest envoy they could send to the Great Spirit with the annual tidings of their own fidelity; and though directly from the Latin word for white, all Christian priests derive the name of one part of their sacred vesture, the alb or tunic, worn beneath the cassock; and though among the holy pomps of the Romish faith, white is specially employed in the celebration of the Passion of our Lord; though in the Vision of St. John, white robes are given to the redeemed, and the four-and-twenty elders stand clothed in white before the great white throne, and the Holy One that sitteth there white like wool; yet for all these accumulated associations, with whatever is sweet, and honorable, and sublime, there yet lurks

an elusive something in the innermost idea of this hue, which strikes
more of panic to the soul than that redness which affrights in blood.

That bit of color meditation runs 469 words, of which the main clause comprises only the final 28. I would apologize for the length if the passage weren't so darned wonderful. Besides, there's really no way to get the sense of just what Melville is capable of without total immersion. If you think it is easy to accomplish all that in a single sentence that holds together, I urge you to try it sometime. Just don't expect us to sit here waiting on you to finish. It is what book reviewers are wont to call "a bravura performance" or "a tour de force," which it certainly is. That sentence, seemingly, has *everything*. It packs in religion, history, anthropology, superstition, aesthetics, semiotics, and most of all humor. But it's more than just jam-packed: it's beautiful. The lists alone—"marbles, japonicas, and pearls" for instance, or Pegu, Siam, Austria, Rome, Greece, the Iroquois—are worth the price of admission. The structure, the way in which he keeps adding long, involved items, each striving to be more exotic than the last, but always hearkens back to the main intent, is astonishing. You can almost hear old Herman laughing as he wrote it, crying out, "Look what I can do." At least, that's what I would be saying were I capable of such a sentence. Modesty was never my long suit.

All bad things, like all good, must come to an end, and Ahab's obsession, along with the demented hunt it inspires, reaches its finale in a cataclysmic encounter in which the White Whale smashes the *Pequod* and its boats, all being sucked down into the vortex created by the dying ship except Ishmael in Queequeg's coffin. When Melville is finished digressing, he really knows how to get down to business. The ending of the novel is one of the great action sequences in all literature. At the same time, there's very little mystery; this quest has been doomed from the outset. That much was foretold by a prophet named Elijah while Ishmael was still ashore.

In Ahab's tragedy there is something of an American cautionary tale. Like his friend Hawthorne, his dark romanticism remains suspicious of both the pursuit of knowledge and manias religious and otherwise. The novel itself, or at least Ishmael's narrative, seems intent on knowing everything about the whale and whaling, yet no amount of knowledge can forestall the calamity that befalls the ship. The forces of the ocean remain beyond the reach of human understanding, just as Moby Dick remains beyond the power of Ahab. There is no striking through this mask; the whale is too big, too powerful, too unknowable. Whether he is a symbol of some greater mystery or a vast mystery in himself, he is immune in the face of mere human efforts. Nor can Ahab solve the larger mystery he attempts to chase down: life and death, being and nothingness, divine Presence and Absence—whatever coloring we may place on his larger obsession—cannot be mastered by will, however insatiable. The effort is as hopeless as attacking a whale with a belt knife. Ahab's pursuit of something that much larger than himself, his overreaching toward the godly, may well remind readers of certain other endeavors in Melville's still-new country. Manifest Destiny, like the earlier City on the Hill, cannot be pursued without courting disaster of body and soul. The costs are bound to be high. There have always been, since the first ship landed on the shore of the New World, leaders absolutely convinced of the rightness of their vision and willing to drive their followers to perdition to achieve it. As Ishmael says of Queequeg's daylong "Ramadan," "we are all somehow dreadfully cracked about the head, and sadly need mending." Not only may visionaries and madmen be difficult to tell apart, but their impacts may be identical.

Melville is America's patron saint of complex and even mad narrative. Faulkner praised him extravagantly, and I'm sure he meant it.

But from him to Thomas Wolfe and Robert Penn Warren to Thomas Pynchon and Tom Robbins to Don DeLillo and Jane Smiley and Toni Morrison to Jonathan Franzen and Louise Erdrich, there is a thread of writers unafraid to go too far, willing to embrace extravagance. That would explain the kinship claimed by Salman Rushdie, by no means American but certainly in the spirit of Melville. A few, not many, novels have tackled the book directly. Most notable on that list is Sena Jeter Naslund's prizewinning *Ahab's Wife*. But direct influence is only one measure of a book's impact. Even those with no overt connection may owe it a debt, as in the case of Derek Walcott's epic poem *Omeros*. And although he claims to be influenced by no writer—suggesting strongly that "influence" is a word we might well retire from literary discussions, Peter Matthiessen wrote the twentieth century's most Melvillean novel, his underappreciated *Far Tortuga*. Of course, being underappreciated is also a trait inherited from Melville. Pynchon, who mentions the sea but rarely, writes his *Moby-Dick* again and again, with no novel Mobier than *Gravity's Rainbow*. He even out-Melvilles Melville in digressions. Oh, and that de Vries parody-with-pause? It's from his 1967 novel with a title that could have been appended to almost all his novels, *The Vale of Laughter*: "Call me, Ishmael." Be careful with punctuation.

SIX

THE GOOD GRAY POET, MY EYE!
Leaves of Grass

There's no written rule anywhere that I know of stating this, no First-teenth Amendment to the Literary Constitution, but there might as well be: you get *one* national poet. And you don't get a lot of say in the matter, which was probably settled well before you came along. The process is a lot like national dishes or drinks. If you're a Scot, it matters not a whit if you like Robert Burns or how you feel about haggis; he's your guy, just as it's your dish even if you canna stand the stuff. Happily, "Auld Lang Syne" or "Comin' Thro the Rye" goes down rather easier than sheep's lungs and oatmeal soaked in whisky and stuffed in a sheep's stomach. And no matter how much I might wish, for personal and professional reasons, that Seamus Heaney were the national poet of Ireland or how much traditionalists might plump for O'Carolan or Thomas Moore, none of them is, or will be, the go-to guy as long as William Butler Yeats remains in the public record. It doesn't matter if one has read him or not; he's in the water, in the air, in the quoted lines that brush past one's ears ten times a day. "The Lake Isle of Innisfree," "Easter

1916," "Among School Children," and "Under Ben Bulben" are part of the fabric of the existence of individual and country alike. He's too big to ignore. He's more than the standard by which other poets are measured; he's the figure with whom they must wrestle, whose echoes flit around every page of verse of every Irish poem.

That wrestling is a key component of being a national poet, that quality of being so infused into the cultural and literary life of the country that no one can set pen to paper (or finger to keyboard or touchscreen, perhaps) without butting heads with you. Subsequent writers may not wish to be of your camp, may not even like you, may wish to throw you over—it doesn't matter. What does matter is that they have to deal with you, go through or over or around you, to get where they're wishing to go. Yeats, for instance, can be a suffocating influence, one to be escaped or rejected; no one else can be Yeats, and one cannot be *like* him without falling into lame imitation or parody. No, the only way to deal with such a presence is to take him on directly, to go *through* him and come out the other side, new metal forged in the heat of the encounter.

Which brings us to the shaggy, bardic, yawping presence brooding like Milton's God over the brink of all subsequent American poetic creation. No, not Bob Dylan, although he might never have existed in the form he took without this singular example, just as all modern poetry would look different without this line, "I celebrate myself and sing myself." There would be an American poetry without Walt Whitman's *Leaves of Grass*. It simply wouldn't be the one we have. Or nearly as interesting. Some poets have followed his example, heading down roads toward which he only points. Others have chafed against him, finding even that the clothing of complete freedom can be a straitjacket. Maybe it's because he's always getting naked in the poetry. Whitman only wrote one poem in his lifetime, and only needed one: it contains everything. He first published it in 1855, when he was thirty-six years old, although one of the more famous lines gives his age at thirty-seven. He added, emended and amended, deleted, altered, reshaped, changed, reinforced, moved and removed pieces for the remainder of his life, but it always remained the one poem, responding to the events of the time, calling forth a spirit of a nation and the soul of a single man, claiming authority from the *demos*, the people of the (lower-case) book.

Still, it's easy to oversell the democratic nature of the book, since his is a *demos* with a difference. His "people," even his "you" is a projection of his "I," as in the properly famous opening of "Song of Myself," the first line of which I quoted earlier:

> I CELEBRATE myself, and sing myself,
> And what I assume you shall assume,
> For every atom belonging to me as good belongs to you.

That's a largish set of assumptions, a sort of *e unus pluribum*, out of one, many. Yet that, too, is very American. We tend to be a people who generalize from our own experience about American-ness: this is what Americans think because this is what I think and maybe what the people around me think here in the Salems of Massachusetts or Oregon, the Fredonias of New York or North Dakota, or the Charlottes of North Carolina or Michigan (which don't even agree on which syllable gets the accent). Whitman, however, adopts a strategy of generosity that makes his presumption acceptable—I will speak for you because I give myself to you, all of me to the last atom to the all of you singly and collectively. Since I am now in you, he declares (and you, by extension, in me), I can speak for you. And in truth, we were waiting for that. We just didn't know it. We had glimpsed it in the ordinary-man pose of Franklin's autobiography, in the rough-hewn frontiersman-soldier posturing of Andrew Jackson, in the native subjects of poetry by Longfellow and the so-called schoolhouse poets—John Greenleaf Whittier, James Russell Lowell, and Oliver Wendell Holmes—in the self-mythologizing of Davy Crockett. None of those, however, were the complete package of homegrown subjects, form, and language. None of them were telling *our* democratic story in *our* demotic tongue. None were native right down to the ground. And the native ground is what matters.

Autochthonous. The word means something like, "sprung from the soil" or maybe a little deeper than the soil, from the earth itself; it's the perfect word to describe Whitman's language, his verse, his poetic project. He consciously rejects European models, classical references, global aspirations, embracing instead the local, the immediate, the homely. He has much to say about the soil beneath his feet and the plants springing from it. He is himself not only sprung from but eager to reconnect with the soil: "I will go to the bank by the wood and become undisguised and naked, / I am mad for it to be in contact with me." Although he would never use the classical reference, he's an Antaeus figure, drawing strength from repeated contact with the ground. Moreover, his roots run deep:

> My tongue, every atom of my blood, form'd from this soil, this air,
> Born here of parents born here from parents the same, and their
>   parents the same,
> I, now thirty-seven years old in perfect health begin,
> Hoping to cease not till death.
>
> *Song of Myself*, I

He positions himself as pure American—not new immigrant, not colonist, not a child of either, but a fourth-generation son of the soil and therefore someone with no connection to any place or any tradition but this one. It's a strategy that could be meant to exclude those who are newcomers or outsiders but is not. Rather, it says, I speak as one who comes from this place, whose authority to speak for it and about it arises from my not being from anyplace else. The chief credential in that genealogy is not lineage but geography, not, my parents were from this or that class or achieved that or this success, but, they and I were "form'd" and by extension *inform'd* by this place. His attitude here as elsewhere is welcoming: please come with me, since it is your place as well as mine. Not only that, but he has placed the reader above him— literally. Before singing of himself, he sings of the "Modern Man" and ponders at the very outset the odd marriage of the "simple separate person" and "the word Democratic, the word En-Masse": I may be me, he suggests, but I am also of you, of *us*. And all three parts of that equation matter, the "I" and the "you" and the "us," or more particularly the "I" and "you" in "us." Whitman sometimes sounds a bit of an egomaniac, but he always intends for us to accompany him.

Whitman is sometimes referred to as America's Homer or Dante; a better comparison would be Virgil. It's not about who is "greater." I have the highest possible respect for Homer and Dante and in many ways prefer *The Iliad* and *The Odyssey* to *The Aeneid*. Homer is so clean, so direct, so spare; he's all narrative. On some level, *The Iliad* is the great national epic and raises a Greek identity out of all the competing local identities from all those little kingdoms, places like Sparta, Mycenae, Ithaca, and the delightfully named Phthia. But there's an unselfconscious quality to that identity building. Anything like a theme emerges almost accidentally from the web of narrative. Virgil, on the other hand, knows exactly what he's about. He's looking for a handout from his intended reader, who just happens to be the Emperor of All the World (Roman style), Caesar Augustus. Augustus has a problem that would sound familiar to denizens of Whitman's America: growing greatness but no history, no *inheritance* of greatness. Virgil, on the other hand, comes up with an elegant solution to the lack of a history: he makes one up.

Compare the shield of Achilles with that of Aeneas. The shield made by Hephaistos for Achilles is cosmological in nature, articulating the universe of the Greeks in bronze—the sun and moon and earth, humans in peace and war, the agrarian cycle of plowing, sowing, and reaping, the entire fabric of life in the world. The shield of Aeneas, on the other hand, tells an elaborate, if completely bogus, story of the founding, settlement, and history of Rome, tracing it from the defeated Trojan Aeneas to the magnificence of that greatest of all possible rulers, Augustus. (Virgil operated on the principle that flattery can get you everywhere.) The Romans knew they were a new nation, relative to the Greeks or Persians or Egyptians, so an ersatz genealogy of the ruling family served them perfectly. See, they could say, not only are we powerful, but we're ancient and therefore significant. So that's one solution to an upstart's anxiety over legitimacy. A little baroque, perhaps. When Achilles looks at his shield, both it and his cosmos make sense. When Aeneas looks at his, he's mystified by a story that lies entirely in the future, most of which he will not live to see.

Never a big fan of mystification, Whitman solves his problem by saying it doesn't matter. We don't need history or names or genealogy to legitimize our existence; we have each other:

It avails not, time nor place—distance avails not,
I am with you, you men and women of a generation, or ever so
     many
generations hence,
Just as you feel when you look on the river and sky, so I felt,

Just as any of you is one of a living crowd, I was one of a crowd,
Just as you are refresh'd by the gladness of the river and the
bright flow, I was refresh'd,
Just as you stand and lean on the rail, yet hurry with the swift
current, I stood yet was hurried,
Just as you look on the numberless masts of ships and the
thick-stemm'd pipes of steamboats, I look'd.

This is from "Crossing Brooklyn Ferry," although it could be from almost anywhere. *We* see the same things looking at the river and sky. *We* feel the same things, being part of a crowd larger than ourselves. *We* experience the same things, all of us on this boat together. And we are in the same boat. I can speak for you, then, as one who shares in your experience. I can even be your Virgil.

And like Virgil, Whitman becomes the guide for so many subsequent writers, and not only poets (not that there's anything *only* about poets). Who, you ask? Take your pick.

William Carlos Williams, Robert Frost, Ezra Pound, Allen Ginsberg, Hart Crane. Lawrence Ferlinghetti, Brother Antoninus, Jack Kerouac, Henry Miller, Woody Guthrie. Clearly the Beats profited immensely from the example of *Leaves of Grass*. Ginsberg saw himself as the logical inheritor of Whitman, with Williams as the intermediary, his *Howl* a rant to Whitman's rave. Kerouac's *On the Road*, while prose, perhaps most nearly captures the spirit of its great predecessor. The openness to experience of the poetry finds its novelistic equal one hundred years on, Whitman's celebration of the common person and ordinary experience becoming Kerouac's assembly of outcasts, excluded groups, peripheral figures, alternative lifestyles—a narrative of finding America's fringes by driving straight through the middle. Whitman, I believe, would have loved that.

For design, however, there are two poem sequences that, while significantly different from one another, marry the Whitman model with the modernist enterprise. The first one may have contributed to a certain confusion about Whitman's interests. He's often associated in the public mind with the Brooklyn Bridge even though he never wrote a word about it in his poetry and the evidence is sketchy at best that he ever set foot on it. So whence comes this mistaken impression? He did write the aforementioned "Crossing Brooklyn Ferry," which is justifiably famous in its own right, but that poem predates the bridge's completion by more than a quarter century and puts the speaker in much nearer proximity to the waters of the East River, which was seriously foul in those days, than one might wish to be. Yet he, being Whitman, doesn't mind, or even particularly notice:

> Flood-tide below me! I see you face to face!
> Clouds of the west—sun there half an hour high—I see you also
>   face to face.
> Crowds of men and women attired in the usual costumes, how
>   curious you are to me!
> On the ferry-boats the hundreds and hundreds that cross, return-
>   ing home, are more curious to me than you suppose,
> And you that shall cross from shore to shore years hence are more
> to me, and more in my meditations, than you might suppose.

Think of the subway at the end of the day. Now think of a similarly crowded conveyance on which people did not bathe nearly as often. See if it brings you to this pitch of ecstasy. That's the thing about old Walt: he just loved the world around him. Partly it's about ego; that is, he loved the world because it had him in it. But he also loved it simply because it existed. Had the bridge existed when he wrote this poem,

I have no doubt that he would have been equally ecstatic at the thousands streaming across it at day's end, at the crush of humanity going about its business unaware, locked as they would be in private thoughts, of presenting a collective picture, of being part of something so much larger than themselves.

But it didn't exist. Which brings us back to this popular misconception.

There is a poem sequence, long and every bit as ecstatic as anything Whitman ever wrote, celebrating the Brooklyn Bridge and everything about this country that went into defining it, and everything it defined in turn. It just happens not to be by Whitman; it's called *The Bridge*, and it's by Hart Crane, published in 1930. Crane lived within view of the bridge for a considerable period while writing the poem, in fact at 110 Columbia Heights in Brooklyn, the address where Washington Roebling, the structure's chief architect, was confined by ill health during its construction (although Crane seems not to have known about that coincidence until after the book appeared). It's safe to say that no one has ever waxed quite so rhapsodic over braided steel cables:

O harp and altar, of the fury fused,
(How could mere toil align thy choiring strings!)
Terrific threshold of the prophet's pledge,
Prayer of pariah, and the lover's cry.

It's art! It's music! It's religion! We love it! And of course, we did, and do, love it. The Brooklyn Bridge was the first and, at the time of the poem's composition, still the only signature suspension bridge in America. That's the sort of celebration Whitman could appreciate. And he was far from a Luddite where technology was concerned, reveling in the new innovations brought about by this Industrial Age he was born into. This particular modern marvel, however, came a little late in the poetic day, completed less than a decade before his death. It would have to wait for a younger enraptured poet.

Crane's poetics are different from Whitman's in significant ways. He is much more conventional in his lines and stanzas in terms of structure and meter; not for him the free verse or those Old Testament repetitions and thundering rhythms. He is much more allusive and "difficult" or "academic," a sort of Whitmanesque sensibility filtered through T. S. Eliot and Ezra Pound, whose influence he can no more avoid than he can the master's. He's also given to obscurantism, so much so that readers often despair of taking any definite meaning from given passages. Thematically, he may be democratic, but stylistically and formally, he's elitist through and through. It's also worth noting that his difficulty and pedantry set him off from his truly democratic predecessor as well as being the weakest aspects of his poem.

It's in spirit and enthusiasm, however, that he most shows himself Whitman's heir. And in ambition. Just as *Leaves* takes us to all sorts of places its creator had not seen at the time of composition, so *The Bridge* carries Crane to all sorts of places and times. And sometimes just carries him away. Whitman's is definitely a poem of Manifest Destiny, yoking coast to coast and gulf to border, aggressively laying claim to everything between Mexico and Canada at a time when the shape of the country was only recently a settled question, and when it would soon be contested anew. Crane's strategy is equally grand and perhaps even more stunning. At a time when much of the nation's travel still took place on rivers, his East River imaginatively becomes all rivers, most significantly the Mississippi, his Brooklyn Bridge all bridges, all crossings. But they also acquire a mathematical identity, becoming the X and Y axes running, depending upon his needs, north-south and east-west or through space and through time, each one simultaneously connecting and dividing. The river joins all points along its axis from source to mouth but separates land on one side from the other; the bridge connects those sides but visually at least (and he's all about vision) bisects the river's course. This mathematical device allows him to wander from coast to coast and top to bottom of the country while at the same time treating the whole of our history as an entity that exists all at once along the stream of time in a sort of perpetual *now*. The effect is breathtaking and at times overwhelming, the delivery often breathless, so that poet and reader seem to be equally astonished by the miracle and tragedy that is America. Whitman might not have approved of the language but would have loved the reach and struggle, the mix of disembodied love and raw sexual desire, the sheer energy of Crane's masterpiece.

The second Whitmanesque epic? It's small in all the places *Leaves of Grass* is big. It insists on the local as the source of the universal—one of those modernist paradoxes. It dwells resolutely in the physical, the immediate, the nonspiritual. It eschews the grand gesture and the grandiose pronouncement, believing its credo, "No ideas but in things." It says the American experience can be found in a single New Jersey city on the banks of the Passaic River: *Paterson*. William Carlos Williams is one of three huge New Jersey voices that benefited from the existence of *Leaves of Grass*, and his epic is one of the major constructions of the modernist era. Those other two? Allen Ginsberg and Bruce Springsteen, who inherits the tradition via so many sources—Whitman himself and Woody Guthrie and Bob Dylan and the Beats among them—that one can't even begin to detail them all.

There's something else Whitman celebrates that makes him distinctly modern. He is the first American poet to speak frankly of the body and its functions, and one function in particular. His depictions of sexuality were immediately decried by the censorious, especially in

Boston. Odd how those who would not otherwise notice his poem had no problem finding things objectionable in it. A highly developed olfactory sense in those bluenoses, one supposes. Boston DA Oliver Stevens threatened criminal action, prompted by the New England Society for the Suppression of Vice. But critics who mattered—Emerson (although he too had trouble with the sexuality) and William Michael Rossetti (comparing it to Shakespeare and Dante)—approved. One woman (Susan Garnet Smith) declared love and offered to bear his child, who "must be begotten on a mountain top, in the open air. Not in *lust*, not in mere gratification of sensual passion, but in the holy ennobling pure strong deep glorious passionate broad universal love. I charge you to prepare my love. I love you, I love you, come, come. Write." Clearly, from the beginning the poem inspired overheated prose. And other things.

And what was the source of all this hyperventilation pro and con? Not so much by today's standards. A sweaty armpit, an acknowledgment that sex exists and that perhaps people enjoy it. Mentions of babies being born. Most alarmingly, an attitude: "I sing the body electric." Well, we can't have that, now, can we? But it gets worse:

If any thing is *sacred*, the human body is sacred,
And the glory and sweet of a man, is the token of manhood un-
    tainted;
And in man or woman, a clean, strong, firm-fibred body, is beauti-
ful as the most beautiful face.

That could be somewhat shocking in a repressed age. How much more, then, the scene in "Song of Myself" in which a woman, repressed herself, watches from behind her blinds the scene of twenty-eight young men bathing and imaginatively joins them in the water. Scandalous!

It's not exactly Henry Miller, is it? But then, Miller wouldn't be Miller, whatever you may think of that eventuality, without the signal example of Whitman. That's what happens with trendsetters; they seem old hat after a while, but they never are. Even if the material isn't shocking, we can feel the intensity of his commitment to it, the *need* to express what he senses and feels and believes. And that is still slightly unnerving.

Now, about that national-poet business. You want to know what makes me so sure, don't you? It's a fair question, one I asked myself early on in thinking about *Leaves of Grass*. Not whether Walt Whitman is really the guy; that's long since settled. Rather, how do we *know* he is? I've pummeled you with evidence of the Whitman influence on America's poetry, fiction, music, pretty much everything in the culture. You could probably make a fair case for his influence on Aaron Copland, although I'm not enough of a musicologist to do that. But this is one case where positive evidence may not do the job. If you want to see the power of Whitman, go to the water's edge and look east. Read British and Irish literature of the past century, particularly the poetry. Spend time looking for his influence. Go ahead, I've got a century or two to wait.

The truth is, Whitman's influence hardly registers in writing from the British Isles. Oh, here and there you might get a whiff, in Jon Silkin, perhaps, or D. H. Lawrence's poetry (but not his fiction). Thom Gunn, you say? Maybe, but he lived in this country and particularly in San Francisco for so many years that any connection may have been forged here rather than there. Besides, if you read his early verse, written when he was just coming through the so-called Movement group with Philip Larkin and Elizabeth Jennings, he sounds very different from his more open, looser, mature self. But if we look at the heavy hitters of the British and Irish poetic mainstream—Yeats, Heaney, Louis MacNeice,

W. H. Auden, Larkin, Geoffrey Hill, Patrick Kavanagh, Edward Thomas, Thomas Hardy—where are the Whitman echoes? Nowhere to be found. And what does that sound like? Nothing like their American counterparts. That, dear readers, is my point: American poetry in particular and American literature more generally looks and sounds the way it does because of exactly one person. I said in discussing Cooper earlier that American writing can be dated BW and AW, Before or After Whitman. Before him, our writing sounded something like British writing of a few years before. Emerson, Bryant, Longfellow, and Whitman himself learned much from the romantics, chiefly William Wordsworth, I think. But 1855 is year one in American literature; after that, we begin to have our own sound, the sound we believe to be our own and appropriate to our experience. After that, we learn from a different WW. After that, *we* become *us*. Whitman teaches us to become Americans—open, positive, assertive, confident, forward-looking, unafraid, boisterous, contentious, passionate. What more can you wish for in a national poet?

SEVEN

GIRLS GONE MILD
Little Women

I'm going to exercise my constitutional right to be a geezer here, so I hope you'll forgive me this outburst of old-guy envy: KIDS TODAY HAVE IT SO EASY. If you were born after about 1965, you have no idea how blessed you are. No, this isn't about walking five miles to school through snowdrifts, uphill in both directions, and it's not about writing my school lessons in charcoal on a shovel by the firelight, although I'm pretty sure I did both of those things. And it's not about corporal punishment, even though I *know* I did that one. Or had it done. This is about something far scarier and more threatening to the dignity of young persons.

School guidance films. The original horror movies. Trust me on this one.

Sometime after World War II the government got into the behavior-modification business and produced thousands—and that is no exaggeration—of films meant to cause all of us to behave properly and follow sound hygiene and generally be fit to live in suburbs, which the GI Bill had caused to come into being all over the country. It's not that the intentions weren't laudable, at least some of the time. There were films on resisting peer pressure to drink or otherwise misbehave, on driving with caution (this was before universal driver education), on sound toothbrushing technique, and on just about every desirable social quality or skill (for) and every undesirable one (against). They were opposed to premarital sex and the Red Menace, in favor of politeness and clean shirts. In other words, it was a lot like watching a movie made by your parents, which, since we went to school partly not to be with our parents, stank. Also, the acting was so bad that even a generation raised on *Gilligan's Island* cringed. It made us wish we were on a three-hour tour.

I'm not sure where the Youth of America learns to seek these virtues and abjure those vices today as all that acetate crumbles into dust in ten thousand school storage rooms. I'm pretty sure it's not YouTube. I do know, on the other hand, where the YOA got its training in a simpler age. It came from a book for young persons written by someone whose chief outward qualification for the task was a history of writing thrillers full of blood and selfish aims and at least a hint of bodice ripping. The situation was a little like Ian Fleming, having set his superspy, James Bond, on a course of mayhem, suddenly undertaking a book called *The Young Adult's Guide to Clean Living*, which I'm pretty sure he never did. So who was this blood-and-thunder novelist who threw over potboilers for wholesomeness?

Louisa May Alcott.

Hey, I just tell 'em; I don't explain 'em.

The novel, needless to say, was—and still is—*Little Women* (1868). Even when it came out it had a placid, nostalgic quality, which the reading public very much wanted. After four years of the most terrible war imaginable, after the assassination of the president, who needed more Sturm und Drang? The crises are for the most part small, private, domestic, not large or geopolitical. This is not to say that it lacks drama.

There is heartbreak, humiliation, exhilaration, death and the threat of death, but all are handled with a certain decorum and even tranquility, as if Alcott intuited that readers would prefer a very measured narrative pace and tone.

The March family, four sisters and their mother—their father being conveniently but quietly away at the war—live an idealized and mostly idyllic existence. While they are a good deal like the Alcotts on whom they are modeled, there are significant differences. Marmee, the preternaturally wise and calm *mater familias*, is a good deal more placid and mild-tongued than Abigail "Abba" Alcott, who by most accounts could occasionally be hard to get along with. And Bronson Alcott, a transcendentalist and pacifist, did not need to go off to war to be unavailable to his family, unlike "Father" March, who is a chaplain to the Union Army. The elder Alcott cared more for his ideas than his family's material well-being and at one point seriously—and openly— considered abandoning them. No such dubious ethics attach themselves to the elder March, but neither is he a tower of strength. Even when the father returns, he is nowhere near as robust a figure as his ever resourceful wife.

The novel is a comparatively upbeat take on life in the middle of the nineteenth century. Yes, the family exists in straitened circumstances. Yes, there is a major war going on, which war has taken their father from them for the duration. Yes, there is suffering and illness and death. Such matters could not be ignored, certainly not by a writer standing at the beginning of the realist period. Alcott insists on the accuracy of her portrayal of life in its small details. If the family she portrays is rather more advantaged than the great majority of families in the country, then so be it. This stance of course is part and parcel of the realist program, which showed a marked middle-class bias; that is—in contradistinction to our contemporary usage of middle class—those people of the shop-owning, professional-yet-not-wealthy, reasonably well-educated bourgeoisie. Even so, the overall tenor of life in the March household is one of sufficiency and even plenty: there is enough, despite the protestations of the girls, of everything required for life and in many cases more than enough. They may have to wear their dresses longer than fashion or pleasure would dictate, but they have sufficient worldly comfort to prepare a Christmas dinner for a less fortunate family. Genuinely hungry people, in the main, do not go without a meal for the benefit of others. This family is not poor but shabby-genteel, a bit down-at-heel rather than needy. And in a great many ways, they are wealthy indeed.

One of their greatest sources of riches is each other. While they may sometimes chafe over the lack of solitude, they never want for company for excursions or partners for conversation. The girls are so close in age—Meg is sixteen, Jo fifteen, Beth thirteen, and Amy twelve when the novel begins—that they can share in one another's lives. The gap between eldest and youngest is neither so wide as Meg imagines nor so narrow as Amy wishes it. Moreover, they all have something to offer. Meg is a beauty, but her real gift is surrogacy. She manages the ménage in the absence of Mrs. March and protects Amy from Jo as a mother would. That Amy needs protecting says much about the inability of the second and fourth daughters to get along and about the oil-and-water mix of personalities in that pair. Of the four, they are the most headstrong and the quickest to anger, or perhaps the least reasonable. Jo's gift is writing, and it's no accident that Alcott slides the family forward in history from her own time line so that Jo can be just the age Louisa herself was when she began writing in earnest. Beth is musical, Amy artistic. They each, therefore, possess means to comfort each other with their abilities, although sometimes also to torment. This closeness must have been a source of either envy or relief to every only child who ever read the novel and a rebuke to those of us who may have gotten along less well with siblings. Add to them the faux brother they find in Theodore "Laurie" Laurence, their old neighbor's grandson, and you have an almost ideal arrangement. Laurie is available whenever needed for whatever sisters cannot provide—male viewpoint, masculine actions or strength (very handy for rescue operations, for instance), romantic possibilities, friendship with an outside entity, an escort for outings—but he can be conveniently tucked away and ignored in order to restore the all-female family circle.

Still, all is not sweetness and light with the March girls. Most, to be sure, but not all. From the novel's famous opening, we see that the girls have shortcomings: "'Christmas won't be Christmas without any presents,' grumbled Jo, lying on the rug." She displays a rather whiny selfishness that is at odds with her behavior more generally, and that lapse seems a way of signaling that the girls will be imperfect. They have their squabbles and tiffs, their foolish errors, and their personal shortcomings. Meg, early on especially, is swept up by vanity and envy: she wants what more fortunate others have. Of this disease she is somewhat cured in the chapter titled, significantly, "Meg Goes to Vanity Fair," when she is taken up by Annie Moffat and given a holiday. Her head is turned by the attention, and on her big occasion, a party, she allows herself to be dressed and made up by the wealthy girls, who go rather too far. She is subsequently mortified when she hears a gentleman call her "a doll" and bemoan the loss of her innocent, cleaner look. Amy's pushiness to be included in all things the older girls do, along with Jo's resentment of her pampered younger sister, nearly gets her drowned when it leads her onto thin ice, literally, during a skating trip Jo had planned for just Laurie and herself. Before Jo even has her skates on, Amy has fallen through the ice and must be rescued by Laurie. The girls return home equally frightened and chastened.

On the whole, however, the March home is a place of security and appropriate, if not exactly model, behavior. Someone is forever dispensing wisdom, and usually actual wisdom rather than the sort Polonius offers up in *Hamlet*. We might expect Marmee to be the font of insight, and to be sure, she has her moments. The profundity she dispenses tends to have solid practical conduct at its heart, "Have regular hours for work and play, make each day both useful and pleasant, and prove that you understand the worth of time by employing it well. Then youth will be delightful, old age will bring few regrets, and life will become a beautiful success, in spite of poverty." Predictably, that conduct is not merely ornamental or external but includes a goodly dollop of existential and spiritual insight: if we moderate our conduct to include both work and play—a major shift from our Puritan antecedents, by the way—we will be better in youth *and* old age, and our lives will be attractive and triumphant irrespective of their position on the usual, dull, monetary scale for success. This pronouncement follows a week's experiment in group failure, where Marmee has left the girls to their own devices, resulting in chaos, sloth, messiness, culinary disaster, and a dead canary. And who isn't ready for a lesson when the canary dies?

But while Marmee gets top billing in the wisdom category, virtually every member of the cast gets a chance to offer up some nuggets. Often those are born of folly, as Meg or Jo or Amy must show that she has learned something from her most recent escapade off the path of righteousness. Jo, the main character as well as the sister who takes longest to master her impulses, probably has more hard-won insights than anyone, although for sheer volume of wise sayings, Beth must surely be the champion. Because she sits quietly and listens to her elders, she seems to have absorbed the most from her parents while having the fewest character flaws to impede her understanding. And because she is so observant, she alone seems capable of learning from the behavior of her siblings without having someone point out the lesson or moral. Indeed, so preternaturally good is she that we are forced to suspect that, like those "young, beautiful, and good" heroines of Dickens's later novels, she must be doomed to short life. It is no surprise, then, when she succumbs to the scourge of the age, tuberculosis, in a deathbed scene that rivals Little Nell's in its affecting qualities. And even poor Beth's dying is a lesson for the others. She does not achieve the dying speech that the narrator claims only happens "in books," instead offering "no farewell but one loving look, one little sigh." She has suffered greatly, complained not at all, thought almost exclusively of others, particularly Jo, and in general had so little sense of self as to demonstrate almost no awareness of what effect her dying may have on *her*. In this environment, it is hardly surprising her survivors find a kind of grace in her passing, "seeing with grateful eyes the beautiful serenity that soon replaced the pathetic patience that had wrung their hearts for so long, and feeling with reverent joy that to their darling death was a benignant angel, not a phantom full of dread." In a world where consumption, as it was then known, could take anywhere from months to decades to carry off its victims, inflicting almost unimaginable suffering during the interval, it is an important lesson that she teaches them and that allows her family to have "thanked God that Beth was well at last."

The novel's narrator, of course, can also disperse wisdom directly, with no intervention by characters, and she does so with considerable regularity:

> It takes people a long time to learn the difference between talent and genius, especially ambitious young men and women.

or

Little cared they what anybody thought, for they were enjoying the happy hour that seldom comes but once in any life, the magical moment which bestows youth on the old, beauty on the plain, wealth on the poor, and gives human hearts a foretaste of heaven.

The apothegms are sometimes a little heavy-handed, especially for more modern tastes, but they are offered in such good humor and with such affection (even if amused or slightly condescending at times) for the characters that we can hardly begrudge their author her right to dispense them.

As the novel progresses, it perhaps loses some of its early charm, particularly in scenes designed to bring Jo into full womanhood and cause her to take the matrimonial plunge. In fact, that choice on Alcott's part, given that she herself never made the same one, strikes later feminists in particular but maybe even general readers as a failure of authorial nerve. Jo is so clearly not in need of male companionship, so able to find fulfillment in her activities as writer and devoted daughter, why must she be married off as a sop to the standards of the day, which Alcott clearly understood as wrongheaded? I am less troubled by either the philosophical or ethical dimensions of that decision than by its aesthetic implication. Those passages where she stumbles into affection for Professor Bhaer seem to me among the most contrived and least convincing of the entire work, something that *must* be done rather than something that *demands* doing. Even so, if we understand the work as a whole to be a sort of guide to becoming a well-adjusted person, marriage is the one big adjustment that must be made. That step is a major part of the human comedy that is *Little Women*.

I've said elsewhere that every novel carries the seeds of its own decoding, and one of those main seeds of Alcott's novel is John Bunyan's

Pilgrim's Progress. For reasons that will likely elude most of those who may have experienced the book in school, it is a favorite of the March clan. It is an allegory of the Christian's pursuit of salvation featuring a main character called, strangely enough, Christian. On his trip from his own City of Destruction to the Celestial City he encounters characters and places such as Evangelist, Obstinate, Pliable, Vanity Fair, the Slough of Despond, House Beautiful, the Delectable Mountains, Wanton, Mr. Worldly Wiseman, and Good Will. Along the way, Christian encounters every sort of temptation and diversion that could possibly waylay the faithful sojourner, but also every sort of helper and aid. Deadly sins and cardinal virtues are much in evidence. Clearly, this is not a book one reads for subtlety. It is intended as a road map to salvation, not a complex interplay of signifiers.

So, too, is Alcott's book concerned with sins and virtues and right conduct. The goal is somewhat more modest than in Bunyan. His is a divine comedy, with its emphasis on matters of the next world as the only truth that counts. Actions in this world only count to the extent that they advance or hinder the cause of salvation. Hers is much more a human comedy, where the emphasis rests on conduct in this world precisely because it matters in this world. That is not to suggest that Alcott was a closet atheist or that the Marches' discussions of heaven and salvation lack sincerity. Rather, it is to say that the distant city where good conduct may avail them is not the celestial one but Boston or Paris; they are learning to be better people because better people improve the world we occupy. The March girls have deadly sins writ small, something like queasy sins: vanity (Meg), anger (Jo), shyness (Beth), and selfishness (Amy). Envy presents itself in nearly all of them at one time or another. Observant readers will note that shyness is not among the classic deadly seven—avarice, pride, anger, envy, lust, gluttony, sloth—but these are girls in a novel for nineteenth-century young persons, so accommodations must be made. Lust is out, although there is romantic desire in the novel. Sloth is out as something unimaginable in the March household; these girls and their mother are always doing something, even when they are doing nothing. And much of the time, their doing drives them toward paradise. In the chapter "Castles in the Air," they discuss their relative chances of reaching that Celestial City, Beth predictably worrying if she is good enough, with Jo assuring her as a shoo-in, while Jo herself may have her work cut out for her. Friend Laurie Laurence interjects that he has just as many labors to come right in the end and promises to accompany her on the more arduous path.

The Pilgrim's Progress also has one other key similarity to Little Women: the absent father. In part one of Bunyan's book, Christian's family refuses to accompany him on his arduous journey. Later, however, they get the message, and part two involves their journey toward the Celestial City. In part one of this novel, on the other hand, the March family must learn to get along and prosper in hardship in the absence of the father. In part two, their journey is toward something much more earthbound—adulthood, with the attendant joys of marriage and children. And that progress is effected, even after Father March's return from the war, by a strongly matriarchal society. So moved is Jo by the strength of women's bonds that she feels Meg's marriage as a sort of death, at the very least a betrayal of what the sisters and mother have become, so much so that she wishes she could marry Meg herself and thereby keep her within the circle. Only after Meg's departure, Beth's demise, and Amy's marriage to Laurie—in other words, after the circle has been blown to bits—can she see her own way clear to romance, however halting. She wishes longer than the others to hold onto the appellation "little," but even she yields to the demands of the adult world.

Little Women stands in the middle of a trio of books published in a mere eleven-year span that could reasonably be claimed as the biggest children's novels ever, or at least until a certain boy wizard came along. Lewis Carroll published *Alice's Adventures in Wonderland* in 1865, a mere three years before Alcott's book, and Twain brought out *The Adventures of Tom Sawyer* in 1876. Throw in L. Frank Baum's *The Wonderful Wizard of Oz* in 1900 and you pretty well define a thirty-five-year period that invented childhood. One has only to look at the lot of all those waifs, orphans, and foundlings in Dickens to understand the magnitude of the achievement. The reality of childhood and adolescence for the vast majority of humans in that century, as in every other, was one of deprivation, disease, hardship, and hard work. These novels elevate childhood to a state of grace, touched by safety, adventure, comfort, love, play, and even magic, qualities about which a great many children of the era dared not even dream. Moreover, they suggested that such qualities *should* be part of childhood, that just maybe our early life should be a privileged time. Maybe not Red Queens and Wicked Witches, but the rest of it. If Tom Sawyer's adventures are less placid than Jo March's, that's largely a product of what activities were permitted boys only and which boys or girls in their time. Or maybe their place. Hannibal, Missouri, after all, was a lot closer to the frontier than Concord. That doesn't mean that girls didn't want to have fun, only that they did so decorously.

The novel has given generations of girls—and boys, too—the means to have that fun, to learn lessons, to see the pitfalls of pride or temper or envy, to found their own newspapers, to take their own picnics, secure in the knowledge that somewhere, just offstage or off-page, a loving familial goddess would be watching out for them. In a society where men are famed for going into the wilderness, for exploring new realms and conquering new territory, for finding ways to be unavailable, in other words, *Little Women* offers another truth: someone else keeps the home fires burning, raises the children, teaches the lessons, keeps the world spinning. If Ecclesiastes is correct that one generation succeeds another until the end of time, Alcott suggests, it does so through the maternal line. I never heard that one in the guidance films.

EIGHT

ABOUT A BOY—AND A RAFT
Adventures of Huckleberry Finn

This was where I was going to make my stand. Go against the grain. Make the surprise pick. After all, I wouldn't be wrong. What everyone thinks they know about growing up in a small town isn't in the book they think it is. Consider the list: untroubled childhood, outwitting slightly dim friends and competitors, the whitewashed fence, the sore toe, the wholesome little girlfriend named Becky, the adventure to thwart a clear-cut bad guy, the innocent mischief, the life almost without grown-ups. I even had a theme all worked up: Tom Sawyer ruined things for every subsequent kid in America. No one can have that childhood experience. It was a perfect plan. I'd have gotten away with it, too. Except for one thing.

I couldn't do it.

Why? Well, there's Hemingway, for one. He said it is, despite the unfortunate final chapters, "our best book." Wait, he goes further: "All modern American literature comes from one book called *Huckleberry Finn*." Then there's Fitzgerald, there's Eliot, there's *everybody*. Even the people who hate it do so because they can't ignore it. Okay, I know when I'm whipped. When so many people, including me by the way, think it's the most important novel in the American canon, it goes on the list.

It's just that the contrarian position was so pleasing, so elegant. *The Adventures of Tom Sawyer* really did teach Americans about childhood, even if much of the lesson was bogus. And as I've said repeatedly and will say again, this list isn't about literary quality or merit. Nor about my preference. If it were up to me, *Letters from the Earth* would be Twain's most influential book, and Americans would be better for it. More disturbed, but better. I even prefer, for reasons that are entirely personal and hardly literary, *Pudd'nhead Wilson* and *Those Extraordinary Twins*. You see why you never want to put me in charge. So sign me up. The book that *matters* among the very considerable Mark Twain oeuvre is indeed *Adventures of Huckleberry Finn* (1884).

The novel is a classic case of a novelist not knowing what he's doing until he does it. I do not believe it is the book he intended to write when he began a companion volume to *The Adventures of Tom Sawyer* (1876). There is plenty of evidence to that effect, not least that he carried over a chapter he chose not to include in the previous book. But as Faulkner famously suggested, a novelist is really a recording secretary, chasing after his characters to jot down what they do in his notebook. In this case, lighthearted adventure went out the window when Huck and Jim climbed on the raft. Lacking propulsion, a raft on the Mississippi in slaveholding times can only go one direction: toward trouble. The result is a darker, more violent book than its predecessor. There are, among other niceties, the murder of Huck's father, a manhunt for the escaped Jim, who is believed to have killed Huck, the slaughter of the Grangerford men, and the tar-and-feathering of the Duke and the Dauphin. There is also every sort of bigotry, skullduggery, confidence game, and threat of violence that you could hope to meet in a day's walk. This is clearly not a children's story.

So what sort of story is it? If this were a film, it would be a buddy caper. Which is interesting, given how abysmally Hollywood has done trying to adapt it over the years. Either they get the buddy part and leave out the social criticism, or they dwell on the social criticism and go all somber, drowning the caper—and nearly the buddies. So it's a buddy caper, sort of. With social criticism. And satire. He ridicules nearly everything—family loyalty taken to extremes, the dimwittedness of the great mass of people, racial attitudes in the middle of the country, hucksters and con men and their victims, the system of social castes, adventure romances of the sort Tom Sawyer favors, organized religion, received morality, and rules. Especially rules. Nearly every one of them that Huck encounters, and especially the important ones, are less moral than his transgression of them. He's been told of the importance of religion, yet nearly every person he meets who is part of organized religion is party to some grotesque immorality, whether it be slavery or mass murder. Religion is the cloak worn by charlatans and humbugs. From whom come rules. Slavery is right and proper; that's a rule. Huck believes in it because he's been told that it is so. He's been told how limited black persons are, which assumption justifies slavery. Yet he finds Jim to be deeper, more honest, more devoted to family than anyone ever suggested. It takes Huck a while to assimilate the lesson, but little by little he comes to understand that Jim is fully human—which is why the later chapters in which Huck acquiesces to Tom Sawyer's dangerous and dehumanizing nonsense regarding Jim are such a disappointment to readers. Indeed, virtually everything Huck believes to be moral, because society has told him it is, turns out to be the exact opposite. He's a straight being in a twisted world, which is the heart of the Innocent's Narrative.

That narrative form, the innocent abroad in a corrupt world, is at the heart of much great literature. The outstanding example may be Voltaire's *Candide*, but the genre would also embrace Dostoevsky's *The Idiot*, *The Catcher in the Rye*, *To Kill a Mockingbird*, and innumerable other works. The innocent, the child, the holy fool, moves through a space he or she cannot understand, and that lack of understanding is commendable. If one can understand that space, one is already among the damned. It may be that Twain's great contribution to the genre is the use of first-person central point of view; that is, the child narrates what he cannot comprehend. He may not have been first to the line on this one—we have the example of Swift's *Gulliver's Travels*, among others, although Lemuel Gulliver is no child—but his use is early and instructive. Hardly surprising, then, that such later avatars as Salinger's Holden, Lee's Scout, and Bellow's Augie all tell their own stories. What's key in these novels is that we readers outstrip the narrators in knowledge of the world. The discrepancy between the external reality, which readers grasp completely, and the young person's version of it produces irony, which in turn produces social commentary, satire, or pathos. In each case, the narrator does not know what he or she is telling us, but we do, and irony lies in that disparity of knowledge. When Huck tells us that the Grangerfords are fine people or that the Duke and the Dauphin are upstanding citizens, he has no idea of the truth of the situation. Twain does, and we do, but not Huck. The results are delicious.

The lineaments of the story are, on one level, quite simple. On another, the episodes come so fast and thick that they represent a torrent of complications. Huckleberry Finn's early life has left him unfit for town living with its school, church, proper dress, and indoor living. Why, he can't even smoke when he wants to. So even though life with Widow Douglas is easier and safer than life with drunken, abusive, and delusional Pap, he chafes against it. Meanwhile Pap sues to recover Huck's fortune (awarded at the end of the prior novel) and is awarded custody by a new judge in town, proving that justice is not merely blind but stupid. He nearly kills Huck one night in a fit of delirium tremens, and Huck fakes his own death and effects an escape. His plan accidentally meshes with that of Jim, the runaway slave of the widow's sister, Miss Watson. When a flood brings them a raft, they embark on a trip downstream toward Cairo, Illinois, and ostensibly freedom for both; in the event, they miss Cairo on a night of fog and confusion, traveling deeper into slave territory. Along the way they have numerous misadventures. Huck puts a dead rattlesnake in Jim's bed as a prank, but its mate comes and bites Jim, who suffers greatly but recovers. When they find the raft, they also find a murdered man, whose face Jim won't let Huck see. The man is later revealed to be Pap. Huck dresses as a girl to gather intelligence but is found out when he can't properly thread a needle, proving that you can fool the law, but you can't fool a matron. Several times, using a variety of means, including feigning smallpox, they must elude bounty hunters or others who would capture and sell Jim. They steal a boat from robbers. Huck becomes involved in a family feud that ends with his new friend, Buck Grangerford, among the murdered. He and Jim become entangled with two malevolent con men, the Duke and the Dauphin, whose first comeuppance arrives when Huck finally decides to do the right thing by their victims, three sisters whom the two hustlers are well on their way to impoverishing. Jim is sold by the Dauphin for forty dollars to Silas Phelps; the occasion for the sale is not Jim's original handbills but the fraudulent ones the Duke and the Dauphin had printed, supposedly to prevent Jim's capture. Silas Phelps turns out to be the uncle of Tom Sawyer, and Huck is mistaken for his friend, whom the family has not seen but has been expecting. When Tom does arrive, he impersonates his younger brother Sid and introduces many ridiculous and dangerous elements into a plan to rescue Jim, one of which results in Tom getting shot in the leg. Eventually, all is made right by two deaths: Pap's and Miss Watson's. It turns out that both traveling companions have been free almost from the start without knowing it, the terms of Miss Watson's will having liberated Jim. Ultimately, Huck rejects Aunt Sally's proposal to take him in and plans to "light out for the Territory." That the wilds and perils of Indian Territory are preferable to being "sivilized" again speaks volumes about what Huck has learned about civilization during his adventures.

This is a world in which "good" people are cruel, immoral, unjust, and benighted. Huck's friend Tom Sawyer is a much darker figure in this novel, citing the "best authorities" from the adventure novels he favors to concoct dangerous adventures of his own; his sense that any other being has rights is shriveled to nothingness. His Aunt Sally Phelps is relieved to hear from Huck that an explosion killed no one, "only a 'nigger,'" as Huck says. That a woman who is basically decent and good can find no room in her heart for the fate of a black person is a major indictment not merely of her but of the society in which she lives. And Miss Watson, the severe churchgoer Huck most fears disappointing, has every opportunity to know that owning other human beings is wrong, yet she does not. Her bequest of Jim's freedom is almost as damning as her owning him in the first place, suggesting as it does that she knew all along that she was committing sin. The Grangerfords and the Shepherdsons attend the same church and hear sermons on brotherly love while cradling their long rifles between their knees. And *these* are the people from whom Huck is supposed to learn right conduct? I think not.

What Twain is after in his novel is a kind of verisimilitude, a fidelity to real life, even if the events are at times farfetched. It doesn't matter greatly that he's fighting a battle long over. This is not an antislavery treatise, nor need it be one. *That* issue is settled. Rather, the issue he takes on is more current, the thoroughgoing attitude of racism, that blacks are inherently inferior to whites, that they are not fully human, that they conform to the stereotypes that make their mistreatment easier to justify. That issue is by no means settled when Twain writes his novel, nor would they be for many, many decades thereafter. Prejudice, it seems, has a long shelf life. One of the author's canniest choices is to give so many of those bad attitudes and ignorant assumptions to his hero. Even after he has been exposed to Jim's humanity for weeks, Huck can still declare that his devotion to his family seems "unnatural" in a black man. The boy who has barely been to school, and hasn't liked it, can make fun of the unschooled man's ignorance. And on and on. Yet what saves Huck, and what distinguishes him from his fellow whites, is his capacity for moral growth. He mostly learns from his mistakes and overcomes the prejudices that society has attempted to instill in him. He is still a work in progress at the end of the novel, but he's also still only thirteen. At that, he's further advanced than most of the so-called adults in this tale.

We can't leave this discussion of the novel without addressing a major concern: so what about the Tom Sawyer subplot? "So what" pretty much covers my response. I'm with Hemingway on this one; we should stop reading when Tom shows up. In a novel that has covered so much ground and been so daring in so many ways, Tom Sawyer's "authorities" and contrivances represent a huge leap backward. Twain had to put the novel away for several years, unable to conclude the thing. That he settled on this device, of massive cruelty to free a man already manumitted by bequest, indicates the level of desperation. I have always found the later chapters of the novel embarrassing, undoing all of Huck's moral development. Even a high school sophomore or junior can tell that something is definitely wrong here. It is the worst sort of betrayal of character; Huck becomes someone other than the person he has grown to be. Would he let himself, after having faced down so many dangers, be so governed by Tom's whims? Can he not see that Tom is the Duke and Dauphin writ small? Can he suddenly be so ignorant of Jim's humanity? I don't think so. Yet there it is in black and white. Readers always have the right to reject some aspect of their novels, and I have come to the point of declining delivery of the late chapters. They're too inauthentic for me.

But I'll defend to the death the greatness of the novel that contains them.

The main thing about Huck and his book is the whole language business. Have you ever considered what life would be like if everyone talked like a character in a Henry James novel? Now don't get me wrong; I have the utmost respect for James. Sort of the way I have the utmost respect for the federal penitentiary. It's necessary for my way of life, but I don't really want to go there. Forget life. Have you considered what reading would be like if all characters talked as if they were in a James novel? No? I'll tell you. It would be decorous but dull. And that's just what *Huck Finn* isn't. Dull, that is. Or decorous, for that matter. Huck talks the way a boy would, if he were ignorant and rough around the edges, if he's been raised by the town drunk in a place like Hannibal, Missouri, if he'd seen the devil and "sivilized" ladies and had been more frightened of the ladies. Huck is ungrammatical, uneven, crude, poetic, beautiful. Here's the famous opening of the novel:

> You don't know about me without you have read a book by the name of "The Adventures of Tom Sawyer"; but that ain't no matter. That book was made by Mr. Mark Twain, and he told the truth, mainly. There was things which he stretched, but mainly he told the truth. That is nothing. I never seen anybody but lied one time or another,

without it was Aunt Polly, or the widow, or maybe Mary. Aunt
Polly—Tom's Aunt Polly, she is—and Mary, and the Widow Doug-
las is all told about in that book, which is mostly a true book, with
some stretchers, as I said before.

What a thing of beauty! "You don't know about me without you
have read a book"! They don't write 'em like that anymore. That's
because they've educated such speech out of almost all of us. Do you
know anyone who could even get their mouths around "without you
have read a book"? I used to, a couple of folks back home in the hills,
but they were very old even then, and that was a long time ago. As for
me, I wouldn't even know how to characterize the parts of speech in
that phrase, except to say they're not behaving in a prescribed manner.
Which is pretty much true of Twain's language throughout the novel.
Also his people. Huck has some great coinages and twists of language,
many of which are regional, like "warn't," that commingling of "wasn't,"
"weren't," and maybe "aren't"—a sort of plural "ain't." To which he also
has frequent recourse. Or "clumb" for "climbed." Makes sense to me.
He even rises to a kind of poetry at times, as when he hides the money
the two charlatans have stolen from the Wilks sisters:

But I knowed better. I had it out of there before they was half-
way down stairs. I groped along up to my cubby, and hid it there
till I could get a chance to do better. I judged I better hide it
outside of the house somewheres, because if they missed it they
would give the house a good ransacking: I knowed that very well.
Then I turned in, with my clothes all on; but I couldn't a gone to
sleep if I'd a wanted to, I was in such a sweat to get through with
the business. By and by I heard the king and the duke come up;
so I rolled off my pallet and laid with my chin at the top of my

ladder, and waited to see if anything was going to happen. But
nothing did.

That's beautiful. The sound alone of "I had it out of there before they was half-way down stairs" can't be improved. It's swift, crisp, and clean. Compared to that, what's subject-verb agreement? The critics of Huck's language have never understood that it is the ideal vehicle for conveying his experience, and his experience is everything to this novel.

One of the great achievements of the novel is freeing writers to make use of dialect and colloquial expression in the pursuit of "serious" writing. Before Huck, dialect was inevitably the hallmark of "low"— low comedy, low class, lowbrow. Like the minstrel show, it was used to make fun of the group it supposedly represented. Twain shows that it can do something else—bring us into the minds of characters who may not be like us, raise serious issues from inside a social or ethnic group, depict without denigrating. He authorizes later writers of all ethnicities to explore the language people around them actually use. Writers as disparate on other grounds as Langston Hughes, Louise Erdrich, and Eudora Welty are beneficiaries of his example. Most importantly, he demonstrates that literary language need not be "literary language." For that alone, we should be most grateful.

The other sort of language issue has caused the book no end of difficulties. When it first came out, *Adventures of Huckleberry Finn* was assailed in some quarters for the coarseness of its language. It was banned in many quarters. A century or so later, it was again one of the most controversial books in the country, according to the American Library Association's list of challenged books, again because of language. The issues are not the same. When the Concord, Massachusetts, Library Committee banned the book, it was because of language that was "beneath" educated readers, suitable only for the slums. This was chiefly because the main speaker was himself uneducated and raised by a ruffian father. It probably also had something to do with Huck's statement when he tears up the letter to Miss Watson and says, "All right then, I'll go to hell." Hell may or may not have lost its sting since 1884, but "hell" certainly has, becoming one of the milder expletives at our disposal. That Library Committee stopped just short of calling the book immoral, although they wanted to, which borders on the bizarre, since in many ways it is the most moral book in our literature.

In the latter half of the twentieth century and the beginning of our own, the language issue surrounds a single word. Yes, Huck, like the people he encounters, does employ the word "nigger." A lot. As he would have. The word troubles us a great deal, as it should, and its history is so varied and fraught that its study would merit a separate book. But Twain was a realist, which is to say, he sought to portray the world as he found it, often satirically but always with a high degree of verisimilitude. To suggest that a common boy from a slaveholding state would refrain from the word, or have any sense that he might need to refrain, is to enter the realms of purest fantasy. Whatever else this novel may be, it is not that. The combination of that word, however, and the attitudes of the characters and by extension its author, ensure that controversy will attend the book as long as we and it hang around. If it were a lesser book, we could simply ignore it. But it is not a lesser book.

This is the book without which a great many other books would not exist. More importantly, a whole class of literature would not look as it does. American satire and a very great deal of American fiction could not be what it is without Twain's singular example. I think you could pretty much remove Kurt Vonnegut, Thomas Pynchon, Tom Robbins, and Peter de Vries from the literary map. Among a hundred or so others. Or you could simply erase that map and begin again with the descendants of William Dean Howells or Hawthorne or James. Where do I go to sign up? The fiction of childhood would not be what it is without him. Scratch Salinger and Harper Lee and probably Judy Blume. And Jonathan Safran Foer's *Extremely Loud and Incredibly Close* (2005), about the Twin Towers attack from a child's perspective.

Let's not forget the armada of critical material. Leslie Fiedler's "Come Back to the Raft Agin, Huck Honey," dwelling on the homo-eroticism of the American male-bonding narrative, set off a firestorm of controversy when it appeared in 1948. Is Fiedler right? I don't know, but the essay remains provocative sixty years on. Then there's *Was Huck Black?* (1994) by Shelley Fisher Fishkin, which stirred nearly as much controversy as the original. *Adventures of Huckleberry Finn* is the American *Hamlet*, an occasion for crackpot theories and wise analyses, and sometimes it's hard to tell the difference.

Treatise on hypocrisy. Indictment of racism. Satire of American foibles. Failed masterpiece. Centerpiece of American literature. We might wish for something other than it is. We might wish it better. We wouldn't wish it away. We'll never escape its long shadow. We don't have to be in Hannibal. Honolulu will do. Or Helena. The Hamptons or Hamtramck. There is one river, one raft, one novel that absolutely matters in American writing. You know its name.

NINE

TWOFER

A Boy's Will and *North of Boston*

O ne of the great pleasures of making up the rules for a game is that, if you break them, who's gonna squawk? So I'll state right here that instead of the customary one book, I plan to discuss a pair. It's okay. Really. These two books are companion pieces that could just as easily have been published in a single cover. Besides, books of poetry are short, mostly. And they really do belong together. Not only that, but I checked with the referee, and he said it was fine.

If you are of a certain age (between, say, 50 and 112), there are some truths you inadvertently encountered in junior and senior high school English classes regarding your national literature. First, it was written almost entirely by men. *Little Women* or *Uncle Tom's Cabin* might have snuck in there somewhere, but on the whole, men wrote "literature." Second, those men (and one or two women) were uniformly white. Third, said white male writers were, on the whole, safely in their graves well before you came along; you knew they were important because they were *dead*. Living writers have the annoying habit of proving one wrong or worse, of writing something either (a) dreadful or (b) so good that teachers have to change the readings. Imagine teaching Eugene O'Neill's *The Iceman Cometh*, say, only to find out ten years after his death that he's been holding out on us and had a masterpiece, *Long Day's Journey into Night*, locked away. Very disquieting. Thoreau never does that to us. But back to our list, and unintended-consequence item four, which is a sort of exception: some literature was committed after 1900. Novels were perpetrated by four people: Fitzgerald, Hemingway, Steinbeck, and Faulkner (if your school was of advanced views); drama by two or three: Thornton Wilder, O'Neill, and maybe Tennessee Williams or Arthur Miller; and poetry by one. His first two books were published, and in large measure written, in England. His first favorable American reviewer was Ezra Pound. He has more misquoted, misremembered, and misunderstood lines than any three poets should have. His name is not T. S. Eliot.

If you want to win money at parties (and probably get in fights over the answer), challenge people to name our most successful expatriate poet. You can do that maybe a thousand times without ever hearing the answer, Robert Frost. Yes, that one. The professional New Englander. The son of the soil (although born in San Francisco). He moved to Old England in 1912 so that, at least according to one account he gave, he could live more cheaply and his wife could fulfill a dream to "live under thatch." While there, he made the acquaintance of several significant English and American poets: Pound, T. E. Hulme, and most importantly, I believe, Edward Thomas. Thomas and Frost, while very different in the specifics of their versification, found reinforcement in each other for a deceptively plain, colloquial style that is held in tension against the rigorous metrical arrangement of the poem. Listen to an amateur read "Mowing" or "Mending Wall," and you'll be struck by the heaviness of the poems' rhythms. Listen to a recording of Frost, and you'll wonder where those stresses went. Many of the poems were composed in America, before he met Thomas, so he didn't find a new direction so much as validation of the direction he was already heading.

That direction can be called "plain style," although such a designation carries dangers. Indeed, Frost's poetry is almost nothing but hazards, a minefield for the unwary. He was fond of saying that he wrote after the fashion of St. Mark in his Gospel "in parable so that the wrong people can't understand them and so get saved." In large measure, it is this quality of parable, of simple statements masking more profound or contradictory truths, that keeps Frost's poetry always vital and even controversial. There is a tendency to take him at his word, to see all the poems about nature and farming as simply about nature and farming; yet there is another level—several others, truth be told—that has to do with existential matters, with life and death, fear and strength, battles against the elements and battles against ourselves. And what is perhaps so remarkable in his work is how those preoccupations were there from the first.

Not that the first was exactly the first. Robert Frost was no *enfant terrible* when he published his first books of poetry. Born in 1874, he was thirty-nine years old the year *A Boy's Will* was published in 1913. Hardly surprising, then, if he sprang on the scene with a mature voice and vision uncommon for first books. His story of creating his first two books was of taking all his poems he deemed worthy of publication and sorting them into two groups. The first group, primarily straight lyric poems, including several sonnets, would go on to become *A Boy's Will*. The second, marked by dramatic monologues and dialogues, would appear a year later as *North of Boston*. Together, they established him as a distinctive, important voice in American poetry. They also gave us some of his most famous poems: "Mowing," "A Tuft of Flowers," "Death of the Hired Man," "Home Burial," "The Wood-Pile," "Storm

Fear," "After Apple-Picking," and "Mending Wall." That's a good career. Happily for us, it was not his career, and there were many more anthology pieces and overlooked gems to come.

Now, about those preoccupations. Let's look at "Mowing" to get a sense of what Frost already knew how to do:

There was never a sound beside the wood but one,
And that was my long scythe whispering to the ground.
What was it it whispered? I knew not well myself;
Perhaps it was something about the heat of the sun,
Something, perhaps, about the lack of sound—
And that was why it whispered and did not speak.
It was no dream of the gift of idle hours,
Or easy gold at the hand of fay or elf:
Anything more than the truth would have seemed too weak
To the earnest love that laid the swale in rows,
Not without feeble-pointed spikes of flowers
(Pale orchises), and scared a bright green snake.
The fact is the sweetest dream that labor knows.
My long scythe whispered and left the hay to make.

The first thing to notice is that this poem is no accident. It is emphatically not the work of an unlettered rustic, a fact that I believe Frost is at pains to emphasize. Not only is it a sonnet, but the fiendishly intricate rhyme scheme—a-b-c-a-b-d-e-c-d-f-e-g-f-g—is something undreamt of by Petrarch or Shakespeare. It not only declares, "I'm a real poet," but also "I'm my own man and something you haven't seen before." Even its turn, the change in meaning for which sonnets are notorious, takes place two lines early, after line six rather than the customary eight. And that sound! A great many commentators have noted the whooshing sound of the poem—all those sibilants and soft sounds that suggest the act of mowing a field by hand. It may well be true that no poem in the English language gets more use from the letter *w* in the initial and second positions: "whispered" (four times), "well," "was," "swale," "sweetest," "weak," "why," "what," "without." Add in all the liquids—the *l* and *r* sounds—to the *f* and *s* sounds, and you've got a poem that, well, whispers. Consider just the first two lines: "There was never a sound beside the wood but one, / And that was my long scythe whispering to the ground." The only sound in this otherwise hushed environment is that of the scythe cutting through the hay, only it doesn't "cut" through anything. Rather, it is "whispering to the ground." The central fact of this poem that is so concerned with facts is missing: there is no mention of the blade encountering timothy or alfalfa or clover (indeed, there is no mention of what this hay is comprised of, a curious omission from a farmer). Instead, the scythe speaks to the ground or lays the entire swale in rows. The hay itself only makes an appearance at the end, left behind by the scythe "to make" on its own.

Nor does he know the nature of that monologue: "What was it it whispered? I knew not well myself." Nature, we understand, is mysterious. Even the author of the activity cannot fully understand the interaction between the inanimate object he wields—the scythe—and the ground. No more can he understand the process by which the hay makes, except that it doesn't involve us. Oh, we can expedite things by turning the windrows over, but the actual curing of the hay is out of our hands. As with so many of his poems, Frost's speaker is both inside the action and in some way excluded from it. He can cut the hay and leave it in rows, but beyond that, he cannot entirely comprehend. That question in the line just quoted is, for Nobel laureate Seamus Heaney, one of the poem's chief miracles. As he said in the old PBS series on

American poetry, *Voices and Visions*, and elsewhere, the question folds back on itself with the doubled "it," particularly since the sentence has such a limited sound palette. Where does the emphasis go? On which "it"? How many possible meanings are contained in that question? It probably means, what was the thing it whispered, but it could just as well be telling us that it whispered the question, "What is it?" Other readings, moreover, are available. And that's just half of a single line of verse in one small poem.

There you have the essential Frost experience. What begins as a stroll down the lane turns into a question of cosmology expressed in some exacting poetics, all wrapped in deceptively simple language, so easy a seventh-grader could understand it. I know this because I understood it in seventh grade. And didn't understand it at all. Our teacher, Mrs. Pyers, was a great fan of Frost, so we got a fairly steady diet of the warhorses, "Mowing" and "Stopping by Woods on a Snowy Evening," "Birches" and "Mending Wall." I don't believe we saw "Home Burial" or "The Witch of Coös" or any of the darker poems. There was a lot of emphasis on Frost as nature poet, very little on alienation from God or man. He was familiar, not dangerous at all. It was the standard schoolroom reading of him then, and it remains a popular reading of him today.

It wasn't necessarily his. He objected to the term "nature poet," noting that he had only two or three poems that didn't have a human being in them. By this, he did not mean a disembodied speaker but someone like the farmer in "Mowing" who is actively present in the scene. His interest is never in nature so much as it is in ourselves-in-nature. In "The Wood-Pile" the speaker comes across firewood cut, corded, and abandoned. Not only is he present in the swamp where he makes his discovery, but in a sense so is the person who did the work but never returned for the reward. His characteristic darkness is on display in this one, too. Why has the person not returned? What terrible thing could keep a person from enjoying the fruits of "the labor of his ax"? What starts out as a poem about a surprising find turns, as so many of his poems do, into a meditation on mortality. He never quite says that the sawyer must have died, but the energy of the poem all points in that direction. It does end, after all, not with the satisfying flame on the hearth but "With the slow smokeless burning of decay."

This countertendency to see the negative led to one of the great controversies in Frostiana. On the old poet's eighty-fifth birthday, in 1959, his publisher organized a dinner in his honor and invited the eminent critic Lionel Trilling to deliver a postprandial talk, which was no doubt expected to be in the form of an encomium. Trilling didn't get that memo. Why he was invited to deliver the address, since he was no great reader of Frost and had never published a word on him, no one knows, but he was. The subject of the speech was "The Two Frosts," that is, the saintly bard of things rural, which nonsense was based on a universal, willful misreading, and the "terrifying poet" of works like "Design," and "Neither Out Far nor In Deep," poems that will not help us sleep at night. His words were a thunderbolt against the complacency of the assembled literati that evening. The following week, the *New York Times Book Review* ran a rebuttal by J. Donald Adams, saying in effect that, no, he really is the poet we thought, and from there, the race was on. Everybody in literary America, it seems, was exercised by the challenge Trilling had thrown down. Or everybody except one. When Frost got a chance to read the text of the speech in June, he was quite sanguine, telling his biographer, Lawrence Thompson, that at least Trilling got the idea of "the badness along with the goodness." Frost saw himself as a "Dualist," by which he meant something like a Manichean thinker, understanding that there are two realities, one good and one evil, that exist beside and compete with one another. He contrasted himself to

Emerson, whom he saw as a "Monist," someone who could see good coming from ill but never the reverse. For a great many readers, Trilling's great crime was suggesting that somehow all was not sweetness and light in a body of poetry where spiders lie in wait within beautifully constructed webs and young boys get their hands cut off by buzz saws, where grieving couples bury their children or itinerant workers come to one's farm to die. For Frost, as for us today, Trilling's error, to the extent that there is one, lay in overstating the case for the dark, dangerous poet. His work clearly possesses both elements, and to overemphasize either is to miss the point.

And that point was there from the very beginning. *North of Boston* contains two of his most famous dialogue poems, both on the subject of death: "Death of the Hired Man" and "Home Burial." Go on; see if you can guess their subjects. Frost was clearly one who was, as the title of another poem suggests, acquainted with the night. One remarkable feature of these two poems is that the central event is nowhere to be seen. Neither the death nor the burial takes place onstage. What is interesting to the poet, and what he makes interesting to us, is not the occurrence itself but the response to it by the living. In the former poem, Warren, the farmer, and his wife, Mary, discuss the reappearance of the former hired man, Silas, who is no prize. Silas had previously been dismissed for his poor performance and for, as Warren puts it, "Off he goes always when I need him most" (18), disappearing in haying time to work for others, then returning in winter when he needs a warm place to sleep. Yet the real drama, the real tension, is between husband and wife. Mary tends to be more forgiving than Warren; moreover, she has seen Silas, whose condition is shockingly altered. Warren only goes to see him at the end of the poem, coming back to report him dead. Something more separates them, however. Warren is all practical action, a series of if-then propositions. If Silas has let him down once too often, then he'll have nothing more to do with him. He always avoided the arguments between the hired man and Harold Wilson, the local boy destined for college and teaching. To him, those exchanges were merely annoying distractions; for his wife, they were part of the human drama of farm life. She has sympathy for Silas despite his shortcomings, or maybe even because of them. *He* thinks Silas should go to his brother, a banker only a dozen or so miles away; *she* intuits why that would not be an appealing alternative for either the well-heeled executive or his ne'er-do-well brother. The conflict of points of view finds its fullest expression in the poem's most famous lines:

> "Home is the place where, when you have to go there,
> They have to take you in."
> "I should have called it
> Something you somehow haven't to deserve."

The first of those statements, by Warren, is the famous one, well remembered and poorly understood, his wife's reply virtually forgotten. Both responses are unfortunate. In a sense, both are true. His is much darker than hers, suggesting that all parties are victims in the equation, although often readers see it as something more forgiving and almost more like hers, which is quite generous, suggesting home shouldn't have to be earned. Almost everything we need to know about the couple is wrapped up in those lines.

For marital discord revealed in response to death, however, nothing can match "Home Burial," a miracle of the theater of dissolution. Every element in the poem speaks to their separation, from the first lines: "He saw her from the bottom of the stairs / Before she saw him." That distance is present throughout the poem. They are at different elevations, or are on opposite sides of a window or door, or are seeing each other from afar, all of which are emblems of the real condition: they are not *with* each other in their mourning. He has watched her parading her grief abroad, going away from the house to share with others, never with him. She watched him through the window digging the small grave, "Making the gravel leap and leap in air, / Leap up, like that, like that, and land so lightly, / And roll back down the mound beside the hole," as if he enjoyed doing so. His great crime, to her, is not so much digging the grave, over which she confronts him, but not feeling the pain deeply enough. Hers, to him, that she is all feeling, all grief, and won't share that pain with him. The poem is a masterpiece of mutual incomprehension. Fittingly, it ends with her unfinished query, "How can I make you—" and his threat to follow her and bring her back by force, also unfinished, "I will—" in response to her "Opening the door wider" to go. There can be no resolution, no solution, for this couple's unhappiness. Frost gives us not a problem to be solved but an agony in its root sense, a struggle between captives in a terrible situation. The poem is a tragedy that is almost Greek: tragic flaws on both sides, caught in a situation beyond their scope, battling against not only themselves but something very like the gods.

That may be what's most characteristic of Frost's work about this poem, the way in which the mythic obtrudes on the commonplace. One may ask if the death of a child is commonplace, but nearly every farm's graveyard had small mounds in the age when childhood diseases were more numerous and frequently fatal. Certainly the couple is ordinary enough. And this perfectly ordinary farm couple—no royalty needed here—enact scenes of suffering worthy of Oedipus or Electra. Those, too, of course, were at root family dramas.

Happily, that mythic quality often comes in less painful forms. In "Mending Wall," for instance, the speaker is engaged in a ritualized annual activity that is at once mundane and symbolic. The yearly rite

of restoring the wall between adjacent properties gives the poet the opportunity to explore mutual suspicion, boundary enforcement, class
difference, and received wisdom. Superficially, the poem has "quaint"
written all over it: these neighbors, one clearly sprung from the soil
and possessed of inherited wisdom, walk the wall to make repairs on
a spring day. Clearly, however, the relationship is adversarial, however
good-natured. "We keep the wall between us as we go," the speaker tells
us. In fact, the phrase "the wall between us" is repeated from the previous line. He tells us that it's "just another kind of out-door game, / One
on a side" (21–22), but little more than that. Since no livestock is involved, there's really no need for a wall other than the insistence of one
neighbor and the acquiescence of the other, but on they go. Yet there's
something deeper separating the two men, something the speaker casts
entirely in his favor. He sees his Yankee neighbor as locked in the past
both physically and intellectually. Carrying a large stone in each hand,
he looks "like an old-stone savage armed" (40), like a relic from the
past. He thinks that way, too, "mov[ing] in darkness, it seems to me, /
Not of woods only and the shade of trees" (41–42). While the speaker
says that before he erected a wall, "I'd ask to know / What I was walling in or walling out, / And to whom I was like to give offense" (32–34),
the neighbor will not go beyond his father's axiom, "Good fences make
good neighbors" (27). In fact, as the speaker delights in telling us, he
digs in his heels against change, repeating the poem's most famous line
as its last. Yet for all his smugness, the speaker repeats himself as well,
twice stating the poem's opening declaration, "Something there is that
doesn't love a wall." He's right: there is something. Him.

What he presents us with is a conflict of world views, or perhaps
more precisely a conflict over what makes such a view valuable. Is it
merely tradition, as the neighbor's statements suggest? Or is it putting beliefs and ideas to the test, as the speaker's statements indicate?

Frost, there can be no question, plumps for a modern stance on such matters. Ideas must prove themselves out, not merely be held over successive generations. Build your wall if you must, but do so for the right reasons. His formal conservatism masks what is often a fairly radical intellectual position. At the same time, one must be wary; the poet is sufficiently arch that he may simply be justifying the speaker's laziness by buttressing it with clever arguments. A Frost poem is a minefield for the unwary, for those who would settle on an easy understanding, and here as elsewhere meaning proves slippery. Reader beware.

One reason Frost is not more emulated in this country is his poetics, which do not fit with the general thrust of modern American poetry. A great one for sporting analogies, he famously said that he liked to write free verse just as much as to "play tennis with the net down." Not for him the loose rhythms of William Carlos Williams or the architectural contrivances of Marianne Moore, but his is clearly a rearguard action. Of the major modernists, only he and Wallace Stevens routinely write in conventional forms, and even Stevens often looks much more "modern" than Frost. Unlike the lyrics, the dramatic poems, monologue and dialogue, are typically unrhymed, but just as metrically regular:

> I'll not *have* the *fellow back*, he *said*,
> I *told* him *so* last *haying*, *didn't* I?

> "Death of the Hired Man"

You'll not find two more conventionally rhythmic lines in a day's walk. True, the first stress pops up without an unstressed syllable preceding it, but from there, it's iambs—that typically English-language pattern of an unstressed syllable followed by a stressed syllable—all the way. The truth is, though, that American verse had already moved in a different direction. Frost is writing AW—After Walt. The general drift of his contemporaries is toward free verse. Williams, Eliot, e. e. cummings, Carl Sandburg, Moore, and even Hart Crane all move away from the formal traditions of English poetry that had been building for the previous six or seven centuries. However indebted they may be on other grounds to Donne or Wordsworth or Shakespeare, they're not following their lead in the matter of metrics and rhyme schemes. Even Ezra Pound, such a contrarian in so many ways, goes with the party line here, picking his quarrel not with Longfellow, who is already dismissed from the stage, but with Whitman.

This quality of being after the fair may explain the relative lack of followers in someone who is as close to a national presence as it is possible for a poet to be in the United States. For most of the rest of the century, poets would move steadily away from closed forms and toward more open poetics. To be sure, there would be pockets of resistance—James Merrill or Mark Strand at times, Dana Gioia more consistently—but this is the century of Ginsberg and Ferlinghetti and the Beats, of Plath and Berryman and the confessionalists, of African American poets like Langston Hughes and Amiri Baraka, who are taking their formal inspiration from other traditions. Oh, there would be a few, among them the New England poet Richard Eberhart, who like Frost had a Dartmouth College connection, or Galway Kinnell or Theodore Roethke, or even in an odd way Gary Snyder, so formally unlike Frost and from the other side of the country. Or universe. But acolytes are not thick on the ground.

The other reason, of course, is that he's inimitable. It's a quality he shares with many of the great modernists. There's no one like Yeats, no one like cummings, no one like Eliot: you cannot write like them without falling into parody or seeming really lame in comparison. You doubt? Look at the first books of poetry by W. H. Auden or Philip Larkin and you'll see why we don't want another Yeats. The only way to be influenced by such a powerful antecedent is to turn that influence into something else, to struggle with it and come out the other side with something quite changed. That struggle is the more arduous if the two poets are of the same nationality. Perhaps that's why in some ways he's had a more significant influence across the water, where his great followers have been Ted Hughes, an Englishman, Russian Joseph Brodsky, Caribbean poet Derek Walcott, and Northern Ireland's Seamus Heaney (the last three of whom won Nobel Prizes in Literature). There are worse poets to have inspired. Each has said that Frost gave a sort of validation to write about nature in its immediate, humble forms, and for Heaney and Hughes especially about life on a farm, in ways that were direct and nonmythologized. Neither was looking for the romantic celebration of the sublime or the classical tradition of the pastoral, both of which are essentially forgeries of nature. And here was this American, writing in simple language about everyday things, and the whole of existence was in there. Life, death, madness, sanity, marital troubles, struggles with nature, struggles with God, struggles with ourselves, all in poems about birch trees and farmyards. The example proved immensely attractive.

At the same time, almost every poet today is a child of Frost. We often get caught up in the formal regularity of his verse and forget the much more innovative quality, the thing he called "the sound of sense." He explains this as the rhythm of native speech, which the poet should capture. If one hears a conversation from behind a closed door, he says, so that no specific words can be made out, one can still hear the *structure* of meaning from the rise and fall of the voices of the speakers even while the meaning itself is lost. He saw himself as first among English or American poets to make a systematic study of this sound of sense, and he applied his findings from the first. Here he is in "After Apple-picking":

> And I keep hearing from the cellar bin
> The rumbling sound
> Of load on load of apples coming in
> For I have had too much
> Of apple-picking: I am overtired
> Of the great harvest I myself desired.

This passage could be turned into prose with no loss whatsoever of meaning and no strain on the ear's expectations of the sound of English. The rhymes come without notice precisely because the lines sound so much like ordinary speech. "I am overtired of the great harvest I myself desired," written as prose, does indeed have an internal rhyme, but it is so quiet as to be almost unnoticeable. And what strikes us in the earlier rhyme is not bin/in but the emphasis caused by repetition, "Of load on load of apples coming in." The line's brilliance lies in its simplicity: anyone might say it. Of course, only Frost does. He exploits great tension between perfectly regular utterance and fairly strict metric practice. What's too often lost in later poetry is any sense of challenge or tension, so that language comes off as merely flat, and flat is something Frost never is.

By way of closing, I'd like to go back to that Trilling controversy over the two Frosts for a moment to consider an implication or two. Yes, there was a good bit of nonsense from some highly intelligent and educated folks, and neither side in the dustup was immune from folly. Who won or lost, who was right or wrong, none of that interests me very much half a century on. What should interest all of us, however, is the fact that it happened at all. Can you name a single poet, even a single literary figure of any sort, in the contemporary frame who could inspire such passion over how we read his or her work? I didn't think so. What's important about Robert Frost is that he was so, well, *important*. He mattered to Americans, to their sense of themselves, to their understanding of what their country was. Does he speak for everyone in all regions? No. Like Hawthorne, like Faulkner or Eudora Welty or Walker Percy or Tony Hillerman, he generally confines himself to what Faulkner calls his "little postage stamp of ground." But what modernism taught us is that the key to the universal lies in the local. Frost's "regionalism" belies a systematic examination of the human condition at large. His appeal is not regional but universal. During World War II, his work was handed out to soldiers in pocket-sized paperbacks in the series "Why We Fight." The army didn't ask whether a soldier was from Nashua or Nogales or Natchez; it knew the poems served a purpose for Americans. Again, it is hard to imagine a contemporary American poet going to war in the pockets of GIs. In fact, it's hard to imagine others from his time. It falls to few poets, perhaps one or two a century, to so perfectly express their time and place, their connection to the land and the people, to embrace the country in such a way that it embraces them back. The American century may have had two. Feel free to nominate the other one.

TEN

IN PRAISE OF PRAIRIE
My Ántonia

Once upon a time there was a land you couldn't ignore. People didn't fly over it in an hour or go whipping by it at eighty miles an hour. It was broad and flat and dusty and hot and freezing and brutal and wide enough to take forever to cross, and, bizarrely perhaps, people went there on purpose. From everywhere, or so it seemed. From Bavaria and Bohemia and Norway and Sweden and Wales and Virginia and New Hampshire and Ukraine. They were Catholics and Methodists and Baptists and Lutherans and Mennonites and Jews, speaking all sorts of different languages. It was like nowhere they'd ever seen before. They couldn't even build houses when they arrived, not houses like they'd ever known. Their walls were stacked sod on one side, a hill on the others. Their wages were often starvation. And somehow they made lives and communities and the great middle of this nation out of the vast emptiness that greeted them.

They "proved up" their claims, breaking sod and tilling land, raising livestock and fighting the elements. Some got on, some got rich, some went crazy. It was a hard life for men, perhaps even harder for women. There was no time for books or poetry or the arts, at least not out on the homesteads. For the most part they left no records of their lives, although sometimes their children or grandchildren did. The prairie gave us cattle and grain and great, open vistas and tales of cattle drives and lawless towns. Cowboy stories. Our native troubadour, Woody Guthrie. Legends of railroads and wagon trains. And one incontestably great novelist.

She wasn't even from the Great Plains but from Virginia, plucked from home in childhood and resettled in Red Cloud, Nebraska. But once there, she caught the spirit of the place. Although she moved eastward after graduating from the University of Nebraska, first to Pittsburgh and later to the wilds of Greenwich Village, Willa Cather never got over her adopted home state. Of all writers in English, only James Joyce wrote more exclusively about a place he never lived as an adult.

Ironically, the prairie she celebrates in her fiction was already disappearing when she moved there; indeed, her arrival was part of that disappearance. Real prairie can only exist in the absence of permanent human habitation. For centuries the Plains Indians had moved lightly over the surface, following the vast herds of buffalo, and even their activities left their mark. In the Great Plains of Cather's childhood, the bison were gone, the land already succumbing to the plow and the network of rail lines. For her, writing was an act of recapturing something in the act of vanishing. Small wonder, then, that her novels are marked by an elegiac tone, memorializing as they do a world and a people that have already passed into memory. For the settlers she describes are as ephemeral and fleeting as the red grasses and the ghosts of the great herds.

In novel after novel she writes of this fleeting moment between unbroken grasslands and the closing of the frontier and of the aftermath of that taming of the prairie: *O Pioneers!* (1913), *The Song of the Lark* (1915), *A Lost Lady* (1923), *The Professor's House* (1925), and even her "war" novel, *One of Ours* (1922), whose best and most compelling passages are those not of the war but of the home front back in Nebraska during the generation after settlement. Nowhere, however, is that elegiac quality more on display than in *My Ántonia* (1918), one of the great novels of the immigrant experience and life on the prairie. Paradoxes abound with this novel. It is largely about the experience of women but told by a man, about immigrants yet centered on someone American-born; it celebrates the lives of those engaged in the destruction it mourns; it revolves around a love that can never be realized. One thing that is not paradoxical: it is beautifully written and was recognized as such from the moment of its publication.

The novel was immediately praised by significant tastemakers of the day, from Randolph Bourne to Carl Van Doren to Heywood Broun to H. L. Mencken, who said, among other things, "No romantic novel ever written in America, by man or woman, is one half so beautiful as *My Ántonia*." In comparing the novel to another by William Allen White, Mencken goes on to say that, "Invading the same Middle West that engages the Kansas tear-squeezer and academician [White], and dealing with almost the same people, she comes forward with a novel that is everything his is not: sound, delicate, penetrating, brilliant, charming. . . . I know of no novel that makes the remote folk of the western prairies more real than *My Ántonia* makes them, and I know of none that makes them seem better worth knowing." Bourne, whom Cather revered as a literary reviewer, was almost equally effusive.

Even so, the early reviewers, like many readers and commentators of the next ninety years, got the novel wrong: they ignored the possessive pronoun in the title. Too often the novel is read as *About Ántonia* or just *Ántonia* but neither of those is the title, and neither captures the narrative strategy. Most readings seem to ignore or conveniently skip the Introduction, in which the unnamed transmitter of Jim Burden's text, what Wayne Booth in *The Rhetoric of Fiction* dubbed the "implied author," tells how Jim came to compose the text. But that introduction makes all the difference in the world. It removes Jim's tale from the realm of the conventional unreliability of first-person narrative and places it in a very specific framework of unreliability. Jim Burden, many years on, many miles removed, successful, and unhappily married—all things we learn in those opening few pages—is looking back at his golden days, a time of innocence and awakening and adventure, in which a girl he loved but, conveniently, could never attain, would lead him from childhood through adolescence to the cusp of adulthood. Four years younger than Ántonia, Jim is distanced from her by reasons of age, religion, nationality, and, strangely, language. An Anglophone native, he is perhaps too distanced from the Slavic and Scandinavian immigrants with whom he shares the prairie ever to be part of their society, but he comes close enough to describe it in fairly intimate detail. In his narrative, then, Ántonia becomes a curious hybrid, part accurate depiction, part projection of Jim's own needs and enthusiasms. But because his narrative is so apparently artless, there is a tendency to see the novel as artless, as an instance of pure realism, with Jim as a mere recorder of event and sensation. It is not. Rather, it is Cather's version of *À la recherche du temps perdu*, and Jim is as much a part of his story as Proust's Marcel—and like him simultaneously an authorial surrogate and a fabrication.

Cather is at pains to set up a frame-tale that in the end she never completes. Like Henry James in *The Turn of the Screw*, although for vastly different reasons, she sets up an initial frame but does not return to it at the novel's close. In the beginning, we meet an unnamed version of Cather who will conveniently vanish after the Introduction, leaving the stage clear for Jim and his narrative. She encounters Jim Burden, an old friend from Black Hawk (one of several Catherian variants of her real hometown of Red Cloud, Nebraska), on a train crossing Iowa, and he expresses his wonder that she has never written about Ántonia, a lively, memorable daughter of Bohemian immigrants. She confesses the limits of her knowledge and suggests they each write down their recollections of Ántonia; her own is never written, and she and the framing device melt away, leaving the rest of the novel to Jim.

That story is broken up into five books: "The Shimerdas," "The Hired Girls," "Lena Lingard," "The Pioneer Woman's Story," and "Cuzak's Boys," which move through Jim's encounters with Ántonia and her world from first sighting in childhood to encounter in midlife after a gap of twenty years. The first section is in many ways the most compelling, encompassing both childhood innocence and its loss. Jim Burden first encounters the Shimerda family on the train west from Virginia after the death of his parents. He is heading for his grandparents' farm outside Red Cloud, while the immigrants are aimed at a nearby property to homestead. Their proximity inevitably brings them together. From the first, Jim is intrigued by the daughter, who is slightly older than he but near enough (four years) to share interests; indeed, he can never quite figure out whether his attachment to her is brotherly fondness or infatuation. Their trajectories, however, are quite different. His grandparents live in a regular frame house with outbuildings, having long since established their farm as a going proposition. The Shimerdas occupy a sod hut cut back into a hillside that first winter; the dwelling is dark and smelly and cramped. Mr. Shimerda, depressed at the separation from the old country, where they were town dwellers and he played music at social occasions, and at the bleakness of their situation, probably kills himself in the depths of January, although there is a hint that he may have been murdered by Peter Krajiek, who sold them the farm and, as their only transla-tor when they arrive, almost certainly cheated them. Jim's grandpar-ents have already extended assistance to the immigrants, and after the suicide they offer more. Jim himself becomes Ántonia's English tutor, and she proves an adept student. At the same time, she has not the luxury of time to attend school on a regular basis; the loss of her father means that she, as second oldest, must assist her brother in run-ning the farm, so her life is nearly consumed with the basics of subsis-tence. That distinction between the friends will be accentuated later, in Book 2, when they move to town, Jim to educational and social opportunities as the grandchild of well-to-do retired farmers, Ánto-nia as a domestic servant to bring more money into the cash-strapped Shimerda household (and to remove one mouth needing to be fed). Still, during their, or at least Jim's, childhood idyll, he and Ántonia find a lot of time to enjoy the countryside, to play, and to be children.

Sexual awakening comes in the form of a dancing craze that takes hold after the protagonists have moved to town. An Italian couple comes to Black Hawk to give dancing lessons, and the town responds enthusiastically with a series of very popular dances that carry on long after the Vannis have moved on to give lessons elsewhere. In the ab-sence of girls from the established families, who are for the most part forbidden to attend, Ántonia and the other hired girls, all from im-migrant families, find themselves much in demand. They are vibrant and high-spirited and attractive, qualities that do not comport with working in some other woman's household. The dances allow the girls to free themselves from the constraints of their working lives, one of which is separation from the young, eligible men of the town. At the same time, the young men, Jim Burden included, experience physical contact with the hired girls forbidden them with girls of their own class. The results are not uniformly happy. When Jim attempts to kiss

Ántonia, he discovers that for all her fondness for him, she has never considered him a romantic possibility but more of a younger brother or alter ego. Some of the young men, however, have more success with the hired girls, who in consequence acquire "reputations," and some, like Ántonia, lose their positions, usually more for general perceptions of behavior and guilt-by-association than for specific actions. Their transgressions have as much to do with caste as with sexuality: the town's middle-class males are off-limits to the working-class females of "outsider" backgrounds. And sometimes the young women are not particularly saddened by the loss. Indeed, given the choice of her position or the freedom her dancing represents, Ántonia chooses the freedom, although that proves to be hazardous.

Throughout this period of maturing and awakening, Jim and Ántonia protect one another. When she leaves the Harlings and goes to work for Wick Cutter, the novel's obvious and rather overdrawn villain, she is clearly in peril. In addition to being the town's unscrupulous moneylender, he has a history of ruining the girls who work for him. When he and his wife leave town for a short spell, Ántonia fears sleeping in the house alone, so Jim stays in her place and she sleeps at his house. Through an elaborate ruse only possible in the age of trains, Cutter has arranged for his wife to be whisked out of his way so he can return home to rape Ántonia. Finding the object of his desire has been replaced by a male, he gives Jim a savage beating. If his protecting of her is costly, hers is solicitous. For her part, she does her best to steer her livelier friends, particularly Lena Lingard, away from Jim, whose studies and future would be put at risk by any serious involvements with girls. Even when Jim moves to Lincoln to attend the university and finds Lena working successfully as a dressmaker there, something of Ántonia's protective charm seems to hover over the relationship, keeping it from advancing too far. Their solicitousness, even their willingness to sacrifice for one another, shows clearly that Jim and Ántonia, although never involved romantically, are in love with, or at least in love with the idea of, each other. Indeed, we might do well to understand that one of the young women from whom Ántonia protects Jim, perhaps unconsciously, is herself.

Steadily, though, the friends grow apart, Jim moving progressively away from the land and toward gentility, Ántonia pulled steadily back to the land, first after the death of her father and later following her failed elopement and the birth of her daughter. She works like a man, works better than many men, yet for all that she is never manly. She remains more robust and more life-affirming than her husband, a wizened, diminished figure, and it is inevitably to her that her numerous children turn for comfort, for support, for strength. If Jim, dislocated, travels lightly over the surface of the earth in his movements from place to place, she becomes the earth, the place she inhabits—rooted in the soil, sustained and buffeted by elemental forces, ever more identified with her locale. If his is the life of the mind, hers is of the body. If his has breadth and scope, hers has richness and depth. But this is not a story of how two friends grow apart; or rather, that is in a sense a mere coda to the story of how they first grow together.

Many of their adventures both early and late have strong symbolic significance. While they are still quite young Jim kills a huge rattlesnake at the prairie dog town they go out to see. That the snake is old and not very vigorous matters little in the incident winning Ántonia's respect, nor in its certifying the prairie as a sort of Eden, at least for the two young friends, as well as an initiation into the realm of adult knowledge. True, death entered this garden before the serpent, and this is more a rise than a fall, but Cather is playing with some extremely well-known biblical tropes. Garden imagery suffuses the text, from Mrs. Burden's garden, where Jim finds comfort and pleasure when he first arrives, to the prosperous farm, complete with orchard, that Ántonia ultimately builds with her husband, Anton Cuzak. In some ways, the motif culminates in a vision of the implement of this garden's transformation:

> *Presently we saw a curious thing: There were no clouds, the sun was going down in a limpid, gold-washed sky. Just as the lower edge of the red disk rested on the high fields against the horizon, a great black figure suddenly appeared on the face of the sun. We sprang to our feet, straining our eyes toward it. In a moment we realized what it was. On some upland farm, a plough had been left standing in the field. The sun was sinking just behind it. Magnified across the distance by the horizontal light, it stood out against the sun, was exactly contained within the circle of the disk; the handles, the tongue, the share—black against the molten red. There it was, heroic in size, a picture writing on the prairie.*
>
> *Even while we whispered about it, our vision disappeared; the ball dropped and dropped until the red tip went beneath the earth. The fields below us were dark, the sky was growing pale, and that forgotten plough had sunk back to its own littleness somewhere on the prairie.*

This passage is a wonderful example of the tricks of perspective, which in a sense is what the novel as a whole is about: what do we see when we are up close? What do we miss? And when we're far away? That moment when the abandoned plough is framed against the setting sun, magnified, magnificent, only to be made small again in the next moment, stands as a major motif in the narrative. On the one hand, the vastness of the land dwarfs human activity, which seems so all-consuming when we're in the midst of it. On the other, the prairie is rapidly succumbing to the plough in the time of the story, as cultivation overtakes the nature and row crops replace native grasses.

That symbolic element extends to the title character herself. It is sometimes said that Ántonia is an Earth mother, but that's not quite accurate. She's far less Cybele than Ceres, goddess of fruitfulness and especially grain (and from whom we get the word "cereal"). On this basis, Cather doesn't miss a trick. Her heroine is shown repeatedly with her arms full of grain, in grain fields, harvesting grain. She seems to know the apple trees personally and runs her hand over their bark. Like the goddess, who resided not on Olympus but on the earth itself, she is resolutely sprung from and anchored to the soil. Her farm is a marvel of fertility, human and agricultural, replete with orchards and fruit preserves and vast quantities of baked bread, of which her many children are proud, worshipping both her and the wheat which seems her special provenance, reminding us that the name Demeter, the earlier Greek version of Ceres, meant "Grain-mother." It is the daughter who is not present, however, who seals the parallel with Ceres. Her relationship with the child born out of wedlock, Martha, is one of near total identification in the way that Ceres and Proserpina are completely connected. And just as Ceres went into mourning at her daughter's abduction by Pluto and relocation to Hades, so too with Ántonia: "I'm reconciled to her being away from me now, but at first I cried like I was putting her into her coffin." That reconciliation, like the joy of Ceres during the six months each year when her daughter emerged from Hades, allows for the profusion of life all around Ántonia.

Which brings us to what is in some ways the main point of the novel—the role of women in taming the prairie. Males in the novel are, frankly, a disappointment. A couple, Wick Cutter and Peter Krajiek, are actively evil, others such as Ántonia's brother Ambrosch merely brutal, but many more are simply nonentities. True, there are some truly good men, such as Anton Jelinek, Jim's grandfather, and the hired men Otto Fuchs and Jake Marpole. On the whole, they are neither particularly good nor bad, but they have the habit of disappearing. Either they die like Mr. Shimerda and Russian Pavel or they drift away in the manner of Fuchs and Jake and even Mr. Burden, who moves off the land and into town, or they are, like Jelinek, who is wonderfully helpful after Mr. Shimerda's suicide but rarely available otherwise, not sufficiently present to make a lasting difference. In such a world, it falls to the women to hold things together, and they do. Mrs. Burden is first to reach out to the immigrant family when they arrive. Her kindness and warmth are also seen in the Widow Steavens and Mrs. Harling, the matriarch of the family that employs Ántonia. It is noteworthy that it is Mr. Harling who forces her to choose between employment there and dancing, and Mrs. Harling who mourns her departure. Their daughter, Frances, helps run the family business and seems to be the real brains of the operation. Lena Lingard herds her family's cattle at a young age, often under the lusting eye of Ole Benson, and later moves to town, eventually establishing a successful dressmaking business. Her friend Tiny Soderball also becomes successful after being deeded a claim "out West" and investing it wisely.

Almost alone among her friends, Ántonia remains poor, although in doing so she is carrying on a family tradition. From the time the family arrives in Nebraska, Mr. Shimerda is lost and demoralized, so his early death comes as little surprise. It therefore falls to his wife to keep the family together and to put it to work taming their property. She accomplishes her task not with an iron fist but with optimism and fondness, traits her elder daughter inherits. When we meet the Cuzak clan, Anton, the father, is away, leaving Ántonia alone at the helm. Even when he returns, he seems peripheral to the operation of the farm—certainly to the life of the family. Everything about the life of the farm—baking, canning preserves, growing an orchard or two, even hard labor—originates with Ántonia. She and her brood may be cash-poor but are rich in the things that sustain life: land and food and caring and love. She is the presiding being not simply of the family but of the plains themselves, the representative spirit of women's roles in settling and developing the heart of the nation. That's what happens when you put women in charge.

ELEVEN

A WHOLE HEAP OF ASHES
The Great Gatsby

If you're going to think much about American literature, you better prepare for irony. Not the sort that's in the books, although there's enough of that, I suppose. Rather, think about the ironies involved in, say, the most important statement about the evils of slavery coming in a book by a writer from a slave state, not from the abolitionist North. Or the funniest writing coming from the gloomiest characters.

Or this. The most penetrating critique of the excesses of capitalism in New York during the Roaring Twenties coming four years before the crash and from a young man who spent every waking hour trying desperately to take part in those excesses, to make sure the times roared. You might think that a fellow who turned himself into an instant success to get the girl he desired would lack the self-awareness to undertake such a project. That someone who one year in the 1920s earned the equivalent of today's $280,000 and by some accounts finished the year further behind than he started it, only to go charging ahead with the same extravagant lifestyle that would ultimately drain his bank account, his health, and his wife's sanity would be able to see what's wrong with conspicuous consumption. Yes, you just might think that.

You would be wrong.

We hear talk from time to time about the Great American Novel, chiefly about why we have yet to see it appear. I've never known what people mean by that appellation or why they think there should be one. More significantly, I don't know why they think they lack one when they have any number of them already. There are several in this survey that can fill the bill, and quite a few that aren't but for which a case can be made. Maybe it's Tolstoy envy; hardly anything can be as all-encompassing as *War and Peace*. Maybe it's a matter of scale and scope: the GAN has to be vast, like us, wildly inclusive, like us, hugely ambitious, ditto. Yet when Thomas Pynchon gives us what we think we want, we run screaming into the night. More probably, though, it's a matter of bad attitude: we don't like the message of this or that novel that wrestles with the problem that is America. So many of our great novels are downers, showing us in an unflattering light. Maybe that's why when a slight novel by a hugely popular young novelist and short-story writer appeared in 1925 while the jazzy age of excess was roaring its loudest, despite huge expectation and good reviews, it went thud. Because it showed us in a bad light. Because it had all those things that should have been fun—wild parties and speakeasies and gangsters and affairs and jealousy—but was definitely not a romp. Because its main character was a fraud, a caricature of our dream of success who ended very badly. Who despite the title was by no means great.

If the universe were just, *The Great Gatsby* would have been F. Scott Fitzgerald's biggest novel. It *is* his biggest. It just wasn't in the moment. Today it sells a great many more copies per year than it sold in his lifetime. Granted, a huge chunk of those sales are to captive audiences, but don't you suppose there's a reason all those professors and high school teachers assign it? Aside from brevity and the eyes of Dr. T. J. Eckleburg? It's his best book by a mile. Oh, I suppose you could make a claim for *Tender Is the Night* and no one would squawk too much, but nothing else comes anywhere close. It's almost as if some force took him over in writing *Gatsby* and made him better than he could be. It avoids the purple passages of overwriting, the infelicitous expressions, and the undisciplined excesses of his early novels and stories. The characters, for once, feel like real persons and not stylized types or convenient plot devices. Fitzgerald knew all this, worked at it, delayed completion to get things just right. He wrote to Maxwell Perkins, the legendary editor who made great novelists of him and Hemingway and made anything at all of Thomas Wolfe, that he was doing something quite different and better than his earlier work, a "consciously artistic achievement." That's a fair assessment. The earlier books were written at great speed and aimed at financial, rather than artistic, achievement. The first, *This Side of Paradise*, was written to get the money to get the girl, and it succeeded. The man who lost Ginevra King because he was too poor, who determined not to lose Zelda Sayre for the same reason, did not have to ransack the imagination too long to come up with Jay Gatsby, the dreamer who becomes rich by any means in order to reclaim the dream girl who declared him too poor. And here's the change: for the first time in his career Fitzgerald knew what to do with that story artistically and was master enough of his craft to get there.

Except for the title. The one we know, the one that works perfectly, was not his choice and was never his favorite. Max Perkins came up with it based on a single phrase from the novel. The author had other ideas. That's okay, you don't have to love the title *The Great Gatsby*. But seriously, *Trimalchio in West Egg? The High-Bouncing Lover? Gold-Hatted Gatsby? Among Ash Heaps and Millionaires?* That one at least has some resonance. This list explains why there are editors. What professor of American literature is going to assign *Trimalchio in West Egg*? Even if we know Trimalchio as a randy upstart in *The Satyricon* of Petronius, and most of us don't, that title's just dopey. What tenth- or eleventh-grade teacher wants to explain to parents that *The High-Bouncing Lover* isn't some sort of porn novel? Say what you will about turning the million-word mess Wolfe gave him into *Look Homeward, Angel*, for my money Maxwell Perkins's greatest contribution to literature is giving this book its clean, slightly ironic title.

The book's story line is pretty simple on one level: boy loses girl, boy goes to incredible lengths to win girl again, boy briefly wins girl, boy destroys happiness for himself and girl and pretty much everyone around him. Which is swell, except that's not the story. This novel isn't about Gatsby. Strange, isn't it, when he's in the title? We'll get to that in a moment. First, let's lay out the story line a bit more fully.

The book begins when Nick Carraway, a young bond trader from the Midwest, moves into a house on Long Island in a place called West Egg. You will no doubt find that name improbable, as I did when I was sixteen, until you know that the author was living at the time in a Long Island town called Great Neck. West Egg is the home to a great deal of what is called "new money," fortunes earned by the persons themselves rather than by their great-grandparents. Those holders of inherited wealth, "old money" in the common parlance, live across the bay in East Egg (like you couldn't see that one coming), which is even farther out the island away from New York. Pay attention to that; geography matters immensely in this novel. In the paradise of parvenus that is West Egg the newest, biggest money belongs to Nick's neighbor, a mysterious creature named Gatsby. Everyone talks about Gatsby, just as everyone, seemingly, comes to his wild parties, but few have even spoken to him, fewer still know him, and hardly anyone has any definite facts regarding his life. This does not stop them from having definite opinions about him.

In fairly short order Nick, despite dwelling in a humble bungalow between two mansions, is invited to one of the parties. It is everything one might hope for, full of wild music and drunken revelry and bootleg liquor (remember, this is 1922) and antics of every description. And people. Lots and lots of them, of every attractive sort. He even meets the woman of his interest if not his heart, Jordan Baker, whom he had first encountered at his cousin's house, but they become separated while searching for Gatsby. Nick seems to stumble upon his host, and after some initial confusion, identities are revealed. Of course, nothing Gatsby does is accidental, and his meeting with Nick, like the invitation itself, is to a purpose: the aforementioned cousin, Daisy Buchanan, is the girl Jay Gatsby loved and lost five years earlier. Everything he has done since then has been accomplished with an eye toward winning her back, however far-fetched and ill-advised that plan might be. Daisy, from money herself, has married the very wealthy, old-money, former Yale football star, Tom Buchanan. What Gatsby cannot comprehend is how difficult that winning might prove and how his newly acquired fortune (he's a bootlegger and associate of mobsters) might not measure up. The parties, it turns out, have been part of that failure of understanding: he throws them to attract Daisy without seeing that his sort of party and his sort of crowd would be anathema to the old-money sorts of East Egg—too tawdry, too frenetic, too common. And maybe too much fun, although he doesn't enjoy them himself. He could learn from his parties, but he doesn't.

Persisting in his folly, he succeeds in getting Nick to arrange a meeting with his dream girl. He must have her; he must. Years before she had let him kiss her, and the universe shifted: "He knew that when he kissed this girl, and forever wed his unutterable visions to her perishable breath, his mind would never romp again like the mind of God." Well, there you go. When your mind cannot romp like the mind of God ever again, you have to get the girl. And he does, for a while. She comes "quite often," Gatsby tells Nick, in the afternoons. But it can't last. Daisy is too shallow and spoiled, Gatsby too romantic and fantasy-driven. It all comes apart on a trip into the city.

This is actually the third trip Nick makes to the city with other major players. On the first, he meets Tom Buchanan's mistress, Myrtle Wilson, the wife of a garage owner. She is coarse and unrealistic, not understanding how Tom is using her in the relationship and truly believing that he will leave Daisy for her. She puts on a party—very tawdry and pompous and low-rent—at the apartment Tom keeps for their trysting, which ends badly when Tom breaks her nose during a row over his not leaving Daisy. On the second, Gatsby takes Nick to lunch with a gangster named Meyer Wolfsheim (modeled on Arnold Rothstein, the man who fixed the 1919 World Series). Nick hears stories of Gatsby's past, all of them deeply suspect, as well as tales of gangsters past replete with mob hits. Each of those occasions affords Nick the opportunity to lose respect for his associates, which chance he grabs more in Tom's case than in Gatsby's.

Neither of those gatherings, however, can match the third for melodrama and disillusionment. Daisy has invited Nick and Gatsby to lunch at her mansion. Both Tom and Jordan are there, and it is decided that they will set off for the city. En route, they stop at Wilson's garage, where Wilson asks to buy Tom's wonderful car—and more importantly where Myrtle sees the car. This scene is the cause of the ultimate calamity: the car is not Tom's but Gatsby's, Tom having insisted on switching cars for the drive to town, then boasted of it to Wilson. In the city, they take a room at the Plaza Hotel for what turns out to be a desultory and ultimately ruinous party. Gatsby and Tom act more and more like rivals, until Gatsby tries to force Daisy to say that she never loved Tom, which she can't quite do, although she insists that she loved Gatsby, too, even while agreeing to marry Tom. Daisy is emotionally stripped bare by the confrontation, "You want too much," she tells Gatsby. "I love you now—isn't that enough." Tom decries Gatsby as a bootlegger, which in other circumstances would be funny, since they are engaged in doing serious damage to some whisky at the time. But this is not a funny gathering. Daisy insists on being taken home by Gatsby, but at the car, we later learn, insists on driving to "calm her nerves." Myrtle sees the car and, believing it to be driven by Tom, runs in front of it. It may be the revenge fantasy of thousands of wronged wives to run over the other woman, but this collision brings no pleasure to anyone. Daisy arrives home in worse shape than ever. Wilson confronts Tom when he, Nick, and Jordan come along later and see the scene of the wreck, and Tom claims innocence, admitting his earlier lie to extricate himself from present trouble. The next day Wilson finds Gatsby floating in his pool and shoots him, then commits suicide.

Gatsby's funeral is as empty as a pauper's. The only mourners for the man who had hundreds at his parties are his father, Nick, a postman, a handful of servants, and the owl-eyed man who at the first party had admired the library. No Daisy, no Jordan, no Wolfsheim, no revelers, no sycophants. Mr. Gatz reveals the ambition of the young Jimmy, who would rechristen himself as Jay Gatsby, the first of many, many self-inventions.

Those of you with strong memories will recall that some pages back I said this novel isn't about Gatsby. That was right before I told you the story of Gatsby. So along about now you're thinking, "So what's it about, wise guy?" Easy. It's about watching. The proper title for this volume would probably be something like *Watching Gatsby*. Just a couple of years before this novel came out, in 1923, Wallace Stevens published his first volume of poetry, *Harmonium*. The book contained a poem called "Thirteen Ways of Looking at a Blackbird," in which Stevens melded the short poem-of-a-moment's-observation program of imagism to his own meditative, philosophical practice of versification. None of the "ways" of looking is definitive; each is partial, momentary, slightly cryptic. There is nothing to suggest that Stevens in general or this poem in particular influenced Fitzgerald in writing his masterpiece; I mention it instead as a way of understanding the design of the novel, which could be called *Thirteen (or However Many Characters There Are) Ways of Looking at Gatsby*. What those characters mostly see is what they need to see, or what they expect to see, or what explains their world to them. The moment he dies and ceases to be an item of contemplation, they vanish. Before that, however, the watchers are legion. And mostly, we're interested in one of them.

Fitzgerald's great coup in the novel, it has always seemed to me, is his choice of narrator. Nick Carraway is rather stiff and snobbish, so he can disapprove of almost everyone, including his main topic of conversation, yet he is young enough and impressionable enough to be won over by Gatsby's—what? It isn't charm exactly, more his need to be charming. Or maybe his neediness in general. Here is a person who seemingly has it all, yet he cannot have the thing he most wants, and his only hope of getting it is through intermediaries. Nick, as Daisy's second cousin, once removed, is well placed for such a role. He knows her, but not well enough to be highly protective; a closer relative might rebuff Gatsby. He also disapproves of Daisy, as well he might, and actively dislikes Tom. He sees the unworthiness of Daisy as an object of Gatsby's obsession yet colludes in the dream. And at every point in the novel, he is implicated in the tragedy that is moving forward. A hundred times he could stop the proceedings with a word but does not, yet in the end as in the beginning, the entire affair is about *them*.

He's with Ford Madox Ford's John Dowell, who declares that "I don't know that analysis of my own psychology matters at all to the story," yet without whose psychology *The Good Soldier* would not exist at all. Nick stands in that line of narrators who deny culpability while seated in the middle of the ruins. If not Nick, then who? He sees the tawdry affair between Tom Buchanan and Myrtle Wilson, sees the cynicism and brutality with which Tom conducts himself. He not only sees but abets the romance between Gatsby and Daisy, even as he knows it can come to no good. He learns things about Gatsby from Wolfsheim that no one else can know. And he can prevent the fatal gathering of the novel's principals, or even bring sanity to the drive home, by leaving with his friend. He does none of these. Yet in his final analysis it is all about *them*—what they did and didn't do, the way they conducted themselves.

What he does do is watch. He's a bystander but no innocent. At times he seems not so much to be watching a slow-motion train wreck as to be watching *for* a wreck. Which he gets. He is the most prominent of voyeurs in a book chock-full of them. Herein lies the brilliance of Fitzgerald's narratorial decision. Nick sees everything in the novel, which on one level is what it means to be a first-person narrator. And what Nick mostly sees is that the object of Gatsby's obsession is unworthy of the herculean efforts made on her behalf. But also perhaps that the efforts are themselves corrupt, the product of a misunderstanding about the nature of the world. Daisy is simply not worth the efforts Gatsby makes to win her, nor are his successes anything to write home about. He's a gangster, ruthless, amoral, willing to do whatever it takes to succeed. We can make whatever arguments we choose that a gangster is merely a businessman without a corner office, that he's Fitzgerald's emblem of American business at large or the frenetic and unprincipled stock market, but the fact remains, he's a gangster. And what Nick sees is that Daisy is not a good enough reason to have become one.

What he does not, perhaps cannot, see is that it's not about Daisy. Yes, Daisy is present as the object of immediate desire, and the speaker who denied the poor youth Jay Gatsby admission into the club. But she's merely a dream stand-in, merely the embodiment of the Unattainable. Poor Jay Gatsby can never acquire social acceptance. His later wealthy avatar fares no better. His new wealth is suspect, along with his garish presentation of himself, his underworld connections, and his protean self-narratives. Besides, as we see with Daisy and Tom and Jordan Baker, privilege and social acceptance are no guarantors of happiness or tranquility. Gatsby's real dream, his Dream, is of something that doesn't really exist. He aspires to some platonic ideal of success. It's not so much dream as fantasy: the Daisy he imagines swooning into his arms forever is a fantasy woman, and his fantasy cannot survive its brutal clash with reality. Ultimately, he dies not of George Wilson's bullet but of a broken dream, of the smash-up of the fantasy he has spent years endlessly constructing. The dream, however, has been broken all along, a fact to which he has been entirely blind.

That's what the book is about, blindness. And vision, of course; you can't have one without the other. And seeing and not seeing, insight and its opposite, and watching, and eyes. That's why the book is presided over by the eyes of Dr. T. J. Eckleburg, an enormous, fading sign for a probably defunct eye doctor. The eyes are enormous, faceless, blue, and creepy, looking out over the Valley of Ashes (we'll come back to that in a moment). That's why there's such emphasis on the man with owl-shaped glasses who peruses Gatsby's library at a party and then, unaccountably perhaps, is the only partygoer to show up at the funeral. Nearly everyone is watching someone else in the novel. Most, naturally, are watching Gatsby. But he's watching Daisy, even when he can't see her and can only see the green light on her dock. Myrtle Wilson watches for Tom to move through her field of vision. George Wilson is so busy watching for a deal that he doesn't see what his wife is getting up to. He does see her get killed but doesn't see what he thinks he sees: Daisy, not Gatsby, is driving the car, so when he goes looking for the owner of the yellow Rolls Royce, he finds him but does not, as he expects, find his wife's killer.

That's a pattern running through the novel: characters see things that aren't there and don't see others that are. And that's another major theme: illusion and disillusionment. Gatsby, of course, lives in illusion and dies, as I suggested earlier, of disillusionment. Before that, he has been a master illusionist, creating spectacles at which hundreds of persons deluded themselves into believing they were happy or celebrated or clever. The Buchanans are so wealthy that "they smashed up things and creatures and then retreated back into their money or vast carelessness" or, I would add, their shared illusions that their money could make them happy or make everything all right. The disillusionment belongs chiefly to Nick, who has come east full of expectations and has them dashed: the "good" people are terrible, everyone is a cheat or a fraud, and the one person who fully embraces the principles of success and advancement is destroyed. Other than that, everything is fine. Seeing things clearly destroys Nick's illusion and sends him back to the West again.

What he sees and dislikes so intently is corruption. The East is a place of dust, rot, and ash. Those fading eyes of Dr. T. J. Eckleburg reign over the valley of ashes, a vast dumping ground of ash and cinders from New York's countless coal-fired furnaces and power plants. The scene is gray and dismal and bears more than a passing resemblance to the Valley of the Shadow, and of course it is the site of one of the novel's literal deaths. Its function, however, is largely symbolic of the more general corruption in the story at large. Wolfsheim, like his model, Arnold

Rothstein, receives credit for fixing the 1919 World Series. Jordan Baker cheats at golf and doesn't bother hiding it very much. Tom cheats on his wife but has no particular fondness for his mistress. The title character, of course, is into every sort of illegal mischief, some of which is so dangerous that people are afraid to talk about it. The parties are decadent, and each drink consumed is an illegal act in Prohibition. Everyone, it seems, is looking for an angle, an advantage, a dodge, a subterfuge. The resulting moral landscape, like the valley of ashes, is a wasteland.

So what's the deal with a bunch of seedy people with challenged ethics? I hate to bring this up, but they're us. In the hothouse atmosphere of New York in the 1920s, when fortunes were made and lost daily and stocks were being sold from pushcarts on Wall Street, greed and corruption were rampant. While Fitzgerald never says very much about the business side of Nick's life, he encodes that immoral behavior in the general milieu. He presents all this as a perversion of the American Dream, which traditionally has had to do with freedom, opportunity, space to build a life, but which has been replaced by grasping, win-at-all-costs materialism. Had this novel appeared in the 1930s, that insight would not be remarkable. But it was published in 1925, more than four years before the crash, about which, I believe, it is prescient. The irony is that Fitzgerald the writer could diagnose the illness but Fitzgerald the man could not save himself with that knowledge. He was as caught up in the materialism of the age, as dazzled by wealth, as susceptible to the unworthy dream as anyone could be. As has often been observed, the person who writes is not the same as the one who eats breakfast in the morning or goes to parties on Saturday or shops at Macy's, and in the case of Fitzgerald, the writer was not only vastly more insightful but evidently incapable of using those insights to save his ordinary self. As I said at the top of this piece, ironies accrue. Add this one to the list.

CHAPTER TWELVE

LIFE IS A CARNIVAL
The Sun Also Rises

In his great poem "Easter 1916," William Butler Yeats speaks of believing, in Dublin before the Easter Rising of that year, that he "but lived where motley is worn." After the rebellion and the execution of its leaders by Britain, he came to realize that Ireland was the place where only one color was worn or ever would be: green—the hue of Irish national identity. Other countries sometimes have that experience as well, when some singular event changes the way they understand something about themselves. Sometimes the sea change is social or political, sometimes spiritual, and, once in a great while, literary.

At the beginning of 1926, Americans wrote the way Americans wrote—every man (or woman) for him (or her) self, catch-as-catch-can. Then a young Yank living in Paris published a novel with the most important editor at the most important house in modern fiction. Nothing much, just some fishing, some alienation, some romantic and sexual difficulties, and a whole lot of drinking. Nothing there to change society, perhaps, but by year's end, America, and especially American writing, would never be the same. Oh, did I mention the bullfighting?

There's nothing special in terms of plot in *The Sun Also Rises*. Ernest Hemingway sends a couple of footloose young veterans, but chiefly Jake Barnes, to Spain, specifically to Pamplona and the Festival of San Fermin. Along the way, they meet up with other Americans, some of whom they like and one, Robert Cohn, whom they detest. They also encounter Lady Brett Ashley, the woman Jake loves but, because of his terrible injury, cannot make love to. Jake and his pal Bill go trout fishing, extol the virtues of Rioja Alta wine and Fundador brandy, drink too much, quarrel with nearly everyone, attend the bullfights, watch the running of the bulls, and even befriend a young matador, with whom Brett takes up for a time. Nothing, however, can assuage Jake's loneliness or improve his disaffection, and he remains at the end of the novel largely as he was at the beginning, if slightly more accepting. An interesting story of the lives of young people after the Great War, it would remain an interesting literary footnote but for one thing: it's the novel where Hemingway, learning as he went, taught America to write.

Never again would fiction be the same. No one can write *like* Hemingway, but we all write after him, and we can only write unlike him through an act of will. Without him, there is no minimalism, no Raymond Carver, its most accomplished practitioner. Without him, there would be no hard-boiled detective novels or stories, certainly not in the form we know. Raymond Chandler, John D. McDonald, Mickey Spillane, or Robert B. Parker—with no Hemingway before them? Unimaginable. Without him, war novels would be entirely different, and *Going After Cacciato* would be virtually impossible, and maybe unnecessary. When an American, especially an American male, sits down to write fiction, Hemingway is the eight-hundred-pound gorilla in the room.

How did it get this way? That's a longer story than the novel in question. According to legend, Sherwood Anderson advised the young newspaperman-turned-literary writer to move to Paris, where the living was cheap. Paris in the 1920s also had the advantage of being where everyone went. While there, Hemingway met and got on well with Ezra Pound, who gave him some early advice about cutting out adjectives and adverbs, as well as Gertrude Stein and Alice B. Toklas, whose salons he attended, James Joyce, with whom he sometimes went over-drinking and whose *Ulysses* he called "a most goddamn wonderful book," George Antheil, the young bad boy of musical composition, Pablo Picasso, Joan Miró, and, well, pretty much *tout le monde*, from an artistic point of view. He was friends with John Dos Passos, and he famously met F. Scott Fitzgerald in the Dingo Bar in April of 1925. Fitzgerald had just published *The Great Gatsby* a couple of weeks earlier, while Hemingway had published nothing much. They did not hit it off at first, but a lunch a couple of days later went much better. Then in July, Hemingway and his wife Hadley traveled to Pamplona with a loose assortment of friends and acquaintances for the Festival of San Fermin, which was virtually unknown to Americans in 1925 but would be world-famous by 1927, all because of the novel he would write. Among the friends were Harold Loeb, who would become the model for Robert Cohn, and Lady Duff Twysden, whose name Hemingway improves to Lady Brett Ashley. He had a bit of a thing for Lady Duff and considerable envy that she went off for several days with Loeb, whom he did not much like (just as Jake Barnes in the novel does not like Cohn yet tolerates him as a "friend"), while poor Ernie was stuck with his own beautiful young wife. Life is so unfair sometimes. There was also a sensational young matador named Cayetano Ordoñez, who would become the model for Romero. The group drank far too much, quarreled and fought, lusted and resented, and generally behaved quite badly; it was perfect. He turned the experience, as he did so many in the early days, into an article on the mayhem and magic of "Pamplona in July." But he also soon realized that he just might have the material for a novel on his hands. He worked on it through the late summer and finished a draft in something under two months, and then, to get away from that story, drafted his satirical *Torrents of Spring*, in which he travesties his mentor, Anderson. Charles Scribner's Sons ultimately accepted that book in order to get the one it wanted, and Hemingway got what every young writer should have, Maxwell Perkins as his editor. Alas, not every beginning novelist can land the greatest editor in the world, only a select few—Hemingway of course, Fitzgerald, Thomas Wolfe. Lucky them.

The novel, by the way, is known as *Fiesta* almost everywhere except in the United States. I guess that's an acceptable title, but nothing so cryptic and marvelous as the one we know, which is drawn from the second epigraph, and that from the Ecclesiastes passage on generations succeeding one another while the earth abides forever. The first epigraph is Gertrude Stein's observation, "You are all a lost generation." We are often inclined to credit Hemingway with inventing that notion, but it belongs to a writer considerably his elder. Taken together, the two tell us nearly everything we need to know about the novel. In a very real sense, the rising generation will not succeed the old one, or not very successfully, because so many of its males were slaughtered in that stupidest of wars that used trenches in place of abattoirs. Yet Stein's remark is not directed at the dead but at the survivors, no "they were" but rather "you are" all a lost generation. I cannot speak for previous eras, but it seems reasonably certain that some older person has said that to someone of the rising generation in every decade since she uttered it. *Fiesta* was the working title while Hemingway was composing the book, but it feels so weightless in comparison with the final title. Besides, his titles are never that short: *A Farewell to Arms* (a corruption of a title and beginning of a poem by George Peele), *Death in the Afternoon*, *For*

Whom the Bell Tolls (a John Donne prepositional phrase), and the thoroughly mythic *The Old Man and the Sea*. Next to that, how can *Fiesta* possibly be the right choice?

The novel is a tragicomedy, although I am not aware of his ever using the term, in three acts. Book 1 consists of seven chapters and confines itself to life in Paris. Book 2 is made up of twelve chapters leading up to and through the riotous festival. The single-chapter Book 3 is the very bad hangover. The damage has been done, the friendships wrecked, the Rubicon crossed. And Pamplona just does not care:

> *In the morning it was all over. The fiesta was finished. I woke about nine o'clock, had a bath, dressed, and went down-stairs. The square was empty and there were no people on the streets. A few children were picking up rocket-sticks in the square. The cafes were just opening and the waiters were carrying out the comfortable white wicker chairs and arranging them around the marble-topped tables in the shade of the arcade. They were sweeping the streets and sprinkling them with a hose.*

That's what an indifferent universe sounds like. Getting on with its own business. Working at its own pace. Ignoring the thrashings and wailing of the self-absorbed actors in the struggle. The message is simple, "I'm done with you now. Find your own way home." But of course, that's what the characters cannot find, a way home. Or a home. They have no place they need to be, nowhere that recommends itself as destination or sanctuary. They won't so much go toward something as simply go.

That passage also demonstrates something else, the vaunted Hemingway style. Historically, we have tended to think of "style" as something added on, florid, with bells and whistles and embedded clauses. That Henry James, now *there's* a style. Or Melville—what a stylist. But Hemingway takes us in the opposite direction, toward something that is almost an anti-style. It is really very straightforward and the rules are simple. Write with nouns and verbs (in the above version, just nouns, the main and almost exclusive verb being "was"). Eschew elaboration. Avoid adjectives and kill adverbs entirely. Strip the body linguistic down to its skeleton. Don't say quite what you mean. Say less. Leave the big stuff submerged, like an iceberg.

Words don't mean what they normally do, especially in the mouths of characters. "Fine" is the typical response to the question, "How are you," but in this novel "fine" can mean any of dozens of possible things up to and sometimes including "rotten," which is probably the second most frequent reply. We can only know what sort of "fine" Jake is feeling from the context and the subsequent conversation. If someone, especially Brett, says something like, "Don't be that way," it was clearly not a good "fine" that was offered. At other times, it can actually mean something like "not actively terrible," "okay," or "pretty good, thanks for asking." Hemingway's point is that we simply can't tell by the words used. Rather, we need to know, need to watch for, how they are used and how others respond to them.

Where William Faulkner is all elaboration, all embedded clauses and run-on sentences and breathlessness, all trying to jam everything in at once, Hemingway is simplicity itself. So easy a child can do it. Except that it is not. A thousand stylistic boats have run aground on those shoals. His is a false simplicity, a thing that looks effortless and even, sometimes, mindless but, as his emulators keep proving, very difficult to accomplish. What's simple and easy is the sentence structure itself: subject-verb-object, or sometimes just subject-verb, over and over. S-V-O. S-V-O. S-V-O. Any numbskull can do that, right?

Try it sometime.

As an example, let's go back to that description of the morning after. Just the first two sentences tell you worlds beyond what they seem to say, "In the morning it was all over. The fiesta was finished." "All over" does indeed mean concluded, completed. But it can also suggest something more like, "killed off." The same with "finished": there's a distinct sense of something defunct here, particularly with some earlier descriptions of the fiesta being most definitely alive. Add to that the residue of the dead rockets and the hosing down of the street, the emptiness of the streets, and there is a strong implication that something has died. As in fact it has. Illusions have been destroyed, possibilities closed down, friendships broken.

Or take the closing passage of the novel, with its famously ironic last question:

> The driver started up the street. I settled back. Brett moved close to me. We sat close to each other. I put my arm around her and she rested against me comfortably. It was very hot and bright, and the houses looked sharply white. We turned out into the Gran Via.
>
> "Oh, Jake," Brett said, "we could have had such a damned good time together."
>
> Ahead was a mounted policeman in khaki directing traffic. He raised his baton. The car slowed suddenly pressing Brett against me.
>
> "Yes," I said. "Isn't it pretty to think so?"

One of his principal techniques is repetition. The "hot and bright" appears earlier in the paragraph, minus the adverb. The simple phrase repeated calls attention to it, suggesting both something uncomfortable (it is hot, not warm) and stark. Jake can see things, and not merely the "sharply white" houses, all too well. In such stark relief, Brett's question is exposed for the safe lie that it is. Her verb tense, very carefully chosen, gives the game away, not "we could have" but "we could have had" that good time. She could, but does not, choose to have that time with him henceforth. Jake's response, "Isn't it pretty to think so," says that he knows it's a fantasy and suspects she does as well, although he'll not contradict her openly. This is all done with no words of any real substance. She neither says what sort of time they could have had, "damned good" being notably empty, nor why they couldn't have it. His "pretty" is so open-ended that it can be taken to mean almost anything, although his meaning is clear enough, that it is safe to say such things after the opportunity has been squandered. What really makes the scene, however, is the punctuating action before his reply. The taxi slowing, Brett is "pressed against" him, evidently without volition. Indeed, the will does not even lie with the driver, for it is the policeman, the complete outsider, who controls the action. If she presses herself against Jake, the meaning is entirely changed. It is one of the great endings in all literature, full of ambiguity and disillusionment and, in Jake's earlier terms, irony and pity. It suggests the hopelessness of the situation of this "lost generation" that has been so damaged by recent world events. When it appeared, it was also shockingly new, not just as subject matter but as prose strategy.

Hemingway's story "Hills like White Elephants" is a favorite of anthologists, and for good reason: it teaches readers how to read. More to the point, it teaches them to read what isn't said. On the surface, the man and the "girl" are merely discussing what to have to drink while waiting for a train on a Spanish railway platform. But they're also discussing something else, some "procedure" that the man claims is "very simple," that they "just let the air in." The girl, as she is called, although it's clear from what's really being discussed that she's much more than a girl, says she knows it's very simple. Each of them tries in several ways to get the other to take responsibility for the decision to have "it" done. And there is a lot of rancor about drinks and hills, much more than landscape or liquor usually invoke, so something else is going on. Everyone I've ever known who has taught the story has the same experience, namely, that a certain number of class members will have read it diligently and still come to class with no idea that the referent that is never used for "it" is abortion. What's going on is that they are learning Hemingway's version of Frost's "sound of sense" theory. Where Frost said that you can discern the sense of a conversation just from the rhythm and sounds of it, even if you can't hear the words, so Hemingway believes that you can intuit major substance words even if they are not used simply by observing how the surrounding conversation is constructed. In this case, students nearly always have a head-slap moment when they realize what they haven't seen but should have. And if one is very lucky, some student will ask, rather apologetically if, you know, maybe that conversation between the lovers is about, um, an abortion? Because she is just amazed that it could possibly have been a topic way back then and even more amazed that it could have been used in a story. Which is his point, really. That it couldn't be used. That, because of censorship rules, it could only be discussed obliquely. And the story is all the more shocking for that.

In our novel, the thing that is never mentioned is the specific nature of Jake's injury. It is clear that he is maimed in some way one can't see when his clothes are on, and clear that the maiming in some way impedes his ability to physically love Brett Ashley, which lack they both believe, at least initially, keeps them from being happy and together. But the closest readers get to an answer are hints and allegations. Brett doesn't want the man she passionately desires, Jake, to kiss her, because it can't lead anywhere. A general who came to visit Jake in the hospital said he gave up more than his life—less than helpful in the circumstances. Jake engages, then ultimately dismisses, a prostitute. After

Brett declines to come upstairs to Jake's flat, he thinks about her sexual proclivities, obliquely of course, and is brought to tears. Hemingway is said to have objected to the term "impotent" for Jake, stating instead that he had all of the desire and none of the mechanism to act on it. In any case, the injury is to the genitalia and renders him incapable of sexual satisfaction, leading him to question his masculinity in numerous ways, the more so because he finds himself in a hypersexual environment of brawling males and matadors—and one very sexed-up woman.

The nature of his injury, or rather its cultural implications, points to a very important feature of the novel. The great myth for the postwar writers is the wasteland, the formerly lovely earth beset by ruin and infertility. The most famous version, of course, is T. S. Eliot's poem that changed everything. But there are lots of wastelands besides *The Waste Land*. Federico García Lorca's play *Blood Wedding* is one famous example, and *Gatsby*, with its ash heaps and broken spirits, another. Hemingway visits this space numerous times, not least in "Hills like White Elephants" and his second novel, *A Farewell to Arms*. This one, however, has everything—meaningless (and nonreproductive) sex, sexual injury, intellectual and emotional impoverishment, emptiness, spiritual barrenness. It even has a reasonable approximation of the Fisher King, when Jake and Bill take off into the Pyrenees in pursuit of trout. As with a great many of the wasteland works of the era, there is much activity but no significance to it. Nor is there hope. The epigraph from Ecclesiastes stands as an ironic commentary on the action. This is the story of one man, but it is also the story of a generation. He will not be succeeded by another generation, any more than will be those tens of millions of the dead from the recent war. That cataclysm disrupted biological and cultural succession, destroying artists and thinkers as well as cobblers and farmers. It laid waste to tens of thousands of square kilometers of land and assured for many decades to come that lives would be lost to previously buried ordnance. It seemed, in so many ways, like the end of the world. Compared to that, what is the waste of a few lives and souls? Hemingway rarely mentions the terrible cost of the larger war, yet almost all the significant players, excepting Robert Cohn, are veterans. Their status reminds us of the unspoken horrors of their near past, and of the unhappy state of the present.

The Sun Also Rises is the defining moment in American modernist fiction. It shows what a new novel can look like, sound like, feel like. It demonstrates what fiction can become in this new, postwar environment. And we do well to remember that even its author didn't know what the novel could become when he began it; composition, in this case, was a process of discovery. This was, after all, a first novel. He had practiced his art in short stories with success, but book-length fiction is a different beast. In his excellent study of how that style became the one we know, Hemingway's The Sun Also Rises: The Crafting of a Style, Frederic J. Svoboda says of this novel that it "demonstrated his mastery over all the skills he had practiced and perfected in his earlier work. The book, perhaps more importantly, shows his maturation into an artist of the first rank in his ability to integrate and interrelate all the varied elements of the novel, subordinating each to the overall effects he aimed to achieve, emphasizing or playing down each as his material required, but never losing sight of the whole." What is equally remarkable is the way he can manage that juggling act with the smallest of building blocks. Not an easy task, keeping your eye on the big picture while turning a magnifying glass on the sentences.

We did not know what Americans sounded like until we read this book. No one knew because no one had ever stopped to listen before. Oh, some regions were charted, and some classes. Twain is very good on the dialects that we might collectively categorize as Missouri Unschooled. And James is all over the opposite, upper register. But before

Hemingway, we had no sense of what Americans might sound like collectively. Of course, these characters are just as small a sampling as any other, and they come out of a shared experience. But Jake and Bill Gorton and Robert Cohn are from different backgrounds, different places, and their rhythms and habits suggest something more universal. Most of all, Jake is from nowhere very specific, and it is his language that teaches us about a sound. Dashiell Hammett, another ambulance driver, will pick it up just three years later in *The Maltese Falcon*. Raymond Chandler will learn it from him and *every* mystery writer will learn it from Chandler. Even the very bad ones. Dos Passos will take it up from Hemingway, with some modifications, for the narrative sections of *U.S.A.* Other writers will pick up the manner, and the mannerisms. The godfather of minimalism, Raymond Carver, sometimes sounds more like Hemingway than Hemingway. His style, and especially his dialogue, is pared down, clipped, elliptical, simple, spare. Tim O'Brien will use Hemingway's style, and his code, and fight against it every step of the way. That's how writers develop their own style. S-V-O. S-V-O. S-V-O. If you hit a rut, use an "and." Don't land on the meaning; land on the silence next to the meaning. Trust the subtext. Give nothing away. Follow the iceberg. You'll be fine.

THIRTEEN

IT TAKES A WEARY MAN
TO SING A WEARY SONG
The Weary Blues

The point of a literary conversation is that it is a *conversation*. Back and forth. Not merely accomplishment and influence but ongoing dialogue. Sometimes the nature of that talk is pretty subtle, so much so that we have to work pretty hard to see the signs and intuit what's being said. At other times, there is no mistaking the intent, the complaint, the reply. It can be something like this, "I, too, sing America." Now that's how to throw down a marker. Nothing to it, just call out your national poet for leaving you out. Stake your claim for recognition as a spokesman for your people.

The man who wrote that was twenty-four years old.

Here's the poem in question:

I hear America singing, the varied carols I hear,
Those of mechanics, each one singing his as it should be blithe and
        strong,
The carpenter singing his as he measures his plank or beam,

The mason singing his as he makes ready for work, or leaves off
  work,
The boatman singing what belongs to him in his boat, the deck-
  hand singing on the steamboat deck,
The shoemaker singing as he sits on his bench, the hatter singing as
  he stands,
The wood-cutter's song, the ploughboy's on his way in the morn-
  ing, or at noon intermission or at sundown,
The delicious singing of the mother, or of the young wife at work,
  or of the girl sewing or washing,
Each singing what belongs to him or her and to none else,
The day what belongs to the day—at night the party of young fel-
  lows, robust, friendly,
Singing with open mouths their strong melodious songs.

That's Whitman, of course, from 1855. It's robust and hopeful
and, in intent, inclusive. Lots of different occupations and places, lots
of persons. And here's the question: who's missing? If you're Langston
Hughes, the answer is pretty simple: me, us.

This is not to say there are no persons of color in *Leaves of Grass*, only
that the assumptions Whitman makes tend to be pretty white. That
fact is not all that astonishing; the great majority of African Americans before the Great Migration in the early twentieth century lived in
the South. In 1855, they were down on the farm, and it wasn't theirs.
By 1926, their numbers were much greater in the North than seventy
years earlier, and Harlem had become the great city of black America.
So maybe the times called for a reset on some of those assumptions:

I, too, sing America.
I am the darker brother.

They send me to eat in the kitchen
When company comes,
But I laugh,
And eat well,
And grow strong.

Hughes calls this poem "I, Too," but he could just as easily call it "Hey, Walt." That's more or less what another obstreperous son, Ezra Pound, does, saying he makes a pact with Whitman so that he can get over or around the great predecessor. Of course, Hughes's audience is considerably broader than just Whitman. In fact, and this is a hallmark of the poetry in his first volume, *The Weary Blues* (1926), there are multiple target readerships in the poet's mind. One is Whitman and those of his followers who might be blithe enough to believe that in speaking for white folks they speak for "Americans." Another is white audiences more generally who, should they stumble across these poems, will discover that there is another race with both shared and opposing concerns in historical, social, and literary arenas. Finally, his main targets are readers in the African American community. This audience is the toughest nut to crack, so he walks a very fine line. He will make use of dialect, church rhythms of call-and-response, and nontraditional art forms, especially jazz and blues, to make his points, and even in his own time, dialect in particular was a ticklish subject. Familiarity has not always bred favor.

But to return to the poem in question, the two words in the title are equally significant. The "I" is claiming its natural right to speak for itself, answering back not merely to Whitman's poem cited above but to *Whitman* at large. Everywhere we look, it's a song of Walt's self, "I celebrate myself and sing myself," and so on. Hughes's poem says, hey, wait a minute, I get to do that, too. That's where the "too" comes in: it asserts that while this is in some ways an echo, it is also a rebuttal, a correction, an erratum slip inserted into the master text of these United States. Yes, Walt Whitman, you have that right, but then so have I. Then he takes us somewhere that may surprise us with the line, "I am the darker brother." It may be hard for contemporary readers to grasp, but the choice of the word "brother" in this context was deeply radical at the time. The notion of universal brotherhood was by no means universal, and not only below Mason and Dixon. And it is meant to draw that other line, the one based on color that decided who ate where and who could use the front door. I suppose it is fairly well known but it is nevertheless worth mentioning that during the 1920s, the most famous venue for black performers in the country, Harlem's famed Cotton Club, did not admit them as patrons. When the poem addresses the question of who eats where, it is not an academic exercise. None of that matters very much, says the speaker; even if you hide me away when company comes as something to be ashamed of, I eat and grow stronger, and one day you will not be able to deny me. One day, when company comes, "They'll see how beautiful I am / and be ashamed." This may be the first overt statement in our history of the later declaration, "Black is beautiful." One can almost hear the chorus of '60s support, "Right on, brother." Or at least an amen. Hughes closes the poem with an even more provocative statement, "I, too, am America." He has moved far beyond the opening line. Not some small part of America. Not a junior partner or domestic servant to be pushed out of sight. The real deal: "am America."

Hey, Walt, are you getting all this?

The simplicity and directness of this poem contrasts nicely with Hughes's first and probably best-known poem, "The Negro Dreams of Rivers." Sonorous, deliberate, full of detail, it provides a complete argument about why the "Negro" of the title must be taken seriously. "I've known rivers," the speaker says twice, along with "My soul has grown deep like the rivers." The rivers he dreams of are the big ones of history, the Euphrates, the Congo, the Nile, the Mississippi. In the words of Johnny Cash, "I've been everywhere, man." The speaker, the voice of a race, really, has the collective experience of having been present since the beginning of human time, of being tied into the deepest knowledge of the world. We do well to recall in this context that, following Heraclitus, rivers are time; Hughes flips that from a river being our individual experience of time to a river being the time of human experience. It's a beautiful thing.

We would also do well to recall that this position is again very radical. When he was writing this poem, he did not have the benefit of Louis and Mary Leakey, whose work proved that humankind got its start in Africa. The Piltdown Man hoax in 1912 demonstrated that much of the world was prepared to believe the fiction that early humans arose in East Sussex. The hoax was not completely debunked until the 1950s. The reason such a thing was possible was that many early paleontologists and Darwinians firmly believed that the white race must be more highly evolved and therefore older than the darker races in general and the black one in particular, so therefore they must have got a head start by evolving in some northerly clime. The history of science is not always an edifying sight.

Hughes, however, doesn't care about all that. He's less interested in the science of the matter than in the morality, less in the morality than in what we might call the logical inevitability. He isn't saying, "We got here first." Rather, he suggests that, "We've been here long enough." Assuming forever is enough, which seems fair enough. "The Negro Dreams of Rivers" argues for acceptance of the claim that black people can make for full membership in the brotherhood of humanity. Not three-fifths of a person but a whole one, an equal one, a respected one. I told you he was radical.

It would be wrong, however, to suggest that the entire volume is concerned with human rights. What it really takes as its subject is human beings. Which as we know are much more interesting. The book is full of all sorts of little poems on a host of topics—the death of an old sailor, for instance, or a sick woman lying "between two lovers— / Life and Death." These poems often come very close to the imagism of Pound, Williams, and H.D., little gems that shine for a mere moment. There are seascape and landscape and sunset poems, the stuff of much poetry in many traditions. Which is part of the point. Hughes is demonstrating that he is indeed a poet, not an essayist in verse. And he *is* a poet. Even at a very young age, he has an understanding of poetic traditions and forms. He also shows that he's willing to break those forms or, more dramatically, invent his own, when the occasion calls for it. One poem is called "To a Little Lover-Lass, Dead," and it is about just what it sounds like. It evokes rather than describes, offers hints rather than certainties. This is part of Hughes's method in the book. He shares with his white modernist contemporaries the belief that a wink is as good as a nod, so there are winks aplenty. At the same time, he occasionally takes on those contemporaries, as when he replies to "Danse Russe" by Williams with his own "Danse Africaine," with its "low beating of the tom-toms, / The slow beating of the tom-toms." He then plays off "low" and "slow," "soft" and "slow," "beating" and "tom-toms" in a brilliant play of word textures augmenting meaning.

Not surprisingly, Harlem pops up in a number of poems. He captures not merely the scene but the rhythm and feel of the place in "Harlem Night Club":

Sleek black boys in a cabaret.
Jazz-band, jazz-band,—

Play, plAY, PLAY!
Tomorrow. . . . who knows?
Dance today!

If that sounds something like, "Eat, drink, and be merry," it should. But it isn't just that. That run of the word play, with its progressive capitalization, drives the poem forward and seeks to capture the frenetic pace of the music. This is not cool jazz. This stuff is *hot*. Harlem also pops up in "Lenox Avenue: Midnight," "Harlem Night Song," "Disillusion," and "Summer Night." One notices that very little of the Harlem material has to do with daytimes, shopping, or stores. This is the Harlem of nightclubs, streetwalkers and nightwalkers, musicians, art, and JAZZ.

If one thing predominates over all others in the book, it is music. Imagine that, in a volume called *The Weary Blues*. In "The Cat and the Saxophone (2 a.m.)," he interweaves the lyrics of the song "Everybody Loves My Baby" with the background club noises of drinks being ordered and served, flirting, and kissing, with the effect that we feel the "impurity" of the performance. No song in a club is ever offered to a silent audience. There are also the previously mentioned "Danse Africaine," "Song for a Banjo Dance," "Jazzonia," "Cabaret," "Young Singer," and "Negro Dancers," as well as the title poem. It is a poem about a blues rather than a straight blues itself, but it captures the thumping rhythms and wholesale repetitions. The poem is about the music but also about the man making it: "With his ebony hands on each ivory key / He made that poor piano moan with melody." Those blues, which he describes as "sweet," are "coming from a black man's soul." This music, in other words, grows out of a very specific racial experience. Already in the mid-1920s there were beginning to be white performers of music that had come out of the black communities in New Orleans and Memphis and the Delta, so Hughes feels the need to stake a claim on the music before it becomes mainstream, homogenized. But he also wants to explore the ways that this music expresses something of the African American soul. When the player is finished and goes to bed, he's all spent, a thing no longer alive. His living self was poured into "that sad raggy tune." Part of the program of the volume is to chart the nature of the contemporary black experience. The poems do not concern themselves directly with slavery or rural living. This is the city, one city-within-a-city in particular, and a big part of that life is musical. Harlem in the 1920s was defined by jazz, by dancing and singing and playing, and by the beat that underscored the frenetic pace of urban life, and it's all here in these poems.

One of the most musical poems in the volume has nothing to do, overtly at least, with jazz and blues. "When Sue Wears Red," which we can call not so much a love poem as one of desire, plays like a song, verse and refrain:

When Susanna Jones wears red
Her face is like an ancient cameo
Turned brown by the ages.
Come with a blast of trumpets,
Jesus!

Susanna lights a fire in the speaker, "a love-fire sharp like pain," to be specific. When she wears red, she's hot all right, but she becomes more than just that. She is transformed, like the speaker about rivers, into the product of her people's entire history, a bearer of witness to the antiquity of the race, coming down untold ages from some "time-dead Egyptian night." Not to mention a religious experience with a brass chorus. That's a lot of freight for one woman with a red dress, not to mention one small poem, but Hughes thinks she can handle it. She is all those things: embodiment of the race, individual being, emblem of desire, inspiration for poet and musician, source of ecstatic fervor. So, too, is the life of black folks many things at once. Spiritual and physical, sacred and profane, artistic and workaday, ancient and new. Why be just one, any more than Susanna can be only one?

Always, at root, the poems are anchored in racial consciousness and racial aspirations. The poem we most associate with Hughes, thanks to Lorraine Hansberry's *A Raisin in the Sun*, "Harlem [2]," with its dream deferred, is not in this volume, but the dreams are, in "Dream Variations" and "The Dream Keeper." In the latter, the speaker invites the dreamers to bring their dreams to him for safekeeping "Away from the too-rough fingers / of the world." In the former, he takes up one of his favorite themes, that of luxuriating in the freedom of doing what he wants, in this case dancing and whirling through the day, out in the open under the sun, until night comes and sleep takes him. His dream has two stanzas, culminating in "Dark like me" and "Black like me," which is the title of another famous book. Hughes is the Shakespeare of African American writing, a wellspring of potential titles with ready-made associations.

Years later, Hughes would go on to write one of his most anthologized poems, "Theme for English B," about a student whose response to the assignment, write an essay about yourself, challenges the assumptions of the white instructor. He is very much like the instructor in hopes, dreams, likes and dislikes, and all the basic human qualities, but somewhat different in terms of the experiences handed to him by segregated society. It is a great poem. It should be: he had already been writing it for years. That's the message of *The Weary Blues*. African Americans are fully human, he tells us again and again—loving life, celebrating and mourning, dancing and reflecting, embracing the dualities of day and night, land and sea, earth and sky, life and death. They differ from white Americans experientially, as the descendents of slaves and victims of racial discrimination. Put together, the two strains paint a picture of black life that few white Americans had seen. The poems make it impossible to fall back onto the stereotypes of the day. This is work of intelligence, insight, sensitivity, rhythm, music, social criticism, and joy. Together with his fellow writers in the Harlem Renaissance—Claude McCay, Countee Cullen, Nella Larsen, Jessie Redmon Fauset, Alain Locke, Jean Toomer, and all the rest— along with the hundreds of musicians and visual artists and actors and dancers, Hughes helped provide the most complete view of black life that mainstream America had ever seen. And the mainstream ate it up. Fitzgerald told us as much when he coined the term "Jazz Age" for the era. The age may have chiefly benefited white people in his stories, but the soundtrack came from Harlem. When Paul Whiteman and George Gershwin and Bix Beiderbecke made their forays into jazz, they came to it as outsiders, learning from black composers and performers. And when white poets and even English poets such as Mina Loy tried their hands at free-form jazz poetry, they were walking paths blazed by Hughes and Cullen and McCay. Oh, they definitely had an impact.

Is it possible for a writer to be too successful, too much the face of an age? If so, then Langston Hughes suffered from that malady. His was the poetic voice of his age in black America, but all ages pass away. By the time of his death, younger writers of the Black Arts movement could openly dismiss him as passé, as insufficiently radical or too willing to accommodate the mainstream view. As much as anything, it was a sign of the times. Jesse Owens, the man who humiliated Hitler at the 1936 Olympics where he openly disproved Aryan supremacy— four times—was called an Uncle Tom by the dissenters in Mexico City in 1968. Louis Armstrong, who confronted racism younger musicians never even witnessed, was similarly ridiculed by that same later generation. In each case, what the younger performers failed to understand was that their radicalism, their strength, was made possible by those belittled forebears. Amiri Baraka would not have been possible without Langston Hughes. A lot of writers would not have been possible without Hughes. He showed us things we hadn't known before. He opened doors we hadn't realized were closed, or that had something on the other side. He made poetry—not black poetry or minority poetry or even American poetry, but poetry—more vibrant, more full of delight and wonder, than it had been before. The function of poetry is to renew the language, to make us see with new eyes, to offer fresh possibilities for the form, to fight against what the English poet Geoffrey Hill calls "the inertial drag of the language." Or as Ezra Pound put it, "Make it new." Poetry restores us by restoring itself. Great poetry changes the game completely, showing us possibilities we never knew existed. That is the achievement of Langston Hughes in *The Weary Blues*. We didn't know what was possible, didn't know the world around us, didn't know some part of the beauty of our world, until he showed us. His greatness is the greatness of Mozart or John Coltrane, bringing us up short to exclaim, we didn't know a human being could do that. And we're so glad to have been shown they could. Pound had no idea how new *it* could be.

FOURTEEN

THE BIRD IS THE WORD
The Maltese Falcon

I have read many—and I do mean many—English mysteries. They're very interesting, these brainteasers with lots of potential suspects, almost none of whom behave very well toward police and almost all of whom are quirky, eccentric in some way or even several ways, with tons of clues both false and real, with loads of atmosphere in manor houses. Have you ever noticed how British mystery writers seem to want to level the playing field by killing off the aristocracy? Talk about class warfare! Oh, and the detectives. All shapes and sizes and backgrounds. They give us slumming noblemen with plummy accents and loyal retainers who go sleuthing as a hobby. Displaced little Belgians retired from official policing who have somehow pitched up on British shores. Village spinsters armed only with knitting needles and superhuman powers of observation. Parish priests using Catholic logic and police inspectors writing sensitive poetry. And on and on. Yes, and that Sherlock fellow, whatever he might be. It takes all kinds, you might say. But that's okay, because they have all kinds.

We have one.

That's okay. One is enough if it's the right one. Which this one is. He (although he's sometimes a she these days) is pure American. Tough. Unafraid. Good with his fists or his gun. Adept at street lingo and wisecracks, especially in the face of danger. Ethically ambiguous. Barely legal. Aloof. Better at confrontation than puzzle solving. However many avatars he may have, he's really just one guy. And he has just one name.

Spade.

Sam Spade may be an odd figure to start a movement, but he did. The guy who launched a thousand series-detectives appeared in only one novel. In a genre where almost all protagonists narrate their own story, he doesn't. In some ways, he's more mysterious than his book, since we know almost nothing of his background, his thoughts, or his real opinions. Dashiell Hammett had already created one very tough character in the Continental Op, who had made numerous appearances in the pulp detective magazine *Black Mask* through the late 1920s. The Op, however, isn't fully human—he even lacks a name, going only by title, an operative of the Continental Detective Agency, which is a caricature version of the Pinkerton Agency for which Hammett himself had worked—lacking such human basics as fellow feeling, tenderness, morality, or warmth. He will break any rule, cause any mayhem, to protect the agency and get results for the client. In this regard, Spade is a huge step forward. His amorality may be more pose than fact, and in any case it is tempered by some measure of human feeling. Even if that measure is very small. *The Maltese Falcon* (1930) is the detective's first manifestation, and he would subsequently figure in several stories, but never again in a novel. That he appeared so fully realized is a testament to Hammett's genius; that he failed to return in a novel, perhaps to his dissipation. As one can tell by this novel or even

more so by *The Thin Man*, Hammett was a drinker of heroic dimensions; in fact, that novel would be his last, in 1934, although he would
live another twenty-seven years. Spade's creator said of him that he was
not modeled on any individual but on an ideal that the detectives he
knew had for themselves as "a hard and shifty fellow, able to take care
of himself in any situation, able to get the best of anybody he comes in
contact with, whether criminal, innocent by-stander or client." This
statement came from the introduction to a 1934 edition of the novel.
At the time, the detective novel was by no means an exalted form, so
the fact that a new edition with an author's introduction was produced
a mere four years after the original is a testimonial to the power and
popularity of the novel. It is no exaggeration to say that Hammett in a
single stroke elevated the mystery novel in the public mind from pulp
trash to serious art form. And this with a hero about whose past or
thoughts we know next to nothing.

Here's what we do know about Mr. Samuel Spade. At the beginning of the novel, he's half of a detective agency, Spade and Archer. He's
sleeping with his partner's wife. When Miles gets murdered on a case,
his chief emotion is neither grief nor outrage but a need to avoid further entanglement with the widow. He thinks nothing of using people,
as when he calls his secretary in the middle of the night to have her
break the news to the bereaved wife. Physically, he is described as "wolf-
ish," as having a face composed by a series of V lines. He's large, almost
bearlike, fully six feet tall (which was slightly more impressive in 1929
than today), and hairless on his torso. He looks "rather pleasantly like
a blond Satan." He gives nothing away—to the police, to associates, to
suspects, to lovers, to clients. Indeed, when Brigid O'Shaughnessy appears at their office with the fatal case, Spade politely holds back, while
the doomed Miles, a womanizer in his own right, plays the gallant to
the supposed vulnerability of the attractive client.

Unlike Archer, unlike almost everyone, Spade can compartmental-ize. He's not above a sexual liaison with a suspect, but it's on his terms, not hers. When he tells her that he's handing her over for murder, he says, "Chances are they'll give you life. That means you'll be out again in twenty years. You're an angel. I'll wait for you. . . . If they hang you I'll always remember you." What a guy! It's the description of her as "an angel" that makes the passage. The timing of it is perfect, separating the prison sentence and his declaration to wait for her. He also knows it's a promise he'll never have to fulfill: what woman will come back to the man who sent her up the river for two decades?

The plot of the novel, which is overlaid with all sorts of complex-ity and murkiness, is almost ridiculously simple. Spade has to solve a murder, and he does so with a ruthless single-mindedness that would do Captain Ahab proud. Since the victim is his business partner, Miles Archer, he has multiple reasons. For one thing, suspicion almost imme-diately falls on those closest to the victim, and almost no one is closer than a detective agency partner. On top of that, as he tells the killer, failing to solve the murder of a colleague is very bad for business if one is a detective. So he solves it. Simplicity itself. It's only the embellish-ment that gets complicated, with a host of interconnected and squab-bling villains, the exotic bird statue of the title, a wild tale of artistic provenance full of murder and duplicity and intrigue stretching back to the Knights Templar (many decades before *The Da Vinci Code*). The cast of characters is wonderful, from the femme fatale Brigid to the vi-cious but ineffectual (and obviously gay) Joel Cairo to the hair-triggered bodyguard Wilmer Cook to the "fat man" bearing the delightful moni-ker of Caspar Gutman. Each is trying to cheat the others and is more than willing to kill to gain his or her objective. But all that is window dressing and mystification, brambles Spade must fight his way through to achieve his real—and really simple—objective. The bird, it turns out, is what Alfred Hitchcock called a MacGuffin, the device that impels the action, while turning out to be of little actual significance in itself.

Spade's technique is to pit every player against every other player, to exploit fractures in relationships, and to split alliances, while seeming sometimes to obstruct, sometimes to abet, their plans. In this regard, his main talent isn't for solving mysteries but for psychology-on-the-fly, for sizing people up and playing on their weaknesses. Hammett, his creator, knew from his own Pinkerton's experience and from watching his colleagues, that they were not master sleuths but, if they were good, canny readers whose text was other people. Spade reads his texts brilliantly, analyzing for chinks in the armor. Half of what he does is pure bluff, and he usually gets away with it. There are dangers to this approach. When Gutman drugs him to get him out of the way, the Mickey Finn could just as easily be poison. When he goads and taunts Wilmer, the bodyguard, he could easily push him too far. Wilmer wants to shoot someone, anyone, and Spade nearly provides him with the opportunity. That Wilmer's victim turns out to be someone else is as much a product of luck as of Spade's brilliant strategy. The point is, in this game of reading with risk attached, the hero is willing to incur the risk, so certain is he of his ability to read the people and the situation. What's more, he's right.

In the I-suppose-you're-all-wondering-why-I-called-you-here scene, in which the British or ratiocinative (meaning, approximately, solving things with brainpower) detective would reveal the astonishing power of deduction and sleuthing; Spade causes mayhem. He knocks out Wilmer, the two-gun punk, and then marks him out as the fall guy, convincing Gutman and Cairo that there is no other way for them to escape. The plan has the advantage of being true—Wilmer is the murderer of Brigid O'Shaughnessy's associate Thursby as well as of Captain Jacobi—but Spade makes that seem like a mere technicality.

This stratagem, like so many others he devises, has the effect of setting the crooks against one another. When the statuette proves to be a fake, Wilmer escapes in the confusion, but the plan is still sound: the dissension Spade has sown will bring about the downfall of the group and provide the police with a literally smoking gun. He knows as surely as Hercule Poirot or Sherlock Holmes who has done what and where guilt lies, but not being sure of the efficiency of the police, he elects for his own rough justice. In the end, everyone will get what they deserve. Having evidently allied with Brigid, he keeps her behind, and she complies for her own well-being, but then he rounds on her and hands her over to answer for the murder of Miles. It's at this point that he utters his famous line about never forgetting her in the event of hanging. And they say chivalry is dead!

Sam Spade is a catalyst. He comes out of the affair unchanged, while making a great deal happen. Yes, he's poorer one partner, but that has happened before he goes into action. He doesn't get the girl, the bird, or the money. He hands over the proceeds from the case, a thousand-dollar bill, as evidence of attempted bribery. And even he, the great detective, must face justice. Unlike the film version, which ends with its famous misquotation of Shakespeare that the bird is "the stuff dreams are made of," in the novel Spade is in his office waiting for Iva Archer, grieving widow and would-be Mrs. Spade, to be shown in.

The basics of every hard-boiled detective novel of the subsequent tradition are present. There's the long-suffering, devoted, and quite probably smitten secretary/Girl Friday, Effie Perine, who can handle almost any situation nearly as well as her boss. She, for instance, discerns that the widow, Iva Archer, is harboring secrets of her own about the fatal night, and does so in a way that a man would not likely notice. Iva herself is destined to be a stock figure in mysteries, the less-than-bereaved spouse who evinces more interest in the future and possibly in the detective than grief at her loss. The official police are represented by Lieutenant Dundy and Sergeant Tom Polhaus. Dundy is entirely by-the-book and therefore hostile to and suspicious of Spade and his rather looser dealings, with Polhaus as hapless mediator in their disputes. Well, how would we know what to think of the detective's methods if someone didn't disapprove? At the same time, he needs information that only the police have, so he needs an informant on the inside, even if, as in this case, the informing is quite public. So, Dundy and Polhaus. It's noteworthy that when Spade solves the case and calls the precinct, it's Polhaus rather than Dundy to whom he gives the information. Virtually every print, film, or television private eye ever since has encountered those two figures of officialdom: the policeman of superior rank who acts as a blocking character, interfering and usually harassing the hero, and the officer or sergeant who facilitates his business. And let us not forget the colorful cast of crooks. Those elements aren't original in Hammett, but he brings them together in a way that is original and that hardly any novelist can hope to better.

Two other features manifest themselves in *The Maltese Falcon* and will persist down the years. The first is the moral fog in which the novel takes place. The detective of necessity finds himself rubbing elbows with seriously fallen human beings, and aspects of the fall seem to rub off. Spade lies, cheats, double-crosses, and misleads as well as any bad guy. He trusts no one and, in truth, doesn't merit much trust himself. He displays no feeling upon the death of his partner, whom he did not like and with whose wife he has been dallying. He sleeps with Brigid O'Shaughnessy even while harboring significant doubts about her, and he speaks lovingly to her even while sending her up the river. He's not even a little discomfited by causing Gutman's death or by ruining any other lives, as long as they aren't his. He winds up doing, more or less, the right thing, but we can never be sure whether he does so for the right reasons or for personal expediency. Of course he has no patience with the homosexual Joel Cairo, but then, neither does his creator. In 1929, the year the novel was serialized, this was not remarkable. But he's equally contemptuous of the police, even to the point of calling Dundy Tom Polhaus's "boyfriend." He's not so much bigoted as thoroughly misanthropic. On the other hand, there are precious few human specimens in the novel who inspire any sort of admiration for the species. By my count, there is one, and it's not Spade but his secretary, Effie Perine.

The moral fog is rather like the miasma in the Court of Chancery in Dickens's *Bleak House*: it finds its objective correlative, its equivalent state in the physical world, in the darkness of the setting. The novel is full of nighttime assignations, meetings in darkened rooms, walks down alleys, and, this being San Francisco, a sufficiency of fog. Its depiction in the Bogart movie version is one of John Huston's chief accomplishments. He, perhaps more than anyone else, taught American film how to be *noir*. The film stock is so dark it's barely visible at times, which is why Turner Broadcasting's efforts to colorize this particular film back in the 1980s was such an abomination. Not only did they introduce color into a monochromatic masterpiece, but the effort necessarily made the film lighter and brighter. This will not do. It violates not only the spirit of the original movie but that of the book as well. Nor do I think the French critics and New Wave directors appreciated the extent to which *film noir* is an extension of *roman noir*, the dark book. Yes, as practiced by Huston and Hitchcock and Orson Welles and Billy Wilder, the films captured a look and mood, but much of the groundwork had already been done in the books that provided source material, novels by Hammett and James M. Cain, Raymond Chandler and Patricia Highsmith. It simply is not possible to adapt their novels and let in a lot of sunshine.

The second defining feature is employing English as a foreign language. One of the chief pleasures of reading mysteries is encountering the lingo, which is partly a function of class. Make no mistake about it: Spade, like his later avatars, is definitely low-rent. He's a man of the streets, with an advanced degree from the College of Tough, and it shows in his attitudes and his language. The cops and the villains all seem to have attended the same school, for no one is taken aback by his colorful locutions. Indeed, several others make their own contributions. When Miles plans to make a romantic play for the seemingly fragile "Miss Weatherly," Spade warns him, "Don't dynamite her too much." When the sexual intrigue turns out to be a fatal setup, Tom Polhaus tells Spade that his partner took the bullet "right through the pump." Spade, however, gets most of the best material, calling the statuette a "dingus" and the gun-toting Wilmer a "gunsel," which again carries disapproving homosexual overtones. When Wilmer tries some tough talk of his own, Spade laughs him off with a great line, "The cheaper the crook, the gaudier the patter." He also has plenty to say about women, or at least plenty of tough-guy lines and epithets, but he can also be tender, as when he tells Effie, "You're a damned good man, sister." You can't say fairer than that. This is language that is exotic to the vast majority of readers—a sort of locker room talk from a sort of locker room most of us will never enter. It's very stylized and heightened, of course, but also rooted in the kind of language Hammett heard in the army and especially during his time with the Pinkerton National Detective Agency. His language is great fun and a source of insight into characters and a certain way of life, but it's also why you'll never see a Hammett novel used as a reading primer.

Is it any wonder, then, that the novel was instantly and repeatedly attractive to Hollywood? The first film version came out in 1931, a scant two years after the *Black Mask* serialization and one year after the book hit store shelves? That first version was played straight, but then in 1936 a comic version called *Satan Met a Lady* hit the silver screen briefly. And not well, according to most accounts. Then in 1941, Warner Brothers decided to produce a new version, possibly because the Hayes Office, having arrived on the scene in the interim, banned the first one from re-release for what it termed lewd content. What luck. Instead of a rerun of a merely adequate film, the world got a masterpiece. The studio chose the young John Huston to direct. He chose, by his own account, to have his secretary cut the novel up and paste it on script sheets. Whether that's literally true or not, the film is one of the most faithful adaptations ever made. It starred Humphrey Bogart, physically all wrong but entirely perfect as Spade, with his cool attitude, his quick wit, his toughness, and his cocksure carriage; Mary Astor as Brigid O'Shaughnessy; Sydney Greenstreet in his film debut; Peter Lorre; Ward Bond without a horse as the long-suffering intermediary Tom Polhaus; and, in an uncredited cameo, the director's father, Walter Huston, as the dying Captain Jacobi. Sometimes the stars, if you'll pardon the expression, align. These aligned so well that several of them would work together again a year or so later in a little number called *Casablanca*. Or a few years later in *The Treasure of the Sierra Madre*. But our film on its own merits is one of the great accomplishments in film history, one of the earliest—and best—instances of *film noir*. And much of its greatness is by the book.

When we talk about literary influence, that discussion often tends to be rather tenuous. Yes, that work *may* have influenced this other one; maybe this new character draws on that older one, or this theme seems to be answering that of some prior work. That's the way the discussion usually goes. Not here. Even if you've never read Sam Spade, you've met him. He's Philip Marlowe. Lew Archer. Spenser. Mike Hammer. Travis McGee. Easy Rawlins. Carlotta Carlisle. Kinsey Milhone. V. I.

Warshawski. Yes, tough guys come in both sexes. And those are just a few of the literary versions. Most of them have appeared on screens large and small. Raymond Chandler's Philip Marlowe, for instance, has been played by, among others, Dick Powell, Humphrey Bogart, George Montgomery, James Garner, Elliott Gould, James Caan, Danny Glover, and, on radio, Robert Mitchum. But the transition to other media doesn't just include adaptations. The movies gave us John Shaft crossing the color line and "Dirty" Harry Callahan taking the figure into the official police. Blake Edwards developed both Richard Diamond and Peter Gunn for television, which would also give us Garner as Jim Rockford, Tom Selleck as Thomas Magnum, and David Janssen as Harry Orwell. Each in some way redefines the role—some are more suave, some rougher around the edges, some are funnier, some more introspective—but all follow the basic template. And that template is Spade.

The hard-boiled detective doesn't trust anyone—not the cops, not his clients (especially not them), not his sources, not the suspects. In this game, trust gets people killed. He (although these days *he* is just as likely to be *she*) doesn't show fear. He makes wisecracks all the time, even in the face of danger. *Especially* in the face of danger. Which is good, because that's where he spends most of his time. He doesn't let his opponent know who has the upper hand. He always holds something back, whether it's evidence or emotion. He's not a person you could trust or relax around or even particularly like, but that's not in his job description. He—or she—may go by a thousand different names in a thousand different guises, but there's really only one name and one real identity: *Nemesis*. I don't know about you, but when we studied Greek mythology back in sixth grade, Nemesis didn't come up, what with all the major gods to memorize and weighty questions, such as why Hera only has one name but Pallas Athena or Phoebus Apollo two. Too bad, because, for a minor figure, she has a major effect as the implacable bringer of punishments. Two situations call for her introduction, crime such as murder that might go unresolved and *hubris*, that overweening pride that brings the tragic heroes to such grief. She comes, she sees, she destroys. Sounds like a detective to me. As it did to Agatha Christie, who used that name for her final Miss Marple novel. Not the hardest of boilings there, but I digress.

This attribute as Nemesis, far more than the spinoffs and crossovers and homages and latecomers, marks *The Maltese Falcon* as one of the shaping works of American letters. Sam Spade stepped out of the pages of seedy pulp stories and into the mainstream of national consciousness for a reason, and it seems to me that reason is a desire for justice. In a world where justice tends to reside with the wealthy as part of a more general package of privilege, we want to believe that there's someone out there who cannot be bought, who cannot be stopped, whose aim is true. We want someone who will stop the robber-baron from stealing our ranch, who casts a cold eye, as Yeats said, on life and death equally, who is utterly merciless. We want an avenging angel, a Nemesis, a Michael with a sword of flame. But we'll settle for an earthier model. Someone not bound by rules if those rules get in the way of justice, who brings retribution with a touch of desolation. A man with no name bearing a serape and a six-gun. A Marlowe, a Spenser, an Archer. Most of all, that desolation angel, Sam Spade.

FIFTEEN

SO BIG
U.S.A.

Oh, right, like I would skip a work with our name on it. The name that is splattered all over T-shirts and that makes its jingoistic, inappropriate appearance at all sorts of international sporting events. Who else does that? Deutschland, Deutschland, Deutschland? I don't think so. Don't even consider trying it with Canada; whenever that one pops up, it's a dismal bust. And the Brazilians can think of way more interesting things to chant, sing, and shout. And shake. No, it's always the same: USA, USA, USA. The three stressed, single syllables. U-S-A. That is the address, right? It's also the title.

What's that? You didn't know there was a book called *U.S.A.*? There isn't. It's the name of a trilogy. Oh, you didn't know that existed, either? Okay, now that I understand. You should. Everyone should. If I had my way, it would be required reading for citizenship, and not just for new citizens, either. You want a passport? You'll need to answer a few questions about *The 42nd Parallel* and its sequels first. Otherwise, we'll let you out, but you can just forget about coming back in. It's huge, sprawling, multivocal, experimental, thrilling, depressing, and highly contradictory. But before I get carried away singing its praises, I sense that you have another question. Please, go ahead.

What kind of maniac would grab at such a title?

Well, one with lots of privileged schooling, for one thing—a classy prep school, followed by Harvard, trips to Europe. And maybe also some hard-knocks education, as well. War experience would be good, driving for the Norton-Harjes Ambulance Corps in France even better. One would see a lot there, and not all for the best. One might even see one's best friend and Harvard classmate, e. e. cummings, imprisoned for sedition by the country he'd come to help, all based on paranoia and the barely existent English skills of French censors. And it might help to come to that privilege via the wrong side of the sheets, as the illegitimate son of a successful, right-wing lawyer who refused to recognize his son as such until he was fourteen years old. Nothing like a soupçon of resentment, class-based or otherwise, to spice up the mix. If all those would be helpful, then John Dos Passos was singularly well suited to write such a work.

He was already an old hand at writing when, in 1930, he published *The 42nd Parallel*, which was followed by *1919* (1932) and *The Big Money* (1936). The set was published as a trilogy with a prologue that was called "U.S.A." in 1938. His first work, a genre-busting memoir-cum-novel of the Great War, *One Man's Initiation: 1917*, appeared in 1920, followed the next year by the more conventional and less successful war novel, *Three Soldiers*. He would publish three more books before his big breakthrough novel of New York, *Manhattan Transfer*, which came out the same year, 1925, as *The Great Gatsby*. In it, he made extensive use for the first time of stream-of-consciousness techniques. Indeed, Dos Passos is in some ways the forgotten stream-of-consciousness novelist. When the names of James Joyce, Virginia Woolf, and William

Faulkner come up in that context these days, he, along with Dorothy Richardson, usually goes without mention, curiously, since he probably introduced those techniques to more readers than the more famous three combined. The winds of literary fashion, however, blow fickle, and he has been largely left behind. Too bad, because he has so much to offer as diagnostician of the American disease.

Why this mainstay of American fiction for half a century (his last novel appeared in 1970, the year of his death) should sink from view so thoroughly is a complex story. Almost certainly part of the explanation is that he does not fit smoothly into the curriculum. He was not a short-story writer or lyric poet, and the longer works, because of their diffuse nature, do not lend themselves to anthologizing: to excerpt Dos Passos is almost certainly to misrepresent him. Another part is that he lacks the one quality that pushed his friends Hemingway and Fitzgerald to the fore of American fiction: narrative drive. The narrative portions tell stories about characters, but there is no discernible plot, nor are the characters treated with much sympathy. They are presented from a distance, as if the narrator is sitting a considerable height above them and looking at them through the wrong end of a telescope. That lack of compassion is perplexing: for all his love of The People, Dos Passos manifests no great fondness for people. His characters come and go, driven by their appetites and immediate concerns, but seem incapable of real change or growth that would make them dynamic creations. As a result, they meander through the century, or at least as far as the middle of the Great Depression, succeeding or failing, chiefly failing, turning up in the narrative now and again, most of them eventually dying or disappearing. They are less characters with novel-worthy stories than props in some much larger fictional project. And what a project it is.

U.S.A. is one of the great poems, maybe THE great poem, in American fiction. A cubist poem at that. The novel is a series of slices of experience, the American experience. There are four different narrative-rhetorical lines of inquiry at work. Happily, they are all clearly labeled so that even the literal-minded, such as myself, can't get too confused. First, literally, there are the Newsreels, the rapid-fire series of headlines and subheads that roll, montagelike, through the events of the outer world, in *The 42nd Parallel* from New Year's Day celebrations marking the new century, with the old Indian wars campaigner General Nelson Miles being thrown from his horse, to the United States' entry into the World War. Here's the beginning of Newsreel XVIX, the last one in that volume:

U. S. AT WAR
UPHOLD NATION CITY'S CRY

Over there

Over there

at the annual meeting of the stockholders of the Colt Patent Firearms Manufacturing Company a $2,500,000 melon was cut. The present capital stock was increased. The profits for the year were 259 per cent

JOYFUL SURPRISE OF BRITISH

The Yanks are coming

We're coming o-o-o-ver

PLAN LEGISLATION TO KEEP COLORED PEOPLE
FROM WHITE AREAS

many millions paid for golf about Chicago Hindu agitators in nationwide scare Armour Urges U.S. Save Earth From Famine

ABUSING FLAG TO BE PUNISHED

The format is rapid-fire, matching the novelist's attempt to capture the rhythm and feel of newsreels. Like many of the modernists, Dos Passos was infatuated with the new medium of film, and his attempts here to emulate the montages of early cinema pioneers such as Sergei Eisenstein or D. W. Griffith are spectacular. Unlike conventional newsreels, however, he does not limit himself to news events only. Advertising slogans, pamphlets from extremist groups on the right and left, popular songs, virtually any topical material would show up in his segments; they only had to advance a thematic purpose to find their way in. The results are often busier and jumpier even than the original newsreels that were a routine part of moviegoing in the days before television's nightly news. His, also, are more thematically biting. In this one, the hyperpatriotic George M. Cohan tune, "Over There," with its closing vow, "And we won't come back (which Dos Passos misidentifies as "home") / Till it's over over there," announcing the American self-assurance that *we* would get this thing fixed, is matched with aspects of the national scene, about which we could be less proud, such as the obscene profits of arms manufacturer Colt and the passage of Jim Crow laws enforcing racial segregation. Virtually every Newsreel section offers similar contrasts and commentaries.

The second mode is straight narrative involving the twelve named major characters, who form an interesting cross-section of American activities and experiences. Mac is a typesetter, Janey a secretary, Eleanor Stoddard a stage designer, J. Ward Morehouse a public relations man, Dick Savage like his creator a Harvard grad and World War I ambulance driver, Ben Compton a union organizer. Very few of them will come to good ends: death, disillusionment, and what E. L. Doctorow in his introduction to the 2000 Mariner Books edition of *The 42nd Parallel* calls "moral defeat," which sometimes looks like abandonment of values and other times like being ground down. Those narratives are handled with a mix of objective viewpoint and occasional outbursts of *free indirect speech*, a mode in which the language of the narration is colored by the language of the character, so that the result sounds a little like it would sound if they were telling their own story in the third person. He doesn't have them tell their own stories in part because none is around for all that long and in part because his storytelling plan doesn't wish them to be quite so self-aware. While in many ways the main narratives are as modernist as anything undertaken by, say, Virginia Woolf, they pale in comparison to the other three narrative modes.

The third mode is the biographies, typically two- or three-page prose poems on historical figures, most of them gods—for better or worse—in the Dos Passos version of the American pantheon. They range from the completely obscure, the unknown soldier from the recently concluded war whose biography concludes *1919*, to Edison and Luther Burbank and J. P. Morgan and the Wright Brothers and Isadora Duncan. Not surprisingly, many of those featured in the biographies are leftists and social critics—Eugene Debs, Big Bill Haywood, John Reed, Thorstein Veblen, Joe Hill. The last of them, perhaps showing the author's disillusionment with the American experiment, is of Samuel Insulls, the legendary electricity and railroad mogul whose holding company collapse destroyed the financial security of hundreds of thousands of investors in the Depression. Those petite lives are some of the most beautiful writing in the trilogy:

Prince of Peace

Andrew Carnegie
was born in Dunfermline in Scotland,
came over to the States in an immigrant

ship worked as a bobbinboy in a textile factory
fired boilers
clerked in a bobbin factory at $2.50 a week
ran round Philadelphia with telegrams as a Western Union Mes-
    senger
learned the Morse Code was telegraph operator on the Pennsy
    lines
was a military telegraph operator in the Civil War and

always saved his pay;
if he had a dollar he invested it.
Andrew Carnegie started out buying Adams Express and Pull-
    man stock when they were in a slump;
he had confidence in railroads,
he had confidence in communications,
he had confidence in transportation,
he believed in iron.

If ever you want to know where the legacy of Whitman is stron-
gest, look no further. The hammering rhythms, the repetitions, the
strong, simple wording—and the sympathy with the working class—all
come straight from *Leaves of Grass*. What Dos Passos is constructing
here is *Song of Myself—and Everybody Else*. Predictably, in the biography quoted above, he valorizes Carnegie for setting up a foundation to
"promote universal peace / always / except in time of war." When he
is criticized for his characters' failure to live up to moral precepts, we
would do well to recall that in their shortcomings they resemble many
"great" Americans.

The final mode, called Camera Eye, is the most difficult to characterize. One might think of them as scenes from a life—the author's

life, or one very like it. These sections are sometimes described, in fact, as a *künstlerroman*, a story of the growth and development of the artist. Whatever their veracity as autobiography, they certainly suggest the development of a sensibility that lies behind the work. Taken together with the other modes, they suggest an attempt at a complete picture: world events, representative stories, major figures, and private life. Only this last one approaches something like the subjective experience of America. Like the Newsreels, these are numbered, although Dos Passos thoughtfully employs roman numerals for the Newsreels, arabic for the Camera Eye sections. The descriptions are of moments rather than sequences—fragmentary, transitory, incomplete:

> *skating on the pond next the silver company's mills where there was a funny fuzzy smell from the dump whale-oil soap somebody said it was that they used in cleaning the silver knives and spoons and forks putting shine on them for sale there was shine on the ice early black ice that rang like a sawblade just scratched white by the first skaters I couldn't learn to skate and kept falling down look out for the muckers everybody said bohunk and polak kids put stones in their snowballs write dirty words up on walls do dirty things up alleys their folks work in the mills.*

These passages attempt to capture the raw, unimproved moment of being, the sights and scents and sounds of growing up and growing to adulthood in America, or in the parts of it where Dos Passos might have lived. Unlike the biographies, they intentionally avoid seeming to have been constructed. In this passage, the sensory data and received information come rushing all akimbo, and akimbo they stay. The memory isn't even sorted by something like regular punctuation. Instead, we are given the sense of owning that memory from the inside, as if it were ours, bobbing to the surface of consciousness but not being ordered, regimented, pigeon-holed. Because it *is* our memory. This, too, is from Whitman, "For each atom belonging to me as good belongs to you." Those atoms, those experiences, those memories are on offer to be shared in the Camera Eye sections. It is not a matter of being representative, as if one childhood is like all others. Rather, Dos Passos suggests in following Whitman, this one experience may illuminate all others, whether they are quite like it or entirely dissimilar. Everyone may learn from everyone else—if they wish. We're all in this together, says the Harvard man who demonstrated for Sacco and Vanzetti's release, the populist who resided in the artists' haven of Provincetown. If we wish to know each other, to learn from each other, to support each other, we can.

There you have it: world events, a broad cross-section, great figures, and private experience. That pretty well describes what makes up the narrative of a country, doesn't it? And when you spread it out over time so that it covers a little more than a third of something called "the American century," you've really begun to capture the feel of the place. For all the hubris suggested by the title of the trilogy, U.S.A. tries to make good on its implicit claim. Is this THE U.S.A. or merely one possible version? That's a question Dos Passos does not attack. He can only give us his version, full of yearning and possibility and disappointment.

That last point is worth further comment. I listed earlier a couple of possibilities for why his reputation has lagged somewhat over the decades since his death. We can add to those an element not often considered in literary discussions: he committed the only unforgivable sin in the world of fiction: he changed his mind. As the 1930s went on, he grew increasingly wary of leftist politics. In fact, by the time he reaches the publication of *Midcentury* in 1961, he is a confirmed conservative, although his allegiance to the right was ever as shaky as it had been to the left. What he believed in were common men and women, and the evidence is strong that he came to believe that all institutions at all times colluded against them, whatever the stated precepts. It is easy to diagnose his change of heart as directly related to the murder by Spanish leftists, or more probably by KGB agents, of his friend, the academic and activist José Robles, but he was growing increasingly disenchanted with Stalinist groupthink even before that. By the time he writes *The Big Money* to conclude the trilogy, it's clear that, while there is plenty of muscle in the writing, much of the air has gone out of his radical balloon. Every outcome is sad, the overall tone, so buoyant in the first volume, has become depressed, even angrier than before. His last Newsreel, LXVIII, is filled with violence over the Colorado miners' strike and collusion between left and right to keep capitalism in place and workers down, along with Roosevelt's dubious claims (it is 1936, after all) that prosperity is just around the corner. And his narrative piece that closes the set is called "Vag," for vagabond, and contrasts a hitchhiker stuck on an unnamed highway with the elite sailing overhead, despite the occasional turbulence, in the century's great American innovation, an airliner. The plane's route, from New York through or over Cleveland, Chicago, across the Mississippi, Omaha, Cheyenne, Las Vegas to Los Angeles connects the whole shootin' match, while the young man, a knot of needs and aches and problems, stands becalmed as cars whiz by him. He, unlike his airborne doppelganger, is only a hundred miles down the road.

Let's say that some bright morning you're approached by the proverbial Martian, and he has no interest in leaders or being taken to them. Instead, he just wants to know what sort of place he's landed in. Here's what you tell him: "You want to know about America? Here it is."

U.S.A. is a slice of the continent. U.S.A. is a group of holding companies, some aggregations of trade unions, a set of laws bound in calf, a radio company, a chain of moving picture theatres, a column of stockquotations rubbed out and written in by a Western Union boy on a blackboard, a public-library full of old newspapers and dog-eared history books with protests scrawled on the margins in pencil. U.S.A. is the world's greatest river valley rimmed by mountains and hills, U.S.A. is a set of bigmouthed officials with too many bankaccounts. U.S.A. is a lot of men buried in their uniforms in Arlington Cemetery. U.S.A. is the letters at the end of an address when you are away from home. But mostly U.S.A. is the speech of the people.

You'll never get a better description than that. That's the end of the prologue. Had he stopped the trilogy right there, it would still have been enough.

SIXTEEN

THE WINEPRESS OF INJUSTICE
The Grapes of Wrath

It didn't start out to be a great novel. Or any novel. It would be too long by at least a third if it were about anything other than the thing it is about. It has inflated rhetoric that sometimes soars and sometimes just explodes. Its naturalistic scenes are grinding in a way suitable to their subject matter, but also in a way that sometimes pulls like an anchor against the flow of the narrative. Considered aesthetically, it succeeds only partially, which is why some of us have a love-hate relationship with it. It has been accused of everything except global warming, and given the length and the number of copies printed, that's a charge that could be laid at its door.

It is quite possibly the most significant American novel of the twentieth century.

Not the best. Not the most artful. And certainly not the one to which readers are likely to turn for solace or a "good read," whatever that may mean. It may not even be this writer's best. But the most significant. It's the book that won its author the Nobel Prize in Literature;

his other books were so many résumé fillers in this case. It is the American *War and Peace*. The American *Middlemarch*. The American *Les Misérables*. And why? Nothing much. It made us see the world differently, that's all.

There are other works that can bring us into direct contact with human misery, with the devastating effects of poverty and dashed hopes and ruined dreams, with exploitation by the powerful, with the rigged game where moneyed interests always win because they hold the cards. We have, for instance, James Agee's and Walker Evans's *Let Us Now Praise Famous Men*, the photography of Dorothea Lange, the plays of Clifford Odets, and no end of paintings and murals and sculptures created by New Deal WPA artists. But nothing makes us feel the pain of the Okies, trapped by circumstance and tricked by false promises of a Golden West, the way John Steinbeck does in *The Grapes of Wrath*. As the novelist T. C. Boyle said in a 2002 National Public Radio interview on the novel, "You can read (about the lives of migrant workers) in your textbook," he says, "but if you read it in Steinbeck's version, you get to live it and breathe it." "Get to" in this case is relative, since no sane person would *want* to live the adventures of the Joad family, or of any of those tens of thousands of families following that twentieth-century Trail of Tears. Still, Boyle addresses the central point: Steinbeck succeeds because he puts us inside the experience—with all the dislocation, the down-to-the-bone need, the anger, the peril, and the bitterness right against our skin.

Steinbeck succeeds with this novel, in other words, because he didn't set out to write a novel. That in-the-belly-of-the-beast quality isn't so much fiction as journalism, which was the plan. He was sent to write a series of pieces for the *San Francisco Sun* on the migrant camps that sprang up in the wake of the Dust Bowl and the tremendous exodus from the Great Plains. Professional that he was, he filed the stories, seven in all, for the series, but knew that it wasn't enough. The story was bigger than that, and needed to reach a wider audience. The problem was how to tell it. He tried, failed, destroyed the manuscript (called "The Oklahomans" at that point), tried some more. Throughout the process, he kept writing and eventually settled on a plan.

And writing. And writing. By any way you keep score, the final result is a big book. One count I have seen put it at 200,000 words, another at just under 180,000. I'll take their word for it. And it's angry. What Steinbeck saw in the camps and in the way human beings with power treated those without made him incredibly angry, which is why the first attempts at the novel failed. Fiction can only sustain so much outrage; too much and the illusion can't hold together. Even so, he was accused of making things up, of spewing venom needlessly. The truth, he said, was just the opposite: had he written what he truly saw, no one would have believed him. But it's the anger in part that's responsible for accusations of being anticapitalist, of being anti-American, of harboring communist sympathies. And those things got the book banned in his home community. Chiefly, what the book can reasonably be accused of is being hostile to California Big Growers, which is to say, of being against the exploitation of the weak and hungry. Of calling injustice by its name. That's the sort of thing that really gets books banned.

So what's in this marvel of controversy? The story is remarkably simple. The Joads, a poor farming family driven off the land by a combination of drought and mechanized farming practices, follows the migration west to California in hopes of a better life. From the outset, their story is one of disappointment, anger, frustration, and death. Five members of this extended clan die along the way: Grandpa, Grandma, Rose of Sharon's stillborn baby, the preacher Jim Casy, and Mrs. Wilson, the wife in a pair they pick up along the way. And Tom Joad kills a man in the fracas that claims Casy, and having violated parole by leaving Oklahoma, he must flee, so he too is effectively lost to the family. There are short wages and false promises and, at the end, a flood of nearly biblical proportions. Yet despite all the terrible things that happen to them, they are remarkably positive and forward-looking at the novel's conclusion, having found resilience in their collective being that they did not know they possessed.

And that is one of the novel's great lessons: people can be generous and supportive and decent and even civic-minded when the profit motive is absent. Owners, on the other hand, are none of those things. Profit corrupts, distorts, exploits, dehumanizes. Every encounter with owners is bad except for the last one, when they help a small farmer who is being squeezed by the big guys to get his cotton in. The paradise they believe they're headed for doesn't exist in the reality of California except in the government camp. There, poor people make and enforce their own rules, run their own society, share what little they have with one another, and establish a virtual utopia of the proletariat. Which drives the moneyed interests crazy. Knowing that, should word ever get around that these ignorant paupers can manage a peaceful, honest, and just community, their days of tyranny are over, they try everything to destroy or discredit the government camp. The Joads, however, can't stay to see that denouement. Driven by hunger, they push on after jobs, only to find themselves working as unwitting strikebreakers for corrupt owners determined to pay starvation wages to workers. It is here they reencounter their old friend Jim Casy, now inspiring the strikers. Here, too, Casy meets his end, bludgeoned to death with a pick handle, his murder sending Tom Joad into a rage that leads him to kill one of the attackers and nearly be killed himself. He must go into hiding and ultimately into exile, his smashed nose clear evidence of his guilt.

So the poor are mostly honest, decent, and hardworking, the wealthy corrupt, venal, and vicious. Small wonder Steinbeck's novels aroused such hatred in some quarters. Small wonder, too, that he was accused of harboring communist sympathies. On that point, however, his critics were wrong; Steinbeck was no communist.

He was much more radical than that.

What right-wing objectors to the novel could never understand was that the works to which the novelist adhered were not *The Communist Manifesto* or *Das Kapital*, not some European documents of class warfare, but four Gospels and three American sacred texts: the Constitution, the Declaration of Independence, and the Gettysburg Address. Few things are more dangerous than the notion that all people deserve to be free from tyrants, whether of the political or economic sort, that even poor people have rights, and that every person deserves to be treated decently. If we begin adhering to such ideas, where will it end? Worst of all, the Okies and their fellow migrants in the government camp seek to form a more perfect union based on government of the people, by the people, for the people. Well, we can't have that now, can we? No wonder the owners and their hired thugs are driven mad by the proposition. They can't afford to believe in such things. The family's almost irrational optimism at the end, in the face of hunger and a hard winter, offers the promise that such government, and the aspirations it represents, shall not, in Abraham Lincoln's words, perish from the earth.

The novel's Christianity is even more radical in its purity. Jim Casy, his initials hard to miss, is a former preacher who has lost his faith, according to his own account. Yet what he's lost faith in is organized religion and tent revivals. As the novel progresses it becomes clear that he believes—indeed, embodies rather than adheres to—the teachings of Jesus. His own "preaching" in the novel is largely limited to the basics of loving one another and being decent and kind. He speaks up for the meek and downtrodden, for "the least of these," particularly the starving children, and for that, he is put to death, his crown of thorns a crushed skull, his last words, "You don' know what you're a-doin'," a backwoods echo of the first statement of Jesus from the cross, "Father, forgive them, for they know not what they do." And just to show that such knowledge does not die, however strange the means of transmission, Casy's work is taken up by Tom Joad, who has now killed two men in anger. Still, Christ figures are where one finds them, and that's the path Tom chooses. His period of hiding from the law is his forty days in the wilderness; he emerges from it changed and ready to take on the task before him, as he tells his mother in his famous speech:

> "Well, maybe like Casy says, a fella ain't got a soul of his own, but on'y a piece of a big one, and then—"
> "Then what, Tom?"
> "Then it don' matter. Then I'll be aroun' in the dark. I'll be ever'where you look. Wherever they's a cop beatin' up a guy, I'll be there. If Casy know'd, why, I'll be in the way guys yell when they're mad an'—I'll be in the way kids laugh when they're hungry and they know supper's ready. An' when our folks eat the stuff they raise and' live in the houses they build—why, I'll be there."

He's even a little embarrassed at how much he's begun sounding like Casy, but that's what disciples do, take the message of the master and carry it forward, in this case from a James to a Thomas, not to a doubter, but now a true believer. What Tom describes in this final scene is the universal spirit, the sense that Great Soul is in everyone, that all one must do is decide to accept responsibility for its keeping and for applying it in the world. In other words, what he really says is that he will follow the Jesus not of miracles and personal salvation but of social justice and compassion. That's a longer journey than the Joads' cross-country ramble for someone who begins the novel with no more goal than staying out of prison and no more plan than getting through the day. He acknowledges and accepts the possibility and even the likelihood that the mission will cost him his life, yet he vows to undertake it anyway, on behalf of others. His family is no longer merely the Joads but the downtrodden of the earth. What could be more Christ-like than that?

This parallel to the story of Jesus points to one of the signature modernist elements of the novel, its embedding of the mythic in the ordinary. The story of this family takes on universal qualities; indeed, when so many were undergoing the same sort of dislocation, how could it not? It is an American Exodus, a trip not to the Promised Land but to a land of false promises. The language, too, is biblical at times, particularly in the alternating chapters, where the family's experience becomes a mass movement:

> The cars of the migrant people crawled out of the side roads onto the great cross-country highway, and they took the migrant way to the West. In the daylight they scuttled like bugs to the westward; and as the dark caught them, they clustered like bugs near to shelter and to water. And they were lonely and perplexed, because they had all come from a place of sadness and worry and defeat, and because they were all going to a new mysterious place, they huddled together, they talked together; they shared their lives, their food, and the things they hoped for in the new country. Thus it might be that one family camped near a spring, and another camped for the spring and for company, and a third because two families had pioneered the place and found it good. And when the sun went down, perhaps twenty families and twenty cars were there.

The language here is very Old Testament, from the lack of specificity of "the migrant people" and "the great cross-country highway" to the Genesis-inspired phrase, "and found it good." Steinbeck's mythic way is not the lyrical-compressed model, as with Hemingway, or the mythic invention of D. H. Lawrence or William Butler Yeats, or the ironic borrowings of James Joyce. Rather, it is the most democratic of myths, couched in language most Americans would know from church or synagogue. And if it sometimes feels overwrought or overshoots its mark, it nevertheless remains recognizable and familiar to the vast majority of readers.

The great danger with this approach is that the characters become idealized or sentimentalized. Innumerable books and plays have foundered on those shoals. The genius of the novel is that the family, even as it is caught up in this mythic process, is resolutely not mythologized. Its members are sharply drawn, full of idiosyncrasies and failings. Their impulses and longings, while common enough, are very much their own. Tom tends toward anger and violence, Al toward sexual escapades, Rose of Sharon toward adolescent fantasies of ease and comfort. Pa is largely beaten down by the failure of the farm, while Uncle John cannot control his guilt or his drinking, and Ma's efforts center almost entirely on holding together a clan that constantly threatens to fall to pieces. The great lesson of modernism, of Joyce and Faulkner especially, is that the universal can only be shown through the local and particular, that only individuals can become representative. Steinbeck takes this lesson to heart, giving us a family that, if sometimes typical, is never generic. The situation in which it finds itself may be general, but its problems are specific, personal, and vivid.

Now here's the weird part. The novel came out in 1939, at a time when people might well have been expected to be thoroughly sick of the Great Depression, which was still in progress. Busby Berkeley musicals and escapist comedies were the order of the day. Who would want to read about so much misery and suffering? Evidently, just about everyone. The book became a bestseller at once, in part as a *succès de scandale*. The novel was vilified as communist propaganda and a "pack of lies" by the Associated Farmers of California, deplored by conservatives as anti-American and by some liberals as overly sentimental or derogatory toward migrant workers and the poor, castigated by some religious groups as overly sexual and scatological, banned here and burned there. Any book that can outrage so many people can't be all bad. And what was the result of all that indignation? It won the Pulitzer Prize for fiction the following year. Which would be the year it was made into an award-winning film by two staunch conservatives, Darryl F. Zanuck and John Ford. The movie, which toned down some of the more controversial parts and provided a more upbeat ending, won Oscars for Jane Darwell as Best Supporting Actress for her portrayal as Ma and for John Ford as Best Director, as well as Best Film nods from the New York Film Critics and the National Board of Review of Motion Pictures. The American Film Institute would eventually name it as the number twenty-one film in its 1998 *100 Years . . . 100 Movies*, while the Library of Congress chose it in 1989 as one of the initial group of twenty-five films designated for preservation by the National Film Registry. The novel itself has enjoyed similarly high recognition. *Time* picked it as one of the top one hundred novels since 1923, while the Modern Library ranked it tenth on its list of the top one hundred twentieth-century novels (although Modern Library readers downgraded it to a mere twenty-second). Most significantly, the gnomes of Stockholm singled out *The Grapes of Wrath* from the Steinbeck oeuvre in the announcement of his Nobel Prize in Literature.

Perhaps it can claim little credit for changing conditions in the camps, since decades would elapse before Cesar Chavez's United Farm

Workers would successfully organize migrant workers and reach agreements with growers, but on every other front, its impact is undeniable. It has been adapted for the stage and inspired tributes from songwriters from Woody Guthrie to Kris Kristofferson to Pink Floyd to Bruce Springsteen, and even a Canadian alt-rock outfit called The Grapes of Wrath, which lasted from the mid-1980s till the mid-1990s. The book goes on selling in excess of one hundred thousand copies a year as a hardy perennial in high school and college literature courses as well as a favorite of general readers. And as long as people want to understand what America was once like and what qualities continue to animate Americans, it will continue as a major literary presence.

SEVENTEEN

LIKE A HURRICANE
Their Eyes Were Watching God

Here's a question to ponder: can a novel be significant in the intellectual and aesthetic and maybe even political life of the nation if it has to be rescued from the rubbish heap of literary history? If it goes out of print shortly after publication and stays there for decades? If the writer winds up impoverished and buried in an unmarked grave?

There's a fairly predictable arc—an upside-down Bell curve—after a writer dies: however popular she may have been in life, her sales, usually with reputation in tow, go into eclipse. This time in the wilderness may last anywhere from a few decades to forever. In part, since book purchases are driven by new books, death inevitably reduces demand. Literary merit is no proof one way or another against this process of historical sorting. It doesn't matter if the writer is Iris Murdoch or Barbara Cartland; all paths lead to the remainder bin. The other part of the process is more in the oh-we've-already-done-that category. After the obituaries and the wave of encomia that occur immediately after the writer's death, criticism turns, sometimes away, sometimes with fangs bared: "Why did we think this person was so important? She seemed major, but time may prove her merely ordinary." That sort of thing. Critics are so snotty, especially when they fear they may have been duped. The passing of an artist *seems* like the time for sober reassessment, and to some degree it is. But it's also an occasion for self-preservation: woe unto the critic who excessively praises the writer destined for devaluation. At some point the writer's legacy will come up for a new vote. The writer may return as a significant but less major literary force or a much more important entity than had been evident during her lifetime or of no value at all, or may land at any point in between. How long a span of time before a reassessment is due? Linguists speak of getting back to them in fifty years, or even a hundred. Pikers. Check with me in two or three hundred years. Or maybe a millennium or so. I'll be happy to give you an answer. The preacher and metaphysical poet John Donne died in 1631. His rehabilitation was complete by the third centenary of his death. A lot of that delay was due to the romantic poets of the early nineteenth century, who didn't do irony or conceits or very much at all of what was in Donne's poetic toolkit. Now we may look back and wonder what those guys were thinking.

So this particular case, by the usual standards, rolled over in a heartbeat. Just thirteen years after the novelist's death, a young novelist, also female, also African American, went in search of the hidden grave. It was overgrown with tall weeds and protected by snakes in a place in Florida where snakes can be serious business. Yet thirteen years doesn't really cover it, since most of the books in question had been out of print for thirty years or more. The tale of that search appeared two years later in an issue of *Ms*. The second writer was Alice Walker, the article, "In Search of Zora Neale Hurston."

This is almost unthinkable today, but when I went through graduate school, Hurston wasn't even a blip on the radar. *Their Eyes Were*

Watching God (1937) was notably absent (in retrospect, that is) from reading lists for area examinations in modern American writing. How's that for weird?

There's another element to this reputation-murder mystery. Contemporaneous writers attacked her over the qualities in her writing for which she has been more recently celebrated. Those novelists, chiefly African American males, were especially hostile to Hurston's book and its free use of dialect. Richard Wright led the charge, accusing it of being a "minstrel-show turn" calculated to appeal to white readers who could feel smugly superior. The novel, he said, made "no desire whatever to move in the direction of serious fiction." One suspects the lack of a tragic outcome also influenced his pronouncement somewhat. Ralph Ellison employed the word "burlesque" to belittle the book. They had their reasons. Dialect writing had acquired a bad name over the years because of those minstrel shows and demeaning depictions of blacks in fiction and poetry. At the same time, some serious writing had taken place in dialect, most notably in the work of Paul Lawrence Dunbar and Langston Hughes, who was an early associate of Hurston's. Those writers also came in for criticism from those who felt the strategy made the race look bad. Maybe that sort of thing looks worse in fiction, where there will always be so much more of it. Yes, the critics had their reasons. They just got it wrong.

I'm in the habit of saying at this point that the plot is really quite simple. That won't work this time. This novel is one of the most artfully constructed you'll ever encounter. Like *Gatsby*, it's a frame-tale in which all the main action is in flashback, if "flash" isn't taken too seriously in this instance. Like Virginia Woolf's major novels, it relies on free indirect discourse for much of the narrative. It is fashioned with an anthropologist's eye and a woman's heart, but always, a novelist's brain. And it is complex.

The novel begins with Janie Crawford, although she has had three other surnames beyond the one she acquired at birth and is generally known by in the narrative, walking back in a rather bedraggled state to the all-black community of Eatonville, Florida. The occasion, and it prompts much gossip in the town, is the end of her third marriage. The first one ended when she left her much older husband, the second when the man from whom she was largely estranged died. The third she had to kill. And he's the one she loved.

Janie was raised by her grandmother, a former slave. When Janie ambles back to town in considerably less finery than she had been known to wear when she was the mayor's wife, tongues wag that her younger lover, Tea Cake, has likely dumped her. Only her best friend, Pheoby Watson, makes the effort to gather the truth, which allows Janie and the third-person narrator to combine in telling her life's story. Janie was always a dreamy and passionate girl, and those qualities, reminiscent of her absconding mother in her grandmother's eyes, caused the older woman to marry her off for security to a farmer, Logan Killicks. Even his name sounds safe. Logan is without romance but possessed of plenty of ideas about treating a woman like a beast of burden, and soon Janie is disenchanted with that life. A much younger man, Joe Starks (she calls him Jody), comes along, flirting with her in secret and telling her his own big dreams about becoming an important person, someone with "a big voice" in things. They run off to Eatonville, along the way marrying without benefit of divorce, and soon he sets up as mayor, postmaster, store owner, and landlord. Good work if you can get it. One might suppose that the marriage of two people dreaming big would work out, but Jody's dreams preclude her having any of her own, and she finds herself in a slightly higher form of servitude than in marriage one. Worse, in some ways, is that he forbids her from consorting with friends who are "common," or less well-off than he imagines himself to be, so her existence is lonely and dull. Eventually, this marriage too fails, and with it his health. In one celebrated scene, she tears into him verbally for his ugliness and lack of virility, and he beats her violently. Only at the end do they interact again, and it is not a reconciliation. As he lies dying, she rebukes him for his shortcomings on her behalf, but he doesn't hang around long enough to hear how it ends.

For a while, her newfound status as a free woman delights her, and she takes on the role of Penelope in rejecting all suitors. Finally, however, Tea Cake, who is approximately twelve years younger than she, comes calling, and his charm and his beauty win her over. They go first to Jacksonville, where he works on the railroad, and then to the Everglades, where they work together on the muck, the rich, alluvial soil that proves such an agricultural marvel. Along the way, Tea Cake's behavior challenges her repeatedly. Almost at once, he steals money from her and goes out on the town, spending it, he says, on dinner for his railroad cronies. He returns apologetic, and they decide to move to the shores of Lake Okeechobee and share all of their experiences. Tea Cake leaves her more than once, is caught wrestling with another woman in the cane field (he says she has stolen the work tickets that are the basis for their pay, and she accepts it, eventually), throws money around, and, when threatened by her friendship with Mrs. Turner, who does not like him because of his very dark skin, beats her. Yet they stay together because his many good qualities bring out the complete person she is becoming. While Tea Cake cannot complete the journey with her, much less be the goal of that journey, he is an essential element in her completing it. He dies because of the hurricane that causes the lake to surge over its retaining dikes and destroys much of Palm Beach, where they are headed for shelter. At one point, Janie is swept into the raging waters that have begun to resemble Noah's Flood. She sees a cow swimming with a dog on its back, and she grabs the cow's tail in an attempt to reach safety. The dog, however, is rabid, and tries to attack her, and she is only saved by Tea Cake's intervention, but in killing the dog he is bitten on the cheek. As his infection deepens, he tries to shoot her, but she kills him in self-defense. She is put on trial, where all the black people of her acquaintance turn against her, but she is acquitted by an all-male, all-white jury.

After giving Tea Cake a spectacular funeral, she returns to Eatonville and its wagging tongues, completing the narrative frame begun in chapter one. She tells Pheoby that she has achieved her dream, having been to the "horizon and back," and that she has known love and known herself in ways her critics never will.

Whew! And that barely scratches the surface.

Along the way there are a great many topics touched on. There is white racism, seen chiefly in the aftermath of the flood, when white men with rifles force black men to labor as burying squads and white victims get coffins while black ones get ditches and quicklime. But whites are not greatly in evidence in the novel. The chief form of prejudice, instead, is black-on-black in the form of Mrs. Turner, who adores whiteness and thinks it incumbent on black people to breed for light skin. She therefore despises Tea Cake, who is emblematic of blackness for her, insisting that her light-skinned brother deserves to marry the light-skinned Janie. There is also sexism within the black community. At every stage of her development Janie is treated badly by a man. It is true that Tea Cake lacks the brutish sexism of Logan or the desire to squelch Janie that is Jody's hallmark, but he also treats her badly and feels he needs to beat her to prove, more or less, that there's nothing wrong with him as a man. He leads her toward freedom but is always freer than she. His rabies-induced paranoia is largely in keeping with his thought while rational; he fears losing her to another man, especially to Mrs. Turner's brother. And there is the shabbiness of envy and gossip among the African American sisterhood, where every move is criticized and every weakness celebrated. In such an environment, therefore, the only sane course of action is to live for oneself, and this is the ultimate goal of all of Janie's adventures. She is the classic quester, encountering difficulty after difficulty in an attempt to arrive at self-knowledge and fulfillment. If many of the events in her life are excruciating, they are all the more perfect expressions of the genre. Going to "the horizon and back" is an almost ideal description of the quest structure. The person who comes back can never be the same after such a trip.

The town of Eatonville is itself an important feature of the novel. It has the advantage of being a real place and Hurston's home town, so she knew it well. Its status as one of the first black-founded towns (incorporated in 1863) gives it a particular historical weight. This is a place where the experience of being African American can be given as much free play as possible, with virtually no white interference. Such a quality is important for Hurston, whose artistic program in this novel is to explore not "the black experience in America" but of belonging and not belonging in one's own community. Janie is an outsider in Eatonville; she is one of them but not *of them*, so she can never be entirely at ease as a native. Her status is significant, since the real point of the novel is to allow her the chance at self-realization. Toward that end, she can achieve much in the town but not everything; she can find the frustration and blocked paths that make her seek out other trails more open to her needs, just as marriage to the repressive Jody primes her for marriage to the more open Tea Cake. The community, therefore, symbolizes as well as causes one stage of her development.

Similarly, Janie's three husbands represent various stages of her self-realization. Logan can only be her husband in a very embryonic stage of her moral and emotional life. Her grandmother, whom she later says she hates, forces the marriage on her as a means of protecting her from the world and herself. Logan was never her choice, and when she does exercise choice, she leaves him behind. Jody is the one she chooses, but that decision is itself immature: she lacks sufficient knowledge of either herself or the world to understand that his dreams will inevitably stifle hers. She achieves a simulacrum of adulthood with him—acquiring status and respectability and material comfort—but it is never more than an illusion. She is never happy or fulfilled in her marriage with Jody. Tea Cake, for all his several faults, actively brings her out, accepting that she is her own person and not merely an extension of him. He does some growing up while encouraging her to do the same, and sometimes his worst behavior leads to her greatest growth. With him, she not only finds her voice but learns that sometimes she does best not to exercise it. She accepts her beating, just the one time, not because he is stronger but because her greater strength allows her to do so. Finally, however, no helping character ever gets to go the final mile with the hero, and Tea Cake must vanish for Janie to come fully into her strength. Her husbands, even the best of them, are only mile markers, not destinations.

There are a lot of things we might learn from the first page of a novel, but only two are unavoidable. The first is whether or not the fiction is in the first person; either there is an "I" in the narrative line or there isn't, so we will notice. And the other is style. By the time you read three sentences, you know what this novel by Thomas Hardy is going to sound like. True, you might need a few more, maybe five or six, for Ernest Hemingway, but that's because with him you don't get much per sentence. In any case, by the end of one page, you know what Hardy or Hemingway is going to sound like.

Yet when we open this novel, and we're confronted with this, we almost get a wrong idea stylistically, and that's not accidental:

Ships at a distance have every man's wish on board. For some they come in with the tide. For others they sail forever on the horizon, never out of sight, never landing until the Watcher turns his eyes away in resignation, his dreams mocked to death by Time. That is the life of men.

Now, women forget all those things they don't want to remember, and remember everything they don't want to forget. The dream is the truth. Then they act and do things accordingly.

We are not surprised, based on this beginning, when the novel turns out to be about the experience of a woman who cannot be defined or contained by the men in her life.

That would almost be enough for the opening to accomplish. Its major feat, however, is to signal something very important: this author knows how to *write*. So, you ask, don't all authors? No, they don't. Some are better storytellers than stylists, and for Hurston's purposes it is important to establish herself at the outset as a stylist. Much of the novel that follows will be told in dialect. She uses a very literary technique called "free indirect discourse," in which the narrative takes its cues and much of its language from the thoughts and words of its characters, and her characters are barely literate residents of an all-black community in Florida. She knows that writing in their language will open her up to criticism the way it did Mark Twain and other regionalists of the nineteenth century. But Twain had something she lacks when he let Huckleberry Finn speak for himself: a track record. He had written numerous books in more or less Standard English before that, and even so he was derided for the prose in his masterpiece.

Hurston, then, is attempting to forestall criticism by beginning the novel in a fairly high literary style that makes observations worthy of Jane Austen. See, she says, I know what I'm doing. Now that's not the only reason for establishing a primary style that is educated and assured. It will also be a welcome point of return at those times of the novel when she is not echoing her characters, and it creates a distance between one way of speaking in the primary narrative line and a second derived from her characters' language. Such a gap calls attention to her achievement not so much in writing the language we expect in novels as in capturing that other way of speaking. And that achievement is very great indeed.

What Hurston accomplishes in *Their Eyes Were Watching God* is to give voice to the voiceless as well as to silence the usually vocal. It is a novel in which almost no white voice is heard, and in which the "big voice" of the important male is finally quieted. Instead, the quieter voices of women predominate in the conversation of Janie and Pheoby, and it is Janie's voice, which every imaginable force from her grandmother forward has attempted to suppress, that finds fullest expression. She becomes more articulate as the narrative moves ahead. She speaks of her experiences in terms of language and becomes aware that language is power. In the afterword to many editions of the novel, the critic Henry Louis Gates Jr. speaks of the linguistic program of the novel as "the project of finding a voice, with language as an instrument of injury and salvation, of selfhood and empowerment." And here's what that "project" sounds like:

> Janie stirred her strong feet in the pan of water. The tiredness was gone so she dried them off on the towel.
> "Now, dat's how everything wuz, Pheoby, jus' lak Ah told yuh. So Ah'm back home agin and Ah'm satisfied tuh be heah. Ah done been tuh de horizon and back and now Ah kin set heah in mah house and live by comparisons. Dis house ain't so abent of things lak it used tuh be befo' Tea Cake come along. It's full uh thoughts, 'specially dat bedroom."

That her voice is the genuine article made for hard rowing for the novel. Certain conservative forces—in literary terms—responded harshly to her linguistic experiment. What later readers, exposed to Toni Morrison and Alice Walker and a host of other novelists, would take completely in stride was deeply shocking to even the educated readers and writers of her time. The response of her contemporary writers was the greatest jolt. Had not Langston Hughes written in dialect and yet been completely modern? Or Paul Lawrence Dunbar? Yet somehow, Hurston had crossed a threshold. It may be that her master narrative differed from the preferred one, about blacks oppressed by white dominant society, in ways that offended some sensibilities. Certainly her priorities are not those of, say, Wright. Or it may be that her feminism, with its attendant criticism of African American males, excessively undercut the authority of male writers who were seeking redress for other grievances. But it may also be as it seems, that she went beyond where many readers were willing to follow. Sometimes it does not pay to be too far out front.

Yet that vanguardism is precisely what makes Morrison and Walker and Paule Marshall and Edwidge Danticat and all sorts of minority and women writers possible. Would *The Color Purple* exist without *Their Eyes Were Watching God*? Very unlikely. Hurston made us see that negritude is not monolithic, that the "African American experience" is actually made up of many different experiences, urban and rural, pious and profane, censorious and celebratory, agrarian and industrial, and most importantly, male and female. Readers everywhere owe a great debt to that younger writer who went in search of a grave all those years ago. How much greater, then, is the debt owed to the great and forgotten novelist buried there?

EIGHTEEN

HE AIN'T HEAVY, HE'S MY COUSIN
Go Down, Moses

I know they've gotten a bad rap in some quarters, but God bless the French. Oh sure, there's that Gallic obstreperousness and the business with eating snails, but consider their contributions to world improvement and American culture. The defense stipulates its mystification at their infatuation with Jerry Lewis, Mickey Rourke, or Sharon Stone, but we'll set that aside for the nonce. Most of their faults are more than repaid by that promise of a bright future, Beaujolais nouveau, and sauce béchamel, the cornerstone of all things civilized. Not only that, but they very thoughtfully provided the Seine with a Left Bank so that disaffected Brits and Yanks could write and paint and compose there, away from family, Henry Ford, and Prohibition. The welcome and appreciation they gave to pioneering black American entertainers—Josephine Baker, Sidney Bechet, Louis Armstrong, Bud Powell, Dexter Gordon, Ben Webster, Freddie Hubbard—and the tolerance those performers found put their native ground to shame. The greatest French contribution to American letters, however, has been their ability to recognize talent that has gone unnoticed by the writers' compatriots. American critics, if they thought about him at all, dismissed Edgar Allan Poe as a kook who wrote overheated Gothicism until the Symbolist poets took up his cause in the mid-nineteenth century. And it's safe to say that the United States would have one fewer Nobel Prize winners in literature but for the French fascination with William Faulkner.

They love his experimentalism, his modernity, *his* overheated (Southern) Gothicism (perhaps we detect a trend here). He's just so out there. He's also an absolutely brilliant prose stylist. All of which may be why he's never been America's flavor of the month. For reasons that remain obscure, we've never taken to the word "abnegation," without which he can hardly write a book. In early 2009, a survey of French writers on their favorite books turned up the surprising result that two of his titles, *The Sound and the Fury* and *Absalom, Absalom!*, tied for fifth as the most mentioned titles. Overall, Faulkner was the second most mentioned writer, ahead of Flaubert and Stendhal and Hugo and Dumas *père et fils* and Joyce and all the rest of the literary exiles. He was behind only Marcel Proust. That would never happen here. And not just because Proust could never win. However we may feel about his prose, though, we Americans should love Faulkner for his insights into who we are, even if we rarely welcome the portrait he paints.

Novelists who live in times of major transition often feel the weight of changing times very acutely. E. M. Forster's novel *Howards End*, for instance, concerns itself with the question Lionel Trilling phrased as, "Who shall inherit England?" Faulkner's question in his writing more often than not is, "Who shall inherit the South?" Born into post-Reconstruction Mississippi, a place that could stake a fair claim to the position of center of gravity of the Old South, Faulkner was witness to the crumbling of the last remnants of the *ancien régime*, along with the unrest and violence sparked by the early years of the push for civil rights, about which movement he was ambivalent. He consolidates the whole sprawling history of the region into his "little postage-stamp of ground," as he calls it, Yoknapatawpha County.

The Faulkner canon is full of families that illustrate the changing fortunes of the post-Reconstruction South: from the decline of the old aristocratic Compson and Sartoris clans to the annihilation of the nouveau riche Sutpens to the worldly rise of the ne'er-do-well Snopeses and the general mayhem of the Bundrens. One could perhaps make the case, Faulkner being such a consistent writer thematically, with most of these families and nearly any of the novels. But there are problems. *The Sound and the Fury* (1929), ruled over by the decaying Compson family, is one of the most brilliant and original novels in the entire modernist canon, but the narrative is a challenge, and frankly, the sections narrated by Benjy and Jason tend to get in the way of thematic clarity. *As I Lay Dying* (1930) is a nifty parlor trick and a great favorite of instructors who want to give students the illusion that they have "read Faulkner." I wouldn't touch a Sartoris or a Snopes with a bargepole, so the first family rules out *Sartoris* (1929) and *The Unvanquished* (1938) and the second *The Hamlet* (1940), *The Town* (1957), and *The Mansion* (1959). And the Sutpen saga, *Absalom, Absalom!* (1936) is just plain scary. Bolder, more daring, more dense, more labyrinthine, even more experimental, if that's possible, but scary nonetheless. Or perhaps, and therefore scary. I've never met anyone who tried reading that first among his novels and was ever the same afterward. There is, however, another tribe that is perhaps the best illustration of altering fortunes, although they make their presence felt in only one novel: the McCaslin-Beauchamps of *Go Down, Moses* (1942). In the real history of his made-up county, the author staked out the McCaslin plantation as one of the five major ventures of the antebellum period, along with the

Compson, Sutpen, Sartoris, and Grenier estates. The Beauchamps were the plantation's slaves. By the time we meet them, many years later, the families are represented primarily by Isaac McCaslin and Lucas Beauchamp, for whom the legacy of slavery has entangled much more than just their fates.

I'm only going to say this once, so let's everyone pay attention: *Go Down, Moses* is a novel.

All right, I may wind up saying it four or five times, but I'm hoping this will suffice. You will recall that I made no such declaration regarding *The Scarlet Letter* or *The Grapes of Wrath*, for the simple reason that I didn't need to. This book, however, has something characteristically twentieth century about it that those books don't have: a table of contents. Once upon a time, as they say, novels were self-contained, whole, and single. They read like complete adventures with solitary story lines. That wholeness, naturally, was an illusion, an exploitation of readers' expectations of finding unity. It mattered little if the hero was Natty Bumppo or David Copperfield or Tom Jones, his story was complete and unified. The twentieth century seems to have gone out of its way to upend those expectations. From Sherwood Anderson's *Winesburg, Ohio* to the latest book by Louise Erdrich or Julian Barnes, modern novels are just as apt to resemble collections of short stories or amalgamations of story, essay, reminiscence, and laundry list as single-narrative fictions. While this trend picked up pace in the last third of the century, the three novelists who started us down that path, at least in America, are Anderson, Hemingway, and Faulkner. Some readers insist that such novels are always story collections, refusing to bend received definitions of genre. In *Faulkner's Craft of Revision* (1977), Joanne V. Creighton coined the very useful term "short story composite" for such works, and it is very helpful in certain critical contexts and has even gained traction over the years. Simpleminded soul that I am, I tend to take writers at their word, so if they call it a novel, so do I. And Faulkner called it a novel, although Random House was sufficiently timid to append "And Other Stories" to the title when it first appeared. Indeed, there are other stories, a total of seven for those of you keeping score at home, all of which are capable of standing alone, none being overly reliant on its neighbors, and of them the title story not being the preeminent example. Even so, a novel.

Now having made this bold assertion, I find myself in some difficulty. The problem, you see, is unity. Such composite narratives usually cohere around a main character such as Nick Adams in Hemingway's *In Our Time*, or a story line that comes increasingly together, as in Erdrich's *Love Medicine*, or thematic considerations, like the paralysis in Joyce's *Dubliners*. Faulkner does us no such favors. Ike McCaslin is clearly the dominant presence in the book, but he's not present in some of the stories. Nor is there any unity of time, since the stories range from around 1859 for "Was" to 1940 for "Go Down, Moses." Thematic unity? Forget it. He has themes that pervade, but they're not inevitably present in each story. No, none of the usual suspects will help us out here. What we have instead is unity of place, although even there we might wish to expand our definition to include not merely the ground but the people (generally) and gestalt of a very extended family. Even then, "Pantaloon in Black," the third story, isn't helping, since it concerns a young black man, Rider, who is neither McCaslin nor Beauchamp. But since the three unities of French dramatic theory don't encompass either unity of gestalt or unity of community, we're on our own here.

Let us first consider the diffuse structure of the book. The stories are all stand-alones, capable of being read as separate entities with their own plot lines and beginnings, middles, and ends. The middle three, "The Old People," "The Bear," and "Delta Autumn," concern

Isaac McCaslin, the unwilling scion of a formerly great Mississippi planter. The first relates a bedroom farce of how Theophilus McCaslin, "Uncle Buck" in most mentions, stumbles into marrying Sophonsiba Beauchamp through the device of a contested poker game in which the stakes change repeatedly. At the same time, this game has a much darker import, as Buck's brother, Buddy (Amodeus), wins the slave girl Tennie from Sophonsiba's brother Hubert to take back to their plantation so that their slave, Tomey's Turl (or Terrell), will quit running off to see her. The low comedy of Buck stumbling into the wrong bedroom and compromising a woman's sanctity is overrun by the casually regarded systemic evil of owning human beings, as Faulkner cannily places the laughter right next to the horror embedded in the situation. In the course of that card game, all the elements for the subsequent story of the McCaslins and the black Beauchamps (who take their surname from Tennie's original owners) are present. Buck and Sophonsiba will become Ike's parents, while Tennie and Turl are the eventual grandparents of Lucas Beauchamp, who along with his wife, Molly, will figure in the second story, "The Fire and the Hearth," and the final, title tale. While there is much to be explained about these families, the essential forces are arrayed at the end of the first story, and everything thereafter concerns one or both of them.

Except one. "Pantaloon in Black" stands alone as the story that does not connect with any of the others and therefore as a challenge to any claims of unity. But let's take the "problem" here as an opportunity to diagnose the novel's actual cohesiveness. Rider's story is of a man driven mad by grief. While it is often spoken of as the novel's weak link, I would argue that it represents the moral center of the book. The master narrative concerns Isaac McCaslin and his relatives, white and black, and the movement of history, represented by both the destruction of the wilderness and the fragmentation of family. Part of what drives that story arc is the inability of a succession of white men to comprehend black persons as fully human. Obviously, the family patriarch, Lucius Quintus Carothers McCaslin, slaveholder and sexual exploiter, is no model for conduct toward persons of African origin. Nor are his descendants. Ike's cousins Cass (McCaslin) and Roth (Carothers) Edmonds are both callous and paternalistic toward their black cousins, and Roth even repeats one of his great-great-grandfather's sins by taking one of his distant relatives (whose lack of substance in his eyes is reinforced by the absence of a name) as his mistress, then abandoning her when she bears his child. Some family traits die hard. Even Ike, for all his Christ-like tendencies, is simply incapable of making the complete leap to a higher consciousness. So too with Gavin Stevens, the Jefferson lawyer who tries to help Lucas and Molly in the title story. Although he means well, Stevens is locked in the old, paternalistic ways of thinking about and dealing with black citizens. The chief difference between him and the white family members on whom the book mainly focuses is that he is susceptible of enlightenment: at the very end of the story, he suddenly understands the perfectly human and normal desires that drove Molly Beauchamp to ask for a proper return to town for her executed grandson, Samuel. While the local editor remains incredulous at her request to put the obituary in the newspaper, Stevens gets it. He suddenly realizes what her requests have really meant and what he has failed to grasp about her to that point. Although for most of the story he has been merely another of Faulkner's well-meaning but ineffectual protagonists, his closing epiphany brings him to new light.

It is in this context that we must understand the placement of "Pantaloon in Black." Rider is a man of prodigious strength, a sort of black Sampson, but he is brought low by his weakness, which is his overwhelming love for his wife. After her death, he undertakes a series of nearly superhuman efforts, mostly designed to bring him to destruction. At her funeral he digs her grave himself at tremendous speed, which is both a display of grief and a warning of excesses to come. After seeing his wife's ghost that night, he quits his job at the sawmill the next day, but only after throwing an impossibly large log down an embankment. He buys a jug of grain alcohol, drinks far too much, and then accosts a security guard named Birdsong because he is cheating local blacks at dice; in the ensuing fray, he cuts Birdsong's throat. Once arrested, he escapes by ripping the jail cell door from its frame and fighting the other prisoners, who attempt to keep him there for his own safety. The next day he is found hanged, presumably by the dead man's relatives. The story is important for two reasons. The first, naturally, is for the sympathetic if slightly mystified portrayal of his full humanity—passion and despair, love and rage, justice and violence, power and weakness. The second is how these traits are completely lost on the white establishment, as exemplified by the sheriff's deputy who tells the second half of the story to his wife. To him, Rider is simply another crazed, subhuman black who runs amok and gets what he deserves. The energies of the story, however, are arrayed against the deputy's version, since the third-person narration of the first part, up to his arrest, show him to be anything but the creature incapable of human sentiment or emotion. The deputy also acknowledges that there will be no justice for Rider, since the Birdsongs represent "forty-two active votes" that the sheriff counts on. The deputy is a thoroughgoing racist who sees little profit in protecting people who, while they may have ceased being chattel, have nevertheless failed to rise to the status of complete persons in his estimation.

It is against this sort of bigotry that Ike McCaslin must be measured, and the next three stories, which constitute the thematic as well as physical heart of the novel, will do just that. He will show himself to be a man who, while possessed of considerable limitations, wishes to do the right thing. His desire to emulate Jesus is, like all human efforts, flawed. Still, he displays some Christ-like tendencies. "The Old People" shows Ike as a boy just old enough to join the annual hunts into the wilderness owned by Major de Spain. Already fatherless, he finds his spirit guide in Sam Fathers, a half-Choctaw, half-black man whose own father, old Ikkemotubbe, sold the wilderness to the white men and sold Sam and his mother into slavery. This history begins to solidify the trope of broken family relations as well as violence or wrong treatment by family members against one another. It will find several corollaries. Sam ritualistically bloods Ike after he kills his first deer, and together, when all the others are out hunting, they see but do not shoot at a gigantic buck that Sam addresses as "grandfather," establishing the mythic connection between the true hunter and his quarry. In these scenes and in Ike's subsequent lengthy discussion (no Faulkner character ever has a short one) with his cousin Cass Edmonds, he displays his spiritual side: older than his years, wiser than his older associates, instinctively drawn toward the good, if not God.

That spiritual element leads him in "The Bear" to renounce his patrimony, although he's sufficiently a product of his time and place to leave it not to his wronged Beauchamp cousins but to Cass Edmonds, who with his descendants will make of the estate something worse than Ike would have himself. That flawed reasoning is typical of the well-meaning but ineffectual Faulknerian heroes, from Quentin Compson through Darl Bundren and Gavin Stevens, whose overly thoughtful natures typically produce inadequate or even harmful actions. In this case, Ike gives up his claim to the farm, largely as a gesture of his belief that the land cannot be owned, that in fact the real evil is ownership, which in turn caused slavery and other evils. Readers may disagree with his version of the causality of evils in this instance, but the point is that Ike is trying in ways others of his acquaintance do not.

The main prompt for Isaac comes from the ledgers that his father and Uncle Buddy kept in which they try to untangle the history of the plantation. These commonplace business records reveal the atrocious central fact, the record of ownership of human beings, along with the more outrageous fact lodged within that horror, the one regarding how they were used by their slaveholder—and not merely some random owner but his own grandfather. It eventually becomes evident that Lucious McCaslin took two of his slaves as mistresses, first Eunice and then his daughter by her, Tomasina, and that in response to her daughter's pregnancy, Eunice drowned herself. This Tomasina is the Tomey whose son is Turl and whose great-grandson is Lucas Beauchamp. Those figures from the first story with its fateful poker game are slowly revealed in all the complexity of their connections, and their actions, and those of the previous generation or two, echo down the years. Miscegenation and incest, the ledgers almost seem to suggest, are the natural by-products of slavery. Ike may see landholding as the central cause of evil; Faulkner, it appears, has other ideas. After such revelations, how can one believe in ownership of the land? Or the propriety of any aspect of one's family history?

The really fascinating element in these revelations is that they come in the midst of what is perhaps the most famous hunting story in American literature. What is generally remembered about the story is the clash of mythic figures in the hunt for the legendary bear, Old Ben. Ben has a maimed foot from a trap he stepped into years before, seems impervious to bullets, and despite his great size manages to appear and disappear like a ghost. Isaac manages to see the bear twice on his own, one time when he dives in to save a "fyce"—a small but aggressive dog—from accosting the bear, only to see the bruin towering over him, and the second time when he leaves his compass, watch, and gun behind, meeting the wilderness on its own terms. None of the dogs can find or deal with Ben until an equally mythic being, a dog named Lion, is brought on board. The great dog and the great bear engage in a fatal struggle, and while Old Ben is busy attempting to disembowel Lion, Boon Hogganbeck throws himself on the bear's back, fatally stabbing it with his hunting knife:

> It fell just once. For an instant they almost resembled a piece of statuary: the clinging dog, the bear, the man stride its back, working and probing the buried blade. Then they went down, pulled over backward by Boon's weight, Boon underneath. It was the bear's back which reappeared first but at once Boon was astride it again. He had never released the knife and again the boy saw the almost infinitesimal movement of his arm and shoulder as he probed and sought; then the bear surged erect, raising with it the man and the dog too, and turned and still carrying the man and the dog it took two or three steps toward the woods on its hind feet as a man would have walked and crashed down. It didn't collapse, crumble. It fell all of a piece, as a tree falls, so that all three of them, man dog and bear, seemed to bounce once.

Lion dies a few days later, along with Sam Fathers, who suffers something between a stroke and a symbolic seizure in the wake of the fight. The two are buried in the same forest clearing, and almost in that moment the wilderness begins to shrivel. The only one to survive is the decidedly unmythic Boon. The tale is as powerful as any in American writing of the encounter of man, spirit, and nature.

Alongside that hunting story, however, lies this other tale of misdeeds by the McCaslin progenitor. Section four, which was not in *The Saturday Evening Post* version but was added for the book's publication, takes readers in a very different direction. And it is in this section that the verbal pyrotechnics really take over. Readers are sometimes over-whelmed by Faulknerian prose and may even find that prose a bar-rier between them and the story. When he's on his game, however, Faulkner is not constructing those Frankenstein's-monster sentences for light or transient reasons. The problem, you see, is that it all—past, present, history, violence, race, inheritance, slavery, emancipation, God, nature, love, hatred, the world, and the I—come in all at once, each demanding its fair share of recognition. No, that's not it. Each one demands *the* recognition. They're a noisy, grasping, competitive bunch, and the din they make sounds a lot like, well, Faulkner. In a famous quote from a letter to Malcolm Cowley, he says that "I am telling the same story over and over again, which is myself and the world. Tom [meaning Thomas] Wolfe was trying to say everything, get everything, the world plus "I" or the world filtered through "I" or the effort of "I" to embrace the world in which he was born and walked a little while and then lay down again, into one volume. I have tried to go a step further. This I think accounts for what people call obscurity, the involved form-less "style," endless sentences. I am trying to say it all in one sentence, between one Cap and one period." He very nearly succeeds. Somewhere in section four of "The Bear" there is a very long sentence. And I do mean very long, long enough to go on for pages and have its own para-graphs. Many, many paragraphs. There's only one problem.

No one knows where it is. There are those who maintain that the sentence starts about seven pages in and covers another five. Just past the middle of page 261 in the standard Vintage edition, a sentence be-gins, "To him it was as though the ledgers in their scarred cracked leather bindings were being lifted down one by one . . ." and doesn't find a full stop until the bottom of 267: *"But why? But why? He was sixteen then."*

Another theory suggests that the real whopper begins just a few pages later and runs unbroken to the end of the section, a distance of roughly forty-three pages. On page 271, there's a paragraph beginning, sans capital, "that was all." The next utterance, starting with "He would never need look at the ledgers again nor did he," marks the opening salvo, despite interior punctuation to the contrary, of the world's longest single statement. A sentence, if you will. Technically, a fragment, since it ends on page 315 with the words "laughing and laughing" and no full stop. My Strunk and White says that's a fragment, but they're just rule makers; I'm saying if the statement is completed in all senses, a bit of a mark on the page doesn't really make a difference. The sentence in this case covers something like five years and much discussion between Ike and his cousin Cass Edmonds. Much discussion, including a great deal that is prejudiced or ignorant or defensive on the part of one or the other of them, mostly Cass. Or it might end about a page sooner, right before the sentence "He moved," when his new wife has made him promise, or tried to in vain, to move back out to the farm he has given over to his cousin. Which of those endings you choose doesn't much matter; it's still really long. Now some people will tell you that the passage is full of periods and therefore cannot be a single sentence. To them I would say again, those are mere rules, and we cannot be bound by mere rules, which after all exist simply to be broken, when it comes to grammar. And there's plenty of broken grammar here. Besides, all those full stops happen inside dialogue, within quotation marks, as it happens, indicating a pause in the speech but not in the overarching utterance, so that the narrative containing them remains uninterrupted, a single, flowing cascade of words.

I like that interpretation pretty much. But I would go one better: the entire section, some sixty-one pages beginning and ending, like *Finnegans Wake*, in midsentence, is a single, sustained thought, the accumulation of family history and analysis, rumination on the past and guilt and power relations and everything else the master can think of.

In *William Faulkner: Self-Preservation and Performance* (University of Texas Press, 2000), James G. Watson calls it "a multilayered literary performance in the fragmented and typographically differentiated one long sentence of the chapter." I couldn't have said it better myself. Or nearly as well, for that matter. Multilayered it certainly is. Plenty of fragmentation there, too. As for being typographically differentiated, let's just say that there aren't all that many sentences in English or any other language that contain their own paragraphs, that start and stop and move fluidly back and forth through time and make use of italics and insets and dashes and every sort of punctuation that humankind has considered, along with most of the English words. Wherever it begins or ends, however you construe such matters, one thing is clear: that section is one of the two or three most amazing verbal *performances* (to use Professor Watson's term) you will ever read. I think it is the sort of sentence only an American could write, definitely the sort that only an American would need. It's a sentence that tries to get its head around a whole passel of history and wrongdoing and guilt and contrition and failure, that whole world between one Cap and one period. Even if we're not sure which Cap and which period. Or even if they're there.

Come to think of it, maybe it's a little short.

One of the great things about modernism generally, and we can apply the observation to Faulkner specifically and especially to this Faulkner, is the way that it veers toward myth—or charges headlong at it. This is, after all, the era that gave us Joyce's *Ulysses*, a seven-hundred-plus-page novel in which three very ordinary Dubliners reenact, usually in highly ironic ways, Homer's *Odyssey*, so we shouldn't be shocked that other writers are pushing toward very large parallels for their human-scale stories. We've been talking throughout this study about an American myth, a story of ourselves, and that's certainly here, present in all four suits, but this mythmaking is something else, too. When you use titles such as *Go Down, Moses* (or *Absalom, Absalom!*, for that matter), there's going to be an impulse toward the mythic; Faulkner does not resist it. Why should he? The stories he's telling—the oppression and enslavement of one people by another, wrongs committed and the attempt to right them, man against nature but also *in* nature, the destruction of an earthly paradise by humans too shortsighted to keep and protect it—are as old as humanity itself, are woven into our foundational stories, are the stuff of myth.

The most obvious mythic element in the novel is the encounter with the bear, who has already achieved his own legendary status within the novel's frame. Yet the story of the bear and Ike is not the story we expect to encounter. This will not be a conventional hunter-quest tale. Ike has no hand in killing Old Ben; that task falls to the collective effort of Lion, himself a legendary hunting dog, and Boon Hogganbeck, who falls several degrees short of mythic. Almost instantly after the fight in which Boon kills the bear, Lion and Sam Fathers also succumb, followed soon by the wilderness itself, which Major de Spain has sold off to a logging company. The next people to come along will lack a connection to the land or will use it to improper ends; the days of moral (in Faulkner's view) land stewardship, like so many fine things, are at an end. One of the abiding concerns of later Americans is the loss of wilderness. Our relationship with paradise has been fraught ever since the first Englishman put his second boot down on terra firma. We feared the wilderness, sure that it housed the devil and his allies; we exploited it and despoiled it; we cursed it for being in our way; and we fretted that it would run out before we did, that we would lose it. It did. But starting in the latter years of the nineteenth century, we began to worry that the loss of the wilderness, The Wilderness, would steal some essential part of our identity. The Lewis and Clark part. We couldn't be explorers or pioneers if there's nowhere to explore, nowhere to be first to. At the 1893 World's Exposition in Chicago, Frederick Turner Jackson delivered a paper called, blandly, "The Significance of the Frontier in American History." The title may have been a snooze; the substance was a lightning bolt. He pointed out something that hardly anyone had noticed: by the standard definition of frontier, the national census of 1890 had found that such a place no longer existed in the United States. The psychic effect was devastating. This sort of hand-wringing has been going on ever since. Consider: "You paved paradise / And put up a parking lot." Okay, Joni Mitchell's Canadian, but they've got the bug, too. Besides, anyone in any country who doesn't claim Joni as one of his own is a fool. This phenomenon of the vanishing wilderness—or the anxiety about it—is at the root of the story of bear, dog, and spirit guide. Each in his way is emblematic of the larger wilderness; with the death of each, a bit more of the wild dies with him. And its allure is diminished, even before its physical space is diminished.

All that myth, however, is in service to a very large and serious question. Ike realizes with the death of the principals that one cannot own wilderness. Indeed, he goes back to the spot only once, finding the sentimental journey spoiled by a selfish and half-crazed Boon pounding on a broken rifle while screaming at him to leave the tree full of active squirrels alone. Boon has been driven at least temporarily mad by the dangerous allure of ownership. And Ike, upon just reaching his majority, cedes his inheritance of the estate to his cousin Cass McCaslin, choosing to live in town, live simply, and work as a carpenter—all of which is slightly mythic in its own right. The decision costs him a fortune and his marriage. When his new wife fails to cajole or browbeat him into changing his mind, she tells him the sex they've just had will be their last ever and proves good to her word. That's all right, Christ figures are really better off without encumbrances, material or emotional. He does his duty by dispersing the money left in bequest to his black cousins, chiefly Lucas Beauchamp and his sister Sophonsiba. One might argue that a more enlightened soul would hand the property over to the descendants of those slaves on whose backs the fortune was built, but Ike's enlightenment can take him so far and no more. Still, his belief that the children of slavery deserve fairer treatment is a step, as perhaps is his belief that property ownership, like the love of money, is the root of all evil.

There is a kind of naïve nobility in his stance. We can love him for his purity, admire him for his selflessness. On the other hand, that is one principle that will never gain traction as part of the American myth. Some aspects of Christ alarm even Christians.

Of all the authors in the American library, Faulkner is the most likely to remain unique. He edges out Melville by a nose. No one will ever write like him. No one will ever again have quite the same set of obsessions or, happily, the social raw materials to work with. And the truth is, we don't need more than one of him. But lots of writers have learned from him—learned his courage to experiment, his willingness to burrow deep into the psyche, to interrogate history, to explore everything in one's world as if it all matters. You can see his influence in Toni Morrison's clashes with history and Louise Erdrich's multigenerational sagas. Pynchon might be Faulkner with a bad attitude. And I once heard T. Coraghesson Boyle describe himself as a "maximalist," which led me to wonder if Faulkner wasn't the original maximalist. Or the original something else. Or just completely original. He doesn't fit in any school, doesn't conform to any pattern but his own, and couldn't come from anywhere except exactly where he does. The Swedish Faulkner? Not gonna happen. He's the most American writer on any list of American writers. If you doubt me, ask the French.

NINETEEN

AMERICAN CANDIDE
The Adventures of Augie March

Sometimes you just need to rethink things. Let's say you're a young novelist. Hey, it could happen. You're a child of immigrants, Russian Jews who moved to Quebec and then on to the middle of the United States. You're quite bright but not very successful. Your first two novels, not to put too fine a point on it, tanked. They may have had flashes of humor, but they were very serious and, worse, very existentialist. Tactical blunder, that. Too European, too esoteric, too damned gloomy. What you've discovered is something almost any professor of twentieth-century literature could tell you: Americans don't do existentialism, or at least not when it's recognizable as such. So maybe you want to move away from those claustrophobic little novels that feel so Continental and do something looser, rowdier, bawdier even, something more American. My recommendation would be to announce the change of intention right up front, get yourself an opening that unbuttons its collar, displays a little insouciance (but doesn't use the word), maybe even contains a touch of

Twain. And for heaven's sake make it catch the spirit of the nation. Something, oh, like this:

> I am an American, Chicago born—Chicago, that somber city—and go at things as I have taught myself, free-style, and will make the record in my own way: first to knock, first admitted; sometimes an innocent knock, sometimes a not so innocent. But a man's character is his fate, says Heraclitus, and in the end there isn't any way to disguise the nature of the knocks by acoustical work on the door or gloving the knuckles.

If that doesn't make you want to read on, you're either (a) not American, (b) not a reader, or (c) not alive. I suppose a rock could encounter that paragraph and not be moved, but if you're a reader, you've just been promised a good time. Do you have so many of those you can afford to turn one down? That voice—irreverent, self-schooled, Huck Finn with Heraclitus—is inviting us along. He'll be rowdy, impolite, rough-edged, bare-knuckled.

This one, we read. And read. Saul Bellow had his first big hit with *The Adventures of Augie March*. Americans may not do existentialism, but we definitely do rowdy and irreverent. The year the novel appeared, 1953, was a very good year. One week in March, the *New York Times* bestseller list featured Nikos Kazantzakis's *Zorba the Greek* and *East of Eden* by some guy named Steinbeck. The *Times*'s Top Ten for the year was headed by *The Robe* by Lloyd C. Douglas and *The Silver Chalice* by Thomas B. Costain (proving, I suppose, that we don't only do rowdy and irreverent) and also included James Jones's *From Here to Eternity*, Ernest Gann's *The High and the Mighty*, A. J. Cronin's *Beyond This Place*, and *Time and Time Again* by James Hilton, who had already given us *Lost Horizon* and *Goodbye, Mr. Chips*. Pretty fast company. Augie and Bellow won the National Book Award.

And why not? The most characteristic American novels—*Huckleberry Finn*, *Moby-Dick*, *On the Road*, pretty much anything by Hemingway—have featured the search for self and meaning, often with a strongly spiritual component. Humor, as always, is a plus, and *Augie March* has that in spades.

As with so many books on this list, *The Adventures of Augie March* is not heavily plotted. Its structure is loose, episodic, even a little ramshackle. This is not a negative criticism. Formally, it is a picaresque—if one can speak of the genre in terms of possessing form. Literally, the Spanish *picaro* is a rogue or scoundrel, so the story of one, a picaresque, is the tale of a rogue, a rake's progress, in the title of a series of William Hogarth paintings from the eighteenth century. The hero, like Tom Jones or Moll Flanders, is usually drawn from the lower classes, and the story is highly episodic. Such a narrative plan does not lead to a highly structured novel, nor do we expect it to. The novelist, or his surrogate, is more like a recording secretary, trotting, in Faulkner's famous phrase, after his characters to jot down what they do. And to a large extent, what they do is outrageous. The *picaro* follows the dictates of his or her own conscience, which device does not trouble him or her unduly with rules and strictures. This is as it should be; a well-behaved *picaro* would not be a very interesting character. The point of the genre is to see what rules will be bent and what trouble will ensue, since the lack of moral conduct leads directly to scrapes with society and the law. And to hilarity. The picaresque is essentially a comic genre, in part because the hero, with all his faults, is at odds with a corrupt or at least highly flawed society. His triumph is the subversion of social order that is itself immoral at some very basic level. Think of Huck Finn on his raft hiding an escaped slave and getting into assorted difficulties because of his willingness to break rules, all the while floating through country where, among other crimes, owning human beings is accepted and valorized, and you pretty much have the genre in a nutshell.

As Huck demonstrates, the picaresque is well suited to first-person narration, so we shouldn't be too surprised that Augie tells his own story. Nor that his version is extremely colorful. When the young Augie, a high school sophomore, is caught stealing from the store where he's working as a somewhat oversized Santa's helper, he's forced to pay for the goods he has acquired and then a bit extra, and he's threatened with reform school by "Grandma" Lausch, the elderly boarder who is no relation of the March clan. Passing over the anomaly of the type of employment and the gifts for a Jewish boy, he heads straight for the prospect of incarceration:

> Even she [his mother] said a few sharp things to me. I suffered like a beaver. However, they couldn't get me to beg and entreat—though I wasn't unmoved by the thought of a jail sentence, head shaven, fed on slumgullion, mustered in mud, buffaloed and bossed. If they decided I had it coming, why, I didn't see how I could argue it.

That passage may be the most perfectly American thing anyone has ever said. I have no idea how beavers suffer, but the simile is wonderful—aptness aside—for how it reveals the character of the speaker. He strains after the picturesque, seeks after the memorable. Plus, it's just funny. I believe we can take it as a given that Augie, consummate city dweller, doesn't know from beavers. It doesn't matter. The list of humiliations visited upon reform school inmates, likewise, is vivid in its own right and indicative of Augie's nature. He has, as Huck Finn says, a swell imagination, but he also has the language of the streets and of tough characters at his disposal. One imagines that slumgullion—the word or the dish, a watery meat stew or thin soup—rarely features in the posh districts of Lake Forest or the lecture halls of Northwestern. It does, however, in Augie's world. His education takes place on the streets, and rough streets they are, filled with colorful and sometimes dangerous characters. His lessons have to do with "living by luck and pluck," with getting by on his wits and taking the measure of the people he encounters.

With the publication of *The Adventures of Augie March*, Bellow begins his great period, following just three years later with *Seize the Day* (1956), then *Henderson the Rain King* (1959) and the amazing *Herzog* (1964), and finally *Mr. Sammler's Planet* (1970). It's possible that somewhere, somehow, a writer once had a better five-book run than that in terms of quality and variety, but I very much doubt it. A lesser artist would have been tempted to reprise *Augie* in book after book, freeing other rascals to get into other scrapes with other colorful characters along the fictional roadside. In fact, almost any literary student of the period can name several who did just that. Bellow is not, however, a lesser artist. He's the great American novelist after HFF (Hemingway-Fitzgerald-Faulkner) and in some ways an antidote to them; where they have their great subjects and themes—wealth and its desolations, manly conduct in a shattered world, the postlapsarian South—he has his great ideas. For there is no doubt that Bellow is, first and foremost, a novelist of ideas. He seeks to animate those ideas, to stand them up and have them walk around in fancy dress, to set them in motion and put them on collision courses with each other and with the harsh realities of life in the middle of the twentieth century. Faulkner said in his Nobel Prize address that there remains only one real source of anxiety, which he captures in the phrase, "When will I be blown up?" For him it is a new and alien consideration; not for Bellow. He was born too late to be formed, as were the High Modernists, by World War I. For him, it is the Great Depression, World War II, and the Bomb.

And existentialism. We have already noted that his first two books are informed, not always for the better, by the ideas of Albert Camus and Jean-Paul Sartre, Martin Heidegger and Martin Buber. Many of the preoccupations of the rest of his career—alienation and anxiety, absurdity and nothingness, freedom and responsibility, inaction and the problem of meaning—are already in place. The problem is that they still look like ideas: wooden, stilted, lacking dynamism, lacking appeal, without a face. Augie supplies that face, that appeal, that dynamism. He makes things go.

On the surface, the novel is something of a jumble. Every time Augie finishes one escapade, he's swept into another. Often, in fact, he's swept into the next before the current model has played itself out. He grows up in a strange household, fatherless and with a mother who seems weak-minded, or at least weak-willed, an older brother, Simon, and a younger brother, George, who is developmentally disabled. There is also a lodger, known as Grandma Lausch although she is no relative, who actually rules the roost, dominating Augie's mother and intimidating the children into doing her bidding. She decides, for instance, that George should be institutionalized, even though none of the family wants that outcome. Years later, Simon will exact revenge by having her family commit her to a home against her will. Grandma Lausch is only the first of many colorful and slightly crazed characters with whom Augie will have contact. He works through high school for Einhorn, a paraplegic with a fascinating mind and a gift for making money through not quite legal means. He treats Augie more like a son than his actual son, Arthur, or his half-brother, Dingbat. This closeness is based to a large extent on Augie's hustling attitude matching Einhorn's own—an attitude shared to a much lesser extent by Einhorn's offspring or half-brother. Einhorn even treats Augie to a night at a brothel as a high school graduation present; the spectacle of Augie carrying his crippled benefactor on his back into the house of ill-repute is one of the novel's great set-pieces. Einhorn's attitude toward his protégé introduces a recurring theme—whether or not the main character is looking for a father, it seems most of the older men and women he meets want to adopt him. His mother's cousin, Anna Coblin, "adopts" him for a summer, largely to replace her son who has gone away to join the service and to sound him out as a possible future husband for her stuttering daughter, Friedl. Later, another benefactress, Mrs. Renling, offers to formally adopt him and throws him out when he declines the honor.

You need two things to tell a first-person story. One is a story; care to guess about the other? Actually, it's not so much a person you need as a voice. Think about the great first-person novels of our tradition, and specifically about the characters who speak out of their own experiences to tell us their stories. Huck Finn. Jake Barnes. Nick Carraway. Isadora Wing. Holden Caulfield. Humbert Humbert. A fellow calling himself Ishmael. Yes, their experiences matter. A lot. But the thing that draws us in and holds us is the voice. Who is speaking to us and how does he or she speak? We have to buy into that voice to stay with the novel. We have to be seduced by or attracted by or repulsed by or interested in or amused by that speaker, those words in that order, that voice. And what a voice Bellow gives Augie! He's not Moses Herzog or Eugene Henderson or Charlie Citrine, for all their several attractions, but something quite separate and wonderful. Language cascades out of him, matching the profusion and speed and sheer wonder of life in the twentieth century at the crossroads of America:

> So that Grandma Lausch would have thought that the very worst she had ever said about me would have let me off too light, seeing me in the shoeshine seat above the green tables, in a hat with diamond airholes cut in it and decorated with brass kiss-me pins and

Al Smith buttons, in sneakers and Mohawk sweaters, there in the frying jazz and the buzz of baseball broadcasts, the click of markers, butt thumping of cues, spat-down pollyseed shells and blue chalk crushed underfoot and hand-slickening talcum hanging in the air. Along with the blood-smelling swageroos, recruits for the mob, automobile thieves, stick-up men, sluggers and bouncers, punks with ambitions to become torpedoes, neighborhood cowboys with Jack Holt sideburns down to the jawline, collegiate, tinhorns and small-time racketeers and pugs, ex-servicemen, home-evading husbands, hackies, truckers and bush-league athletes.

Okay, we can go home now. *That's* what America sounds like, looks like, feels like. Augie's a hustler through and through, and this passage, like so much of the novel, is pure hustle. It has *go*. That cataract of description that is the first sentence can't possibly come at us any faster or fuller; it seems it must burst and yet, it holds together. There's detail everywhere, but it isn't just random. He picks the telling details, the "frying jazz" and "Jack Holt sideburns." Even if, like me, you haven't a clue about Jack Holt, that's pretty darned evocative. My favorite detail, however, is the hat with the diamond airholes. Brings me up short every time, partly because I'm just old enough to barely remember such things and partly because it's simply perfect.

Every great character illustrates something essential in the human condition—pointing out a trait or carving out a small niche. The essential thing about Augie is his utility to other people, the danger he runs of being excluded from his own existence by someone else's designs on him. Augie is often seen as an Everyman, but in some ways that designation misses the point. He's special, and part of what is special about him is that he's not exceptional in any way. He's good-looking, but not in a movie star sort of way. People like him but not in a way they would follow him. Rather the opposite in fact. Augie seems custom-made to invite others to try to make use of him. Everyone, it seems, is in search of an acolyte. Augie runs through an impressive array of would-be father figures and surrogate mothers. Even his lovers seem to have him pegged as someone they can shape to their own ends. Thea, the collector of raptors and vipers, displays an attitude toward Augie not entirely unlike that toward the eagle she trains but that finally lets her down. Augie, too, lets her down, chiefly by having a mind of his own.

Even his criminal record is very nearly not of his own doing. Augie is nearly arrested when he goes off to commit one crime—helping smuggle illegal immigrants across the border from Canada—with an acquaintance who has already committed another. The car they're using is hot. I'm sure we've all been there. When your life is in danger of being plotted out by others even down to landing in prison or dying in a lifeboat, it's time to light out for the territories. Stella, the woman he eventually finds and marries, gets to articulate the strategy: "But one of the things I thought is that you and I are the kind of people that other people are always trying to fit into their schemes. So suppose we didn't play along, then what?" But he's already been working it out as he goes. And he goes a lot. Fleeing is his most frequent activity. He's no coward, but he spends a lot of the novel running from some person or other.

A lot of those flights involve jobs and women. Education he manages to avoid on his own, although he occasionally comes near it. The world seems determined to hook him up with unsuitable occupations and equally unsuitable females, and he has to keep extricating himself from those. Among his jobs: dog groomer, smuggler, coal-tip operator, thief, labor organizer, boxing corner man. None of them is his idea, and none satisfies. Several carry significant risks to him for reward for someone else. The women are, for the most part, also someone else's idea. Those two threads come together in the person of Thea Fenchel, who wants him as subservient lover and exotic animal wrangler. Augie, as we know, is from Chicago; this cannot end well. In fact, Thea seems to desire Augie because his lower social status suggests that she can use money and position to control him. She is also one of a string of obsessives fixed on an idea, not the last but in some ways the one most dangerous to his freedom. Their Mexican sojourn comes to an emotionally messy end when Augie takes initiative in a relationship and rescues Stella from her unstable and dangerous boyfriend. Their relationship fares better than the rest because they share a type of experience that neither wants to repeat or inflict on the other, as evidenced by Stella's quote above.

What Augie comes to realize in all this is that for most people, life is fantasy. They try to project a world that will be more satisfactory than the one they inhabit, which is a luxury he has never been able to afford:

> Everyone tries to create a world he can live in, and what he can't use he often can't see. But the real world is already created, and if your fabrication doesn't correspond, then even if you feel noble and insist on there being something better than what people call reality, that better something needn't try to exceed what, in its actuality, since we know it so little, may be very surprising. If a happy state of things, surprising; if miserable or tragic, no worse than what we imagine.

He has a chance to test that hard-won wisdom when his ship is shot out from under him during the war and he finds himself in a lifeboat with a certifiable lunatic named Bateshaw, whose delusions are more immediately dangerous than any he has encountered so far. What he arrives at is an understanding that one must face reality head-on and, like Voltaire's hero Candide, cultivate one's own garden. Even if that plot lies far from home. Stella and Augie end the novel in Paris, where she is working as a film star and he is involved in black market operations.

The immediate future is dreary, at least as regards the marriage, but ultimately, we know that Augie will land on his feet and face reality. That's what a hero, American, free-born, will do. He's one of the great creations in any literature, a champion of the individual spirit in the face of almost overwhelming power, a shape-shifter determined never to be caught, an American Adam, newly created and taking it all in. There is a lot to take in, too. Few novels boast such a colorful cast of characters or such a barrage of activity. Through it all, however, Augie stands as our focal point, more than holding his own against those who would dismiss him. He hustles his own meaning, creates his own life, forges his own soul in the fires of midcentury experience. Where hats have diamond cutouts. What more can we want?

TWENTY

ME AND MY SHADOW
On the Road

For this next bit, half of you can check out for a little while and go do something else unless you are (a) innately curious, (b) out of Darjeeling, or (c) interested in the study of that exotic species, the American male. For the other half, I put it to you that when you were fifteen or seventeen or nineteen and first encountered this book, you were deeply moved. It changed your life, almost changed your life, or made you wish you could change your life. It made you sad or angry that you were born at the wrong time or in the wrong place and missed a great adventure. It altered your writing style, your sense of self, your love of cars, and, briefly, your appreciation of jazz. It stirred your soul. If it didn't, you either aren't really American, aren't really a guy, or have never driven flat-out on baked two-lane highways with all the windows down for hundreds of miles as you savored the sweetness and sadness of existence in all its sweaty, masculine, beatific glory. Or have a vocation for the priesthood. Not that there's anything wrong with any of those. There are a very limited number of books that can produce such a profound effect. By my count, the twentieth century had precisely one. And it wasn't *Kids Say the Darnedest Things*. Not that there's anything wrong with that, either.

The word for the day, children, is "Beat."

But the Beats themselves weren't enough. Oh, there would have been a writer named Jack Kerouac had there only been his association with Allen Ginsberg, William S. Burroughs, Gregory Corso, and Gary Snyder. There just wouldn't have been an *On the Road*. Or at least not the one we know, and certainly not of the quality we know. For that matter, the remainder of the Kerouac *oeuvre* would likely not have been as good, as rich, as interesting as it turns out to be. Because he would have remained merely Jack Kerouac. What he became, and what made the novel possible, was Jack Kerouac-Cassady. Even with all the Columbia-educated, determined, hip, proto-counterculture, visionary literati of his experience, he could never become the writer we know without a hopped-up, car-stealing, oversexed hustler from Denver named Neal Cassady. For it would be Cassady who dragged him back and forth across the country, who showed him the low side of high living, who wrecked his health with amphetamine-fueled sleepless weeks, who talked a mix of Eastern wisdom, philosophy, crime, thrills, and pure nonsense in a blue streak like a cross between a Zen master and a Midwest auctioneer. More importantly, he gave the struggling novelist a new way of organizing prose. Headlong. Wild-flowing. Sometimes slap-dash. But always forward:

> *South Main Street, where Terry and I took strolls with hot dogs, was a fantastic carnival of lights and wildness. Booted cops frisked people on practically every corner. The beatest characters in the country swarmed on the sidewalks—all of it under those soft Southern California stars that are lost in the brown halo of the huge desert*

encampment LA really is. You could smell tea, weed, I mean mari-
juana, floating in the air, together with the chili beans and beer. That
grand wild sound of bop floated from beer parlors; it mixed medleys
with every kind of cowboy and boogie-woogie in the American night.
Everybody looked like Hassel. Wild Negroes with bop caps and
goatees came laughing by; then long-haired brokendown hipsters
straight off Route 66 from New York; then old desert rats, carrying
packs and heading for a park bench at the Plaza; then Methodist
ministers with raveled sleeves, and an occasional Nature Boy saint
in beard and sandals. I wanted to meet them all, talk to everybody,
but Terry and I were too busy trying to get a buck together.

Nowadays, every semiliterate sixteen-year-old with a bad attitude
can write like this; in fact, it was the bane of my brief stints teaching
creative writing. But if it has become a cliché that has passed in and
out of fashion a few dozen times and something lightly accomplished,
that's because of what we all learned from reading it, then reading his
successors and imitators. When it appeared in 1957, there was nothing like it. And to achieve that effortless style, its creator sweated
blood. Several of the Kerouac signature moves present themselves
here. Note the ersatz compound "brokendown" in a phrase typically
hyphenated, the superlative coinage "beatest," the mix of the exotic
(marijuana—hey, this was the 1940s) with the mundane (chili beans
and beer) that drags the ordinary toward the exotic and the exotic
toward the commonplace. Most of all, we should note that dynamic
catalog of characters: "Wild Negroes," followed by "hipsters," "old desert rats," "Methodist ministers," and the "Nature Boy saint," who collectively make this a compilation that seems expected in its milieu and
only wild to the East Coast outsider, Sal Paradise, who narrates the
novel. More on him presently.

Now, though, the novel. Or the urban legend of the novel. There are enough myths, folktales, superstitions, and just outright nonsense regarding Jack Kerouac's *On the Road* for ten books. We haven't enough space to deal with all of them, so let's take on one or two of the most persistent and pernicious. The most dangerous to health and public welfare is that the novel was written under the influence of drugs. It would be far more accurate to say that Kerouac wrote it while recovering from the influence of drugs. A great many chemicals, chiefly Benzedrine, were consumed during what we might call the research phase of the book, so much so that the author twice came home to Mémère (did I mention that the legendary "wild man" lived with his mother?), his health shattered from trying to keep up with Cassady in the substance abuse department. The drug of choice during the composition of "the scroll" manuscript, to which we will return, was caffeine, Kerouac imbibing huge amounts of coffee and pea soup (caffeine content unknown) in the three weeks in April 1951 that resulted in the 86,000-word, 120-foot-long, single-spaced paragraph that would eventually become the novel we know, although biographer Ann Charters and others claim he also took Benzedrine to stay awake.

Now, that scroll. Kerouac did indeed trim and tape sheets of tracing paper together into the massive scroll that has moved, with help from the writer himself and Allen Ginsberg, into legend. Over time, he would rework it in other scrolls. The impulse was not, as has often been maintained, to produce a final copy. Rather, it was a response to failure. The April word-barrage represented at a minimum the third or fourth attempt at his "road novel," which he had been carrying around with him for years in skeletal form in small notebooks where he recorded the events of the trips with Cassady. The first effort was scuttled by his too-heavy allegiance to Thomas Wolfe, as had been his first novel, *The Town and the City*. Wolfe may have his virtues, though they've always eluded me, but being a model for a future King of the Beats was not among their number. That was 1948, three years before the scroll and nine before eventual publication. Another version was planned with the narrator a ten-year-old black boy. It takes very little imagination to see why that didn't fly. Still, it took more time and more failure to arrive at a satisfactory solution.

What Kerouac eventually settled on was a narrative alter ego, a character enough like himself to let him swing out the rhythms he wanted but far enough away to assure plausible deniability. What he came up with was Sal Paradise, a metric double—one clipped syllable for the first name and a dactylic surname, one stress followed by two unstressed syllables. That's the first thing you need to accept in dealing with his work, that metrical arrangements and the sounds of words matter as much as what the words say. He may not have been a successful poet, but that doesn't mean he wasn't poetic. Kerouac belongs with Hemingway and Faulkner in that tiny handful of novelists who were great poets of the fictional form and who by their efforts reshaped the sound of modern prose, American division.

Sal is one of the great narrative inventions. Like his creator, he swings between elation and dejection, squalor and ecstasy. He's a sponge of experience and language, very much affected by those he meets along the road. Most of all, he's generous. He doesn't judge the people he meets. Instead, he accepts them as having arrived at a place in their lives for a reason. That's good, because mostly the places his people have arrived at are not on Easy Street. The novel is in that sense the inheritor not of the tradition of Thomas Wolfe but of John Steinbeck.

Dean Moriarty, on the other hand, is not so much a fictional creation as a found poem. Neal Cassady screamed into Kerouac's life like a whirlwind, custom-made to become a character in a novel, if only the novel that could hold him might be invented. He was America's

Jean Genet or Brendan Behan, except that he couldn't remain still long enough to be in the service of art. Late-phase romanticism, Byronic subclass, has been fascinated with the outlaw, the rule-breaker, the transgressor. Hardly surprising that Cassady would wind up as maniac-in-chief among Ken Kesey's Merry Pranksters, since Kesey's own holy fool, Randle P. McMurphy owes so much to the type—and probably to the particular instance. Petty criminal, bigamist, drug user, friend abuser, bisexual, he crossed nearly every boundary and looked for more to be crossed. And he talked a blue streak; indeed, his life was largely an amphetamine-charged monologue that occasionally included spectators. Turning him into Dean Moriarty required less inspiration than transcription. When such a being waltzes into the artist's life, it would be an insult to the gods of creativity not to make use of him.

Now this is a time when one can appropriately say, there is no *plot* worth mentioning. Tons of action, but no structure beyond a loose, episodic sequencing. That's okay, though; we have more than enough heavily plotted novels. Besides, anything resembling an actual plan would have a deleterious effect on our perception of this mad, frantic, desperate racing back and forth across the continent, the pointlessness of which is part of the point. And as you might expect in a novel without a plot, it is equally innocent of subplots. The focus is always on Sal and his problems and his hopes and his disappointments, chiefly owing to his involvement with Dean. In a letter to Sal very late in the novel, Dean mentions Proust; it will no doubt be heresy in some quarters to suggest that this is a Proustian novel, and yet on one level it is. Sal is attempting to reconstruct experience out of disparate and jumbled memories in order to comprehend all that has gone into making him. There is, however, no madeleine to trigger the onslaught of reminiscence.

To untangle the bird's nest of activity would be a week's work to read as well as write, but we can tease out the basic story line. While recovering from illness and divorce in 1947, Sal meets Dean Moriarty, long the stuff of rumor and legend in Sal's circle. That circle is made up of artistic and literary types, including Carlo Marx (modeled on Ginsberg), with whom Dean almost immediately has an all-night talkfest the thread of which virtually no one can follow. Sal's chief affliction is postwar malaise, and in this regard he is very representative of his generation, although his reactions to it scarcely mirror those of the vast majority of his fellow young Americans. He yearns for meaning, joy, affection, adventure. Dean seems to supply or embody all of those, and Sal is infatuated with the idea of Dean. The reality of him is sometimes less appealing. This initial meeting sets off a three-year cycle of cross-country jaunts, some of them jauntier than others. First, in July of 1947, Sal goes to Chicago, then Denver, then on to California. In Denver he meets up with native son Dean and Marylou and their friends, and he works for a while. When Dean and Marylou had arrived in New York, they were just married and full of lust, at least, for one another, but before long Marylou had reported Dean to the police. Their relationship will be marked by similar highs and lows. And by separation. Marylou is the first of three wives over the course of three years, and four children are born to him, although they seem to cause him little enough pause in his frenetic comings and goings. After Sal leaves them he heads to San Francisco where he works as a night watchman at a camp for merchant sailors, but soon he heads south to Los Angeles in the company of Terry, a Mexican woman on the run from an abusive husband. He spends most of a week with Terry and her family in the fields as a farmworker, until the realities of hard work and short pay catch up with him. Unlike the Mexicans, he is at liberty to turn down such an option; for all his complaining about being white and missing out on the minority experience, Sal is not at all shy about accepting the greater range of options available to a white male in postwar America.

The next year he travels with Dean again, this time on a southerly route through New Orleans, where they impose on Bull Lee (William S. Burroughs) and his wife long enough to become thoroughly unwelcome. With a nearly full car of penniless deadbeats, they have to rely on hitchhikers to bring in gas money as they make their way to San Francisco again, arriving broke and somewhat saddened. The spring of 1949, however, finds Sal again seeking out Dean, and together they storm across the country in mostly grand fashion, although his impression of Dean is headed south. Sal goes to Denver, working in a fruit warehouse, which he quickly comes to dislike—there does seem to be a theme emerging here about hard work—and then on to San Francisco again, from where he and Dean set out on their next adventure. It is undertaken in a bit of a crisis: Dean has been stealing cars willy-nilly, and one of them belongs to a police detective. They arrange to transport a Cadillac to Chicago for a wealthy man. Along the way they have two small wrecks, pick up students and hobos, and drive all the way from Denver to Chicago at an average speed (pre-Interstate system) of seventy miles an hour. The car arrives in better condition than one driven by the Blues Brothers, but not by a lot. Then they take a bus to Detroit and another travel bureau ride on to New York, where they stay with Sal's aunt. Dean works hard to make child support payments to two different women, one who is his wife (Camille) and one (Inez) who will be. Sal leaves him there to go back to Denver, and this time finds his friends and has a good time there. Soon, Dean joins him, and together with Stan Shepherd they set off for Mexico. They have various adventures there, including getting stoned with a Mexican family and visiting a brothel that specializes in ear-splitting mambo music and underage prostitutes, although Sal can't bring himself to engage the sixteen-year-old he desires, settling on an older woman instead.

Later on, in Mexico City, Sal finds a new path to delusion and unconsciousness: dysentery and fever. Predictably, Dean abandons him to Stan's care, completing a pattern of refusal ever to take responsibility for another person's well-being. Sal decides Dean is "a rat" but even then excuses him, deciding that no one could really "understand the impossible complexity of his life, how he had to leave me, sick, there to get on with his wives and woes." Back in New York, Sal finds what he has been looking for in Laura, a woman considerably less colorful than his prior traveling companions, and they decide to move to San Francisco. Dean declares that he will come to get them, and he does—five and a half weeks too early. The man who arrives is a shadow of his former self, speaking in broken sentences and seeming broken in some more essential way, as well. His behavior suggests that something, most likely amphetamine overuse or withdrawal, has accelerated his downward trajectory. The impression is reinforced by his taking the train rather than his totem, the car, back to the West Coast. Dean's collapse contrasts with Sal's elevation; he is finding strength and stability and even hope in the closing stages of the novel. If the romance of the road is fading, it is being replaced by something more solid and mature. These changes are reflected in the novel's famous closing rumination:

> So in America when the sun goes down and I sit on the old broken-down river pier watching the long, long skies over New Jersey and sense all that raw land that rolls in one unbelievable huge bulge over to the West Coast, and all that road going, all the people dreaming in the immensity of it, and in Iowa I know by now the children must be crying in the land where they let the children cry, and tonight the stars'll be out, and don't you know that God is Pooh Bear? the evening star must be drooping and shedding her sparkler dims on the prairie, which is just before the coming of complete night that blesses

the earth, darkens all rivers, cups the peaks and folds the final shore
in, and nobody, nobody knows what's going to happen to anybody
besides the forlorn rags of growing old, I think of Dean Moriarty, I
even think of Old Dean Moriarty the father we never found, I think
of Dean Moriarty.

Isn't that something? The only ending I know of that comes close
is *Gatsby's*, and for much the same reasons: the death of a dream, the
ineffable sadness, the mix of hope and disillusionment—hard to miss if
you've got good material. Which he does—"all that raw land that rolls
in one unbelievable huge bulge over to the West Coast"—the same as
Walt Whitman, only more of it.

That's his real family tree. Kerouac is the true heir of Emerson, who
nevertheless could never have recognized himself in the novel. With a
select few others, Gary Snyder and Hart Crane among them, he is one
of the few twentieth-century writers seeking transcendence through
experience of the natural world in ways that follow, loosely, Emersonian precepts. And for Kerouac, as for Whitman, that transcendence
has to do with embracing the country—*the whole place*, as we see in
that closing passage. In *On the Road*, that search is for revelation and redemption. Sal thinks he is looking for ecstasy, for the sort of boundless
joy and enthusiasm he imagines Dean to possess, but what he needs, as
opposed to what he desires, is redemption not for himself as much as
for the country, or for himself as embodiment of the country. And the
revelation is of what the country might possibly be, how it might meet
the promise of its beginnings with its future reality. Kerouac has Sal
embrace every group, individual, social station, and possibility for creative living, even if so many of them end in disappointment. That possibility is what makes Dean—petty criminal, fast mover, drug taker, con
man, jailhouse intellectual—fascinating to Sal. His joy, his capacity for

ecstasy, is huge. But that is also what makes his fall so sad. The disparity between what Dean might have been and what he is forms a basis
for a tragic view of life.

Nor is it only Dean Moriarty who disappoints. Never has a novel
with such a strongly articulated desire for joy and transcendence expressed such sadness and pain. Sal begins in melancholy and winds up
only slightly better, stronger if not particularly happier. The release
proffered by the wildness that is Dean is never realized, although insights into its possibility are seen in jazz clubs, among the downtrodden, with workers and hobos, in nonwhite society, and, of course in
racing along the nation's highways at speeds above the legal maximum.
Kerouac seems to believe—and certainly lived as if he did—William
Wordsworth's lines that although poets begin in youth in gladness,
they "thereof come in the end in despondency and madness." Those
lines are written in connection with Thomas Chatterton, poet, hustler, substance abuser, self-destructive genius. Sounds like someone
we meet in these pages, doesn't it? In Kerouac's case, that dichotomy
plays itself out in the war between the open road and closed avenues.
He wants so badly to believe in it, but that becomes more difficult as
time goes on, and much evidence suggests that society has thrown up
more and more roadblocks.

It's all part of a conversation he's having with his literary, romantic forebears, English and American, but especially with Whitman,
who enjoins us to reach out for the entirety of American experience,
to embrace the whole country and all of its people. Yes, Kerouac says,
but that's a big task and probably overwhelming for a single person.
The sheer effort can break you. At the same time, he provides us with
the romance of that open road, the full-tilt boogie, the trip to the
horizon and back, as Hurston says, and we've been following him
ever since.

TWENTY-ONE

WHEN READING GOT GOOD
The Cat in the Hat

There once was a time not so far in the past
When reading a kid's book did not go by fast.
The books were so boring, the books were so dull
That we did not like them, not like them at all.
Ted had his Sally and Dick had his Jane,
And reading about them gave us all a pain.
They were so nice, and so clean and sweet, too,
But mostly we noticed what they didn't do.
They didn't get dirty and always were nice,
But you can take only so much of this sugar and spice.
They stood around meekly with dogs—all named Spot,
And they never had fun, no, not even a jot
Or even a tittle, since they were not rude,
They did nothing at all but just stood,
stood,
stood,

STOOD.

So it was quite clear, like a dog on a bun,

That when you were reading you did not have fun.

Then into this mess came a figure quite tall

Who made reading jolly for persons quite small.

His real name was Geisel but we knew him as Seuss,

A poet of nonsense with mirth for his muse.

He gave us a couple of real kids, a pair,

No Ted but a Sally, and, yes, "I" was there.

On a cold, cold, wet day all they could do was sit

And being real kids they didn't like it one bit.

Now this Seuss had a plan to enliven their day

And to give children reading that felt more like play

By letting a cat in red stripes and a grin

Bring mayhem and mischief and lots of fun in.

Now, none of us ever had seen such a Cat

With a box full of Things that made other things splat.

They played with such fire and they played with such verve

And made such a mess; why, that Cat had some nerve,

That children forgot to think reading a bore

And read the whole book and then clamored for more.

All this with few words: a mere two-thirty-six,

With rhythm and rhyme, why, those were his tricks.

And who, reading this, would not want another

With so many things that you can't tell your mother?

Okay, I know—going to the same college as Dr. Seuss does not make you Dr. Seuss. Especially if you missed being his fellow student by, oh, half a century. But how can you read him and not think, it's a good day for anapests? That's the unit of infectious rhythm—unstressed-unstressed-STRESSED syllables that go dum-dum-DUM—over and over again in rhyming couplets. There are four of those metrical *feet*, as they're called, per line, making the line something called anapestic tetrameter. Which is Literary for "four funny-looking feet." That's easy. Try explaining Homer's dactylic hexameter (meaning, naturally, six funnier-looking feet) sometime. Of course, not every line is going to have exactly twelve syllables (or, since he worked, like Anglo-Saxon poets, in half-lines, six). No one sticks precisely and slavishly to the dominant meter except greeting-card writers. And no one, probably in the whole history of the world, has made anapests so much darned fun.

Here's what it looks like on the page:

The sun would not shine.
It was too wet to play.
So we sat in the house
All that cold, cold, wet day.

And here's how it scans:

The SUN would not SHINE. It was TOO wet to PLAY.
So we SAT in the HOUSE all that COLD, cold, wet DAY.

Scansion is the technical term for how the metrical arrangement works out in practice. *Meter* is the rhythmic pattern adopted for the poem. Scansion is how the individual poem winds up using its meter. As I said before, Dr. Seuss works in half-lines, breaking the metrical arrangement in the middle so that early readers won't be overwhelmed. Effectively, however, this representation shows what's really going on with the poem's rhythm. In general, the metrical feet have two unstressed syllables ("would not") preceding the stressed syllable ("SHINE"). As often happens, the poem's first metrical foot disobeys, just to show that it can't be bossed.

Modern kids are so lucky. I'm one of the bitter ones. We just missed out on the magic. The Cat was born in 1957, the year that I started kindergarten, but it didn't filter down to West Cornfield, Ohio, until I was past the primer stage of my reading life. Besides, bookstores were not thick on the ground on Sweet Potato Ridge Road. That's a real place, by the way. Everyone should grow up on a Sweet Potato Ridge Road. I read all the Seussyphan works when they started showing up a few years on and my younger brothers were reading them. Lucky sods. You can't freely embrace a book when you're three years "too big" for it. Thirty, or fifty, yes, but not three. My readers had Ted and Sally in them. And Spot, naturally. So what happened, as you might imagine, is that my classmates and I didn't read anything interesting for school until about fifth grade. Those earlier years were taken up with slight variations on "See Spot. See Spot run." I know not what course others may take, but those words still make me want to run. At last, we were saved by inventive teachers and the real reason for which the wheel was invented, the bookmobile. Literary salvation that rolled. From the bookmobile you could get *stories*. From the bookmobile you could eventually get Robert Louis Stevenson. From the bookmobile you could even occasionally get in trouble with your mother. From the primers you got Spot.

So what saved children of a later time from all that spottiness? It wasn't Congress or the state board of education or any of the expected sources of relief. It was *Life*. Just imagine, a magazine interested in reading—what a country! In May of 1954, John Hersey—yes, he of *Hiroshima* fame, published a piece called "Why Do Students Bog Down on First R? A Local Committee Sheds Light on a National Problem: Reading." The chief culprit, he averred, was the reading primer. "Insipid," he said. Full of children no real child could identify with—too clean, too polite, too static. To top things off, Hersey asked why children should be subjected to such drivel—make that *boring* drivel—when there existed a cadre of fabulous children's illustrators. He ticked off the names of three worthies, including one Theodor S. Geisel, who bore his mother's maiden name as his middle name, which he used as his nom de plume. It would presently go from merely famous to extremely so.

Hersey's article was one of several small miracles that resulted in a much bigger one that never goes out of print. First of all, it appeared in arguably the most important weekly magazine of its day, although the editors of *The Saturday Evening Post* would have demurred. And second, he managed to call out the one man best suited to the job. Better still, the man in question was interested. And then something weird and slightly miraculous transpired. Geisel was contacted by an editor. But not his editor. Not even his publishing house. Dr. Seuss was under contract to Random House, run by Bennett Cerf, who was no slouch at off-kilter humor himself, but it would be William Ellsworth Spaulding, a textbook editor at otherwise stuffy Houghton Mifflin in Boston who would come up with the idea. The story goes that Spaulding sent a list of 348 words to Geisel, who pared it to 223 for his working vocabulary for the project. The final list would grow to 236, including a single word of three syllables, "another," which is very nearly mandatory to come up with rhymes for "mother," who, if absent from the scene is never far from children's minds. Another fourteen have two syllables, with all the rest being singles. And you thought nothing could be said in monosyllables! The final miracle is that Houghton Mifflin and Random House decided to play nice together, the former taking school text rights and the latter, as the author's proper house, keeping trade book rights. In Seussland, even dogs and cats get along.

He wanted the title to rhyme, and the first two words that rhymed were "cat" and "hat." The die was cast. Of course, you could give those two words to ten million people—or Whos, for that matter, and not get the present text. But those words fell not to just any old Who but to one very specific *him*. The Seuss sensibility—the Seussibility, if you will—immediately grasped the silliness inherent in putting the *hat* on the *cat*, and making it a striped hat, at that. What it had not reckoned with was the difficulty of writing a story with such a limited vocabulary; the project took him more than nine months, far longer than anticipated. A look at the finished project will illustrate the problem. It's the rhymes. More particularly, it's the murderous shortage of rhyming words. Let's say you have a vocabulary of 236 mostly monosyllabic words. How many of them do you think will rhyme with another? More particularly, how many do you expect to have more than one rhyming option?

Exactly.

And to make matters worse, this is not a short poem. By my count—and counting is deucedly awkward with this book, in which some "lines" straggle out over three or four lines of type—the text contains 274 lines. Only half of those lines rhyme, since effectively the odd-numbered lines are the first two metrical feet of the tetrameter, or four-footed, lines. We can depict the resulting rhyme scheme as it appears on the page like this: x-a-x-a, where "x" is the standard means of representing an unrhymed line and "a" the first rhyme in any scheme. A quatrain (a four-line stanza) in which the odd-numbered lines rhyme with each other and the even-numbered lines form a second rhyme would be represented as a-b-a-b. Fair enough?

What we end up with, then, is a book whose writing is formally quite rigid with its anapests and rhyming couplets but whose subject matter is anarchy itself. The children in the story find themselves shut up in their house on a cold and rainy day while their mother is away, and being exceptionally good children, they do not get into mischief. Nevertheless, mischief finds them in the form of the Cat. He is essentially a bad child—a showoff, a risk-taker, a headstrong individual who will not listen to others or even notice that others are talking to him. Set against him is the fish, a sort of aqueous Jiminy Cricket who acts as the conscience of the children and the foil to our mad Hatter. You doubt? Leaf through the book and you'll find the fish present in every scene that contains the Cat. He's also there a couple of times when the Cat isn't, but the reverse *never* happens. The fish is a scold and a drudge, but he's also right. They're not allowed to do the things the Cat does; their mother will be furious when she finds out. Why, they're not even supposed to have a stranger in the house when she's away, and now look at this mess, and there's gonna be heck to pay, blah, blah, blah. One of the lessons of the book, however, is that being right doesn't make one a lot of fun. In any case, the kids hardly need him, since he's mostly giving voice to their thoughts. *They* don't wreck the house or want it wrecked. *They* don't welcome the Cat's enthusiasm and lack of discipline. On the other hand, it is thrilling to be in the presence of misbehavior, to experience a bad attitude vicariously. As long as you have plausible deniability, that is. And you're not a fish.

The story is simplicity itself, and as old as human storytelling. A stranger comes to town and creates mayhem. He could be the rightful but unrecognized heir to the throne or Beowulf arriving to give the Geats a hand with their monster problem, or the Man-With-No-Name or the Magnificent Seven coming to the village to upend the local thugs. In this case, the unrequested stranger is a Cat with curious taste in clothes promising fun on a sodden day. What he needs, apparently, is an audience. This particular stranger is in luck, if luck it be: he has a captive audience that will be properly amazed and aghast at his antics.

In a very different context, the critic Christopher Ricks identifies a certain kind of rhetorical device common to seventeenth-century metaphysical verse and that of late twentieth-century poets of Northern Ireland as a "self-inwoven simile," by which he means a simile that contains both terms of its comparison. He means it as a term of approbation for poems that are highly self-referential, that is, concerned with their own existence to a very high degree. Without bogging down to explain Professor Ricks's thinking, I wish to steal from him (which, as T. S. Eliot noted, is what great writers do) and suggest that Seuss's book is its own self-inwoven metaphor. There is no better comparison for the activity of writing this book than the activity *in* the book. Is it too much to claim that the story is autobiographical, that the Cat is Ted Geisel himself? For the design of this little book mirrors the shape and intention of his career—stirring things up, taking charge and taking chances, breaking rules only to set things right in the end. The good doctor is a very moral agent masquerading as a trickster, which can also serve as a description of our hatted feline. He gives shape to childhood by shaking things up, like his creator.

So where, you ask, is the shaping? Look around you. Look at the books *your* children bring home from school, from the library. Those books are not dull. In fact, they are expected to be *not* dull. They do not contain empty repetition and formless pseudo-narrative, and they have all but banned dogs named Spot. We often hear of parents or community leaders getting up on their hind legs over some book or other, but if you really want to see riots in the streets, try bringing back *Ted and Sally*.

You want to see the greatest influence that this Seussian masterpiece has had on our culture? Turn on your television. No, not ESPN, although sometimes one does wonder. Go to your local public broadcasting affiliate between the hours of 9:00 a.m. and 4:00 p.m. Much of what you see will be CoS—Children of Seuss. I submit that there would be no *Sesame Street* without the liberating influence of a certain Cat, that the strange beings and wacky logic of America's favorite street would not be possible without the paradigm shift ushered in by the good Doctor. For that's what it was. The paradigm of children's education and children's entertainment was profoundly altered by the series of books that began with *The Cat in the Hat*. Prior to that we had an endless parade of Uncles Orrie and Rory and Captains Al and Hal and Skippers Ryle and Kyle and their inevitable sidekicks. The prime example of the species, of course, was Captain Kangaroo with his gigantic jacket pockets and his entourage of Mr. Greenjeans, Bunny Rabbit, Dancing Bear, and Mr. Moose. The Captain, or Bob Keeshan, who played him, had himself started as a sidekick, playing Clarabell the Clown to *Howdy Doodie*'s Buffalo Bob Smith. Don't get me wrong, *Captain Kangaroo* was a great show and very important to an entire generation of us, to whom it taught many lessons, chief among them that Schwinn bicycles were the ultimate object of desire and had prices "slightly higher in the West and South." The atmosphere of the show, like most of the species, could best be described as slow-motion zany. There were antics aplenty, but they were held together by a framework that tried not to overexcite its audience. And it had an earnestness about it, or at least about its educational aspect, that stopped time. What Dr. Seuss presents us with, on the other hand, is the possibility that we can learn at full speed, right there in the headlong rush of frenetic surrealism. That may be the book's greatest gift to children's education, the license to employ the surreal, even the subversive, in the service of teaching. Anyone who can remember the 1950s will surely understand how impossible it would have been in that world to imagine, let alone get away with, a Cookie Monster or a Grouch who lives in a trash can, much less the absurdist videos teaching children about the letter *T* or sharing. But after Thing

One and Thing Two, to say nothing of the later Voom that proved so effective on pink bathtub rings, they become almost inevitable. Nothing breeds imitation like success, and *Sesame Street* went on to spawn a host of imitators with varying degrees of success. It is disquieting to think that our Cat gave rise to a certain purple dinosaur, but it's not impossible. Merely unthinkable.

The Cat, however, does more than merely influence subsequent culture, although that alone would merit our admiration. No, he brings down to the basic level of childhood the essential conflict that rages always in the American soul, the war between conformity and rebellion. The comparison to the Magnificent Seven is only partly specious; this hero strides in to fight evil, but of a different sort. These children are in danger of becoming adults, J. G. Their mother's strictures, as voiced by that tiresome nanny of a fish, seek to take the child out of them, to make them sit quietly, comply meekly, live out existences of boredom and inactivity, all in the name of domestic tranquility. They have been trained to be good kids. They *want* to be good kids. But you can't spell "kid" without "id." Enter the Cat. He embodies the spirit of misrule, the anti-authoritarian impulse that is probably at the heart of being human and certainly at the heart of being American. From the Tea Party to the tea parties, our national spirit has contained a healthy dose of contempt for rules and a love of disorder. Want proof? I give you two streets, Carnaby and Haight. The swinging '60s in London were chiefly about looking fabulous—in all senses of the word. That same era in San Francisco was about being fabulous: we don't need no stinkin' couturiers. Their decade was swinging; ours far out. And we would have dropped the terminal *g*.

Or take religion. Britain has the Established Church. The first thing someone did with an established church in America (which came here to get away from that other one) was to break away from it. Or get kicked out. I suspect the Puritans and Roger Williams probably had different versions of what happened. From that auspicious beginning, American dissent just exploded. Don't like your church? Start a new one. And always stick to your guns. Diagonally across the road from the house where I grew up is a church of Plain People, one of the various sects that are characterized by bonnets and flat-brimmed hats and eschew some or all things modern and fancy. One of my favorite stories that I heard about them was that a member had once been "churched," as the saying goes, for they would never use "excommunicated," for refusing to paint the red stripe on his otherwise-black Model A Ford. I have always found both positions in that dispute, which may be apocryphal, admirable—and wholly American. That church, by the way, spawned one and perhaps two breakaways, at least one of which underwent another split. That's just so *us*. At the same time, we are fully capable of total acquiescence and perfect docility, sometimes in the face of outrageous restrictions. Yet inside every solid citizen, there lurks an insurrectionist; inside every well-mannered child, a Cat.

TWENTY-TWO

WALK A MILE IN MY SHOES
To Kill a Mockingbird

Here's a word of advice to all you aspiring novelists: make your first novel the best you can; it may be the only one you get. The truth of first novels, as we all know, is that they languish in drawers, failing to find a publisher or even failing to cause themselves to be finished. Or they hit the bookshelves for five minutes and quickly begin the slide to the remainder tables and the pulp vat. Or they may hang around, get mildly good, mildly dismissive reviews: "This piece of juvenilia holds promise, if only the writer can become more serious, more mature, more accomplished." All of those outcomes can effectively silence a budding fiction writer. Failure can take many forms. But you know what's even more dangerous?

Success.

Let's say you're a young writer who has published a few short stories and shows all sorts of potential. Let's say you write about the world you know—*everything* you know—from growing up in a small town. You use up all the colorful and dangerous eccentrics in your home town, pouring your heart and soul into your novel. You give it everything you've got and hope for the best, even if the best is "a quick and merciful death." At least it will have been published, and maybe someone will notice, even if they don't like it all that much. Only that's not how the story turns out.

They love it. Everybody. Critics. Okay, not all critics, because you know how they are, but enough. Readers. Prize judges. Hollywood. Teachers—especially teachers. It goes on to win the Pulitzer Prize and, within two years, become an Oscar-winning film. Your. First. Novel.

Your last novel.

Because how can you possibly top that? And where are you going to find the material to do so? You've used it up, and it you. The answer, of course, is that you can't. Even if you live another half-century.

Ask Harper Lee.

The story goes that in 1958 she received the gift of a year's wages from friends who believed in her talent, with the instruction to "write whatever you please." What pleased her was a tale of life in a small Alabama town, replete with injustice and prejudice and compassion and mystery and madness seen through the eyes of a young girl but told by her adult self. The characters were modeled on her family and neighbors, including a very young Truman Capote. Within a year she had her draft, and within another, a successful novel. A wildly successful novel. She did not go back to the airline counter where she had been working beforehand.

In the Yeats poem I mentioned somewhat earlier, "Easter 1916," William Butler Yeats says, in essence, that he had believed himself to live in a trivial land and engage in trivial conversations, but all that changed with the rebellion, which in effect made nationalists of the Irish, himself included. In a sense, that's what happens to Scout and Jem in *Mockingbird*: they cease to inhabit a trivial, inconsequential place. If you flip *Adventures of Huckleberry Finn* over, you get this novel—shenanigans first, then the momentous business.

Scout (Jean Louise) and Jem (Jeremy Atticus) are the children of an unconventional father, Atticus Finch, a small-town lawyer in Maycomb, Alabama. Their mother is dead, and they are raised in large measure by their black cook, Calpurnia, who provides the needed if undesired strictness in their upbringing. Atticus himself offers insights, the ability to express themselves, and most importantly, the freedom to make mistakes and to learn from them. The story takes us from just before Scout begins school, the regimentation of which she hates, through until she is around nine and Jem thirteen, as we know from its famous opening.

One of the oddities of the novel form is that so many of its examples press forward by looking backward. You can think of it as the after-the-catastrophe effect, since such novels are almost never comedies. *The Great Gatsby* would be such a novel, with Nick Carraway looking back over disastrous events. Or Lawrence Durrell's *Justine*—all those lives wrecked, all that mayhem. There's a second element common to these two books and a great many like them: they have first-person narrators. This makes sense. A godlike, omniscient presence, or even a more limited third-person narrator, need not try to reassemble the pieces of life or memory; after all, it was not his life that was ruined, her friends who were destroyed.

But the stories need not be tragic. Looking backward at the outset can also be a useful device for imbuing a novel with mystery: something has happened, we are told—not going to happen or could happen, but has happened—and from then on, we want to know what it was. We may see this device in actual mysteries, but it probably occurs more often in mainstream fiction where a touch of mystery, less whodunit than what-was-done, is desired. Such is the case with *To Kill a*

Mockingbird. There's so much story there, so much social importance to events, that we sometimes gloss over the opening, but we should pay attention:

> When he was nearly thirteen, my brother Jem got his arm badly broken at the elbow. When it healed, and Jem's fears of never being able to play football were assuaged, he was seldom self-conscious about his injury. His left arm was somewhat shorter than the right; when he stood or walked, the back of his hand was at right angles to his body, his thumb parallel to his thigh. He couldn't have cared less, so long as he could pass and punt.

How was his arm broken? Why? And why does it matter? We want to know, of course, but this is a case of seriously delayed gratification. We have to wait until the very last pages, so long that we have in all likelihood lost memory of the passage, and when the arm is broken, it comes to us as both a surprise and the fulfillment of a promise.

Lee, however, is not finished laying out her clues. With wonderful economy she includes all the principals of the drama—father Atticus Finch, their friend Dill, the Ewell family, and the shadowy figure of Boo Radley—all in the first three paragraphs. The setting, loosely, is established by the first of their Finch ancestors coming up the Alabama River to this locale.

Or perhaps "mystery" isn't quite the word we want here. Maybe the correct metaphor is agricultural, that Lee is planting seeds of the novel to come, dropping names like corn kernels into the newly worked ground of her first page.

Of those, the most important is the kernel she doesn't mention. There are two key, as-yet-unavailable facts about our narrator, unnamed here but later to be called Scout. The first is that she's a female, around nine at the time of the major event she mentions in the first line. The second, much more significant, is that she is no longer nine. "Enough years," in her words, have passed that she can bring a perspective to events that would have been entirely beyond her younger self. That fact will make all the difference in the world to this narrative.

Quietly, it is there right away, to be reinforced by numerous time markers throughout the text. The remarkable thing about the revelation is the almost offhand ease with which Lee plants it. That's what narrative masters do: provide information so subtly and simply that we may not even notice—until it's needed.

One of the things that defines Scout's experience is the presence of their friend Dill in their summer adventures. He comes to Maycomb to spend summers with his aunt; more particularly, he seems to be sent to his aunt to get him out of the way of his parents' troubled marriage. Dill, modeled in large measure on the very young Truman Capote, has a wild imagination and soon takes a fancy to the mysterious neighbor, Arthur "Boo" Radley, a recluse whose existence is little more than rumor. The children get up to a lot of mild mischief in seeking the fact of Boo, and while he remains in hiding, he offers signs. They find gifts in the hollow of a tree on the Radley property. When they trespass and Boo scares them away by firing a gun, Jem loses his overalls in the scramble for safety. Later, they are washed and mended and hanging over a fence for him to reclaim. When a neighbor's house catches fire, Scout, who has been watching, discovers that someone (she believes Boo) has slipped a blanket around her shoulders.

None of this matters very much until much later, when Boo saves their lives. When the hijinks end and the novel turns deadly serious, they will need his friendship. Atticus outrages the racist element in the white community by defending a black man, Tom Robinson, on a charge of rape against the daughter of a notoriously vicious family, the

Ewells. In fact, he defends Tom twice, once in court and once at the jail to protect him from being lynched. The court case is ludicrously corrupt. Despite overwhelming evidence that Tom could not have raped Mayella Ewell as reported, owing to his withered arm that would render him incapable of the sort of force reported, he is convicted. In these two settings, Jem and Scout discover the inequities of life in the Jim Crow South. As children of Atticus Finch, for whom the law is everything, they are amazed that citizens can have so little regard for law as to attempt an extrajudicial hanging. In fact, Scout is chiefly responsible for breaking up the mob when her questions to Walter Cunningham about his son and namesake, who is her classmate, cause him to be embarrassed at being caught out at this unholy gathering and lead him to break up the mob. Their white classmates turn against them so that they have to endure taunts and slanders against their father, who forbids them to retaliate. At the same time, they find love and acceptance at the African American church where Calpurnia, their housekeeper, takes them one Sunday. At the trial, two things occur to underscore the thoroughgoing racism of their community. The first is that brother and sister witness the proceedings from the "colored balcony" to which nonwhite persons are consigned. The children, especially Scout, would not have been allowed entry into the courtroom had they been seen entering the white section, so they sneak upstairs. From the balcony, moreover, the trial looks very different; seen from above, much of the bigotry becomes painfully obvious. And finally, the injustice of the verdict is patent. Jem is nearly undone by his disillusionment at that and at Tom's fate, which is compounded when he is shot while attempting to escape.

Worse awaits, however. Although he should be satisfied with the outcome of the trial, Bob Ewell is just smart enough to see that he has been shown up for the fool and villain that he is and swears vengeance against Atticus and the presiding judge. He attempts his vengeance not on the lawyer but on his children, attacking Jem and Scout as they walk home from a Halloween party, which is where Jem's arm gets broken while he struggles against the full-grown man. In the darkness, Boo Radley saves the children and stabs Ewell to death, although the sheriff, Heck Tate, insists on a version of events—that Ewell tripped over a root and fell on his knife—that will spare Boo public exposure. Even after all this, Atticus can reinforce his message to Scout that most people are basically good, "when you finally see them."

This is a novel that is all about seeing, about looking for things, about seeing things you're not supposed to, about seeing things you are, about perspective and its impact on what we see or what we understand about what we see. And, naturally, about blindness, whether from bigotry or assumption or rumor or "community standards." Atticus shows by example that we need to see for ourselves and not be ruled by the vision of others. He also shows himself to be surprisingly farsighted when called upon. Although severely myopic now, he was a dead shot in his youth, and when a rabid dog wanders down the street, he is called upon to take the shot that cannot be allowed to miss. He removes his glasses, which he needs in every other area of his life:

> With movements so swift they seemed almost simultaneous, Atticus's hand jerked the ball-tipped lever as he brought the gun to his shoulder.
>
> The rifle cracked. Tim Johnson [the dog] leaped, flopped over and crumpled to the sidewalk in a brown-and-white heap. He didn't know what hit him.

Nor, in a sense, do Jem and Scout. This is not the father they believed they knew, simply because they have never *seen* him do such a thing. They assume that what they have witnessed thus far is the whole of their reality, so conclusions can be drawn. This act fits no part of their assumptions. Thus endeth the lesson.

The larger lesson that Atticus insists upon has to do with trying to understand other people without prejudging. His main contribution to Scout's ethical development is this: "You never really understand a person until you consider things from his point of view . . . until you climb into his skin and walk around in it." It may well be that he carries it to a fault, that his attempts to understand people like Bob Ewell—and sometimes getting them disastrously wrong—stem from overconfidence in his precept. Yet it is equally true that in this novel about a child's moral development, there is no more important precept than this one. Scout—the character in the midst of this drama—could never articulate, much less comprehend, all the ramifications of the growth of her ethical being. Because she is telling this story from "enough" years later, she can look back on events and on her own attitudes with a sort of kindly skepticism; she is no longer invested in what that earlier self had thought. There is another subtext at work here: if a child can figure these matters out, what is wrong with adults? For equality under the law and acceptance of all people by all people were far from settled matters when the novel was published in 1960. In fact, I once read that only two years earlier the United States saw the first year since Reconstruction in which there were no racial lynchings.

1958. The first.

To Kill a Mockingbird enters the national discussion of many things, race and place and class and justice, at a time when things are just beginning to change in significant ways. But it is not a call to arms, a sweeping indictment of the nation, or part of a mass movement. Rather, its method is typically American, which is to say typically

Emersonian. Don't worry about "society" or "the community" as the locus of change. Change yourself. Let one person become different, more enlightened, more compassionate. Speak the truth. See clearly. And let the big consequences take care of themselves. That's so crazy it might almost work.

Almost from the moment of publication, Lee became nearly as reclusive as the mysterious Boo Radley. Okay, not quite at that level, but she refused requests for interviews and declined to give speeches or make pronouncements on her famous offspring. And as we know, there would be no more novels. Huge success can be ruinous. Both Thomas Heggen, author of *Mr. Roberts*, and Ross Lockwood, of *Raintree County*, were destroyed by the inability to create a follow-up to their enormous bestsellers. Wonderful sales figures, film and stage adaptations (in Heggen's case, he was reportedly making $2,000 a week from the Broadway play alone), the works. Didn't matter. Both died by their own hands in ways that were almost certainly not accidental. They had the life frustrated out of them by failure. That doesn't seem to have been the case with Harper Lee. She certainly has lived long and, by most accounts, comfortably after the book struck gold. She was on the set of the 1962 film adaptation, and she became friends with Gregory Peck. She accompanied Capote to Kansas for research on the killings that would form the basis for *In Cold Blood*. And she published a couple of essays and letters over the years. But here's something no one ever addresses about Harper Lee and her funny-poignant-powerful-sobering-critical novel: why write another? Why even expect another? The sad truth is that most writers, even very good ones, will never have a novel as profound or as influential as *To Kill a Mockingbird*. If you have been so favored by the gods once, what right have you to expect a repeat performance? For that matter, what right have readers to demand more? Sometimes, just maybe, one is enough.

TWENTY-THREE

NOT IN KANSAS ANYMORE
The Crying of Lot 49

Every once in a while, a novel comes along that puts its finger on the pulse of the country and feels palpitations. It holds a mirror up to our very nature, showing us as we are. And we are afraid. It records the rhythms and melodies and discords of modern life at 33⅓ rpm and plays them back at 78. With a warp. That book captures the surface of the American experience but also lays bare the soul and reveals what Americans are like at their very core.

Wacko.

That book is usually by Thomas Pynchon. Unfortunately for the casual reader, that book is roughly the size and weight of an anvil. *Gravity's Rainbow* (1973), for instance, comes in at a sprightly 760 pages of insane goings-on and paranoid musings on how the machinery of power attempts to crush individual variations. Early on in the book, we see a military spy operation to determine why every single time that a U.S. soldier stationed in London named Tyrone Slothrop (more on Pynchonian naming practices later) sleeps with a woman, in the next few nights a German V-2 rocket obliterates that block of the city.

We've all read books about that, right? It won a share of the National Book Award, along with Isaac Bashevis Singer's *A Crown of Feathers and Other Stories*. His later books *Mason and Dixon* and *Against the Day* have even dwarfed their famous predecessor.

Our book, however, is not one of those hay bales. My old copy with a psychedelic cover checks in at 138 pages. Over the years I've probably had 138 students tell me it's too long. They're wrong. It's the perfect length. But then, cartoons always run short. And make no mistake about it, *The Crying of Lot 49* is a cartoon—a Technicolor, hallucinogenic, Day-Glo, paranoid cartoon in hyperdrive full of every bit of current pop culture nonsense, dark conspiracies of the distant past and the immediate present, insane characters, soul-crushing institutions, outrageous puns, and inspired lunacy that a single human mind could ever make up. And drugs. Lots of drugs, from the casual marijuana use by the Beatle-wannabe band, The Paranoids, to the LSD being peddled by the main character's psychiatrist, Dr. Hilarious, to mescaline and psilocybin, to the ocean of alcohol consumed by a host of drinkers.

What, your shrink's not named Hilarious? I'm so sorry. And welcome to Pynchonland, where no name goes unexploded. The names always mean something, and sometimes the hapless reader can even figure out what that something might be. In this novel, the names have to do with mental states, bodily functions, and female hygiene products (Stanley Koteks, Mike Fallopian, Manny de Presso, Hilarious, station KCUF, for which I have sometimes threatened to bring a mirror to class, Professor Emory Bortz), or with allusions to other historical figures or concepts (Metzger, Genghis Cohen, Pierce Inverarity, his name a combination of a famous stamp collector and a misprinted stamp with the image reversed, an "inverse rarity"), or just cheap puns (Oedipa's husband, Wendell "Mucho" Maas). Trouble is, sometimes the imagination just can't keep up with reality. The murky, insurrectionist mail service, the Trystero, sounds more plausible than Thurn und Taxis, which was the real postal monopoly created during the Holy Roman Empire. Lest you doubt its existence, I have in my files a news wire photograph of the latest Prince von Thurn und Taxis, Albert II, seated on his mother's lap at age seven. The caption identifies him as the world's youngest billionaire. And then there are the head-scratchers, the ones we just can't decide how to process. The alternative mail system using the acronym W.A.S.T.E. (We Await Silent Tristero's Empire) whose receptacles look strangely like garbage cans and whose carriers bear a curious resemblance to homeless men either gathering correspondence or pursuing the art that a later generation would call dumpster diving. And when I think of all the Big Mac wrappers I thoughtlessly tossed in there!

Several times in these profiles I have had occasion to use some variant of the sentence, "The plot of this book barely even exists." This will not be one of those occasions. On the other hand, the plot is nearly impossible to reduce to digest form. The chief difficulty lies in the fact that the events of the novel and the perambulations of the heroine are such that any synopsis may prove to be as long as the book itself. Still, here goes. Oedipa Maas, who has not yet been able to admit to herself that her marriage to Mucho, a disc jockey for an AM station near San Francisco, is a failure, finds that she has been named coexecutor of the will of her ex-lover, Pierce Inverarity. In order to perform her duties, she travels to the town of San Narcisso, near Los Angeles (insert your own joke about Southern California self-absorption here, Pynchon seems to say), where she has an affair with her fellow coexecutor, a lawyer named Metzger, and meets nothing but strange, disturbed, and paranoid characters, from the disgruntled employees of a disgruntled aerospace defense company that can't get government contracts (really? in the height of the military-industrial complex?), to the band called The Paranoids that can't get a record contract, to the theater troupe putting on a Jacobean revenge tragedy, to various characters who only want to sleep with her, to a host of persons pursuing crank obsessions and inventions, to right-wing extremist conspiracy theorists, to moderate conspiracy theorists, to—oh, never mind. I've read it dozens of times and can't keep them all straight. In the midst of all this mayhem, however, she keeps running into evidence—possible evidence—of a vast postal conspiracy that has been going on for centuries. Or of her incipient madness. Or of a conspiracy of a very different sort, whose aim is to drive her mad and whose author is no longer around to witness the mayhem. Those possibilities aren't necessarily mutually exclusive. As the poet Delmore Schwartz once said, "Even paranoids have real enemies." That statement could be the epigraph to all of Pynchon.

But back to the plot. In structure, this is a classic detective novel, amateur-sleuth division. Oedipa has a mystery thrust upon her, can't find any means of avoiding it, and finally settles into her role as ad hoc gumshoe. She meets all the usual suspects. All right, no one in this novel is usual, but hers fulfill the customary demands. They are colorful, highly differentiated, and locked into their own obsessions, which in general do not overlap with hers. When she needs a piece of information, they resist giving it to her or else give her something that turns out not to advance the case. On the other hand, their offhand observations lead to further discoveries and, inevitably, further investigation. Every item of data leads forward toward something else—or perhaps sideways, since there rarely is anything resembling straight-ahead progress. What seems simple at first becomes more and more involved until the detective seems hopelessly mired in contradictory and possibly dangerous information. So far, so good. But at the point where, were she Sam Spade or Miss Marple, she would unravel the threads to solve the case, she is simply overwhelmed by the mystery, as so many clues bombard her that she feels suffocated underneath them.

The actual mystery concerns the possible existence of an alternative mail service that has been around for centuries, periodically challenging whatever official postal carrier was endorsed by the authorities. It is said to have sprung up as a competing venture to Thurn und Taxis, only to go underground when the Holy Roman Emperor chose the other service to carry mail through the empire. Its reputation was as a guerrilla force, ambushing T&T couriers and, later, Pony Express riders, while developing its own mail delivery system for use by those on the margins of society. It turned the emblem of Thurn und Taxis, the post horn, into its own symbol by adding a mute, clearly a stealth maneuver worthy of a shadowy organization. In the California of the novel, the W.A.S.T.E. system is used by the dispossessed of the state—failing organizations, fringe-group theorists, budding insurrectionists, junkies and winos, and above all, the poor. If it exists, Trystero thrives on secrecy, but of a very open sort. It must operate in the shadows and margins of society yet be available—and above all, known—to society's disenfranchised. In that case, it would leave many hints as to its existence, but hints that would be easily overlooked by any but those sensitized to its being. And boy, is Oedipa sensitized. She goes from barely noticing the odd clues that come her way to being flooded by them.

Many of her sources of information and support vanish, leaving her vulnerable and insecure. Mucho becomes involved in Hilarious's experiments with LSD, and his personality begins to disintegrate and merge with his surroundings. Hilarious goes mad, convinced that the Israeli agents have finally closed in on him for his crimes at Buchenwald. Oedipa finds herself caught in a police standoff facing his rifle, only to trick her way out of danger and take him into custody. Metzger runs off with the teenage girlfriend of one of the Paranoids; while

Driblette commits suicide by walking into the ocean. At the same time, others who had been less forthcoming originally—Mike Fallopian, Bortz, her stamp-broker contact Genghis Cohen—now inundate her with information. And she sees signs of Trystero everywhere, especially during a long night visit to Berkeley, when each new scene, from children playing a rhyming game to a young wino going through the trash (or collecting the mail) to a dying sailor who needs comforting, strikes her with another piece of evidence. Far from leading her to a resolution, however, the barrage overwhelms her, makes her doubt her sanity, pushes her closer to the abyss:

> That night she sat for hours, too numb even to drink, teaching herself
> to breathe in a vacuum. For this, oh God, was the void. There was
> nobody who could help her. Nobody in the world. They were all mad,
> on something, possible enemies, or dead.

Oedipa finds herself pushed to the brink and abandons the search. Or attempts to. Circumstances won't let her opt out, short of violence. She tries to. In fact, almost everyone in the novel tries to, through drink or drugs or madness or suicide. Her problem is that she's too sane, too essentially healthy, for any of the alternatives chosen by her male acquaintances. Instead, she pushes ahead, attending a stamp auction where the novel gets its title (the sale that interests her is of lot number 49), despite knowing she probably won't receive definite answers and may only find further complications.

The above passage may be the most perfect experience of the encounter with nothingness in all of literature, at least as good as anything in Jean-Paul Sartre or Albert Camus. Plus, it's way more fun than, say, The Plague. The point is, The Crying of Lot 49 doesn't feel like an existentialist text because it isn't. What it is, is a satire of contemporary America.

The problem with most existentialist works is that they feel like dutiful embodiments of someone's philosophical tract: absurdity, check; fear and trembling, check; nothingness, check. Pynchon, on the other hand, begins with an absurd situation (California circa 1964) and goes from there. If that happens to square with someone's philosophy, so be it. In any event, his concerns are bigger than that. We're all winding down toward death. You, me, every human construct ever invented, the universe itself. Nothing you can do to stop it. Who you gonna call? There's no God and no human on whom you can rely, in whom you can trust. Whatever it is, you can't solve it, can't reject it, can't run away from it. Next to cosmological entropy, what can a little philosophy do?

That's what makes this novel so much fun.

Well, that and the ridicule. Pynchon stands in that line of social satirists from Twain (and maybe that great American, Jonathan Swift) to Vonnegut and Tom Robbins who come to the aid of society by ripping it to shreds, by exposing its follies and excesses and hypocrisies. He finds plenty of material. The book is full of keen observations on the cultural and economic scene circa 1964 or 1965. The first thing we hear of is a Tupperware party at which the hostess used "perhaps too much Kirsch in the fondue." Could there be a more '60s moment? Then there's the cigarette maker who wants to up the ante on healthy smokes by using not mere charcoal in its filters but *bone* charcoal. Human bone. There are all the send-ups of rock and roll, perhaps the richest of which is the group Sick Dick and the Volkswagens, whose current radio hit is "I Want to Kiss Your Feet," which would no doubt be an interesting alternative to a much better known song by the Beatles. Perhaps more to the point, he emphasizes the destructive qualities of youth culture and the worship of adolescence, especially in Mucho's and Metzger's romantic attachments to teenyboppers. Won't anyone grow up? The California he shows us is also full of conspiracy theorists and mad dogs of various stripes. Everyone is pretty sure someone else is out to get them. There's a right-wing group, the Peter Pinguid Society, that sees the John Birch Society as a bunch of slackers. Pretty nervy, naming the target of satire in the act of pillorying it. The workers at Yoyodyne, the failing defense contractor, sing the company song, a plaint about being stiffed by the federal government, which underwrites everyone's research and development but theirs: "We can't get the R&D / On a Piper Cub." To the tune of "Aura Lee," no less. Very touching. The only thing more surreal than Oedipa's trip with a tour group to a gay bar is her encounter in it with someone who has sworn off all relationships and joined a twelve-step program called Inamorati Anonymous, all this before Stonewall, the chastity movement, or the proliferation of a thousand organizations with acronyms whose second letter is invariably "A." Of course, Oedipa at the time is wearing a name tag identifying her as Arnold Snarb, who is "looking for a good time." She sometimes has a hand in making things more bizarre. In almost every case, Pynchon's invention is spot-on, if sometimes outrageous or offensive.

There is also a wonderful parody of a daddy/baby war movie starring a very young Metzger, who has never gotten over being a child star, the flip-flopping of careers (several times) of Manny di Presso between acting and the law, and absolutely the best description of a Jacobean revenge tragedy that you'll ever read. It's really a small matter that the play doesn't actually exist. The novel spends what seems a disproportionate amount of time on detailed plot summary of *The Courier's Tragedy* by Richard Wharfinger, a name that sounds plausibly Jacobean and characteristically Pynchonian, which is to say peculiar and suggestive. Ultimately, however, what appears to be a midnovel digression develops into the crucial source of information and conspiracy. The imagined play is replete with all the gratuitous gore and twisted sexuality of real revenge tragedies; in fact, it seems to have amassed every distasteful element from all the major dramas into a single, unsavory dish. It is also, we should stipulate, hysterically funny in the telling. The tale revolves, as it should, around disinheritance, jealousy, disguise, espionage, and ambush. The mutilations, murder, incest, and kinky sex are merely bonuses. The thing that catches Oedipa's attention, however, is the emphasis on a postal conspiracy and especially the line in act four that includes a mention of Trystero. She finds herself drawn into pursuing this possibly corrupt line, which does not appear in the standard text of the play, speaking to the director, a local bookstore, and a local academic who is a leading authority on Wharfinger. This dramatic revelation drives the action, or at least drives her into action, for the rest of the book, so much so that a real human tragedy—the wrongful handling of human bones that are possibly from ambushed American troops—falls by the wayside. Alleged wrongs from hundreds of years earlier supplant actual wrongs of her own time. Perhaps that's all right, however, since they ultimately make her focus on larger wrongs of inequality and poverty to which she has been oblivious. More anon.

Then there are those sentences! Pynchon may not be the greatest American writer of his era, whatever that might mean, but he may well be the greatest American writer of deranged sentences. Here's a small gem from the first page of the novel:

> She thought of a hotel room in Mazatlán whose door had just been slammed, it seemed forever, waking up two hundred birds down in the lobby; a sunrise over the library slope at Cornell University that nobody out on it had seen because the slope faces west; a dry, disconsolate tune from the fourth movement Bartók Concerto for Orchestra; a whitewashed bust of Jay Gould that Pierce kept over the bed on a shelf so narrow for it she'd always had the hovering fear that it would someday topple on them.

There are several characteristic elements here. Most noticeable, of course, is the density and pace of the references—from Mazatlán to Cornell to Béla Bartók to financier Jay Gould in seconds, with the particularity of "a dry, disconsolate tune from the fourth movement"—in a sort of one-sentence montage. Which is the problem for some readers of Pynchon: the thousand montages in sequence, the unending cascade of information. Make that, of obscure, trivial, arcane, and frequently bogus information. Taken on its own, however, this minicascade is a marvel. Readers find themselves snapping back and forth between the new item of data and the previous one to see if there is some connection, if the first anticipated the second in some unexpected way. Such is rarely the case, but still we check, even after we know better. The great danger, clearly, in reading Pynchon is whiplash. It is a hazard I for one willingly risk, just for the joys of those fabulous sentences. Style in the twentieth century cut two ways. There was the less-is-more school of Hemingway, Beckett, and minimalism on the one hand. On the other there were the people like T. Coraghesson Boyle, who has been known to go over the top himself. Those are the writers—Proust, Joyce, Faulkner, John Fowles, Toni Morrison—for whom the world comes bursting forth, so that the challenge is to capture or contain it in language, to get the whole world, in Faulkner's phrase, "in one sentence, between one Cap and one period." You just have to love that sort of extravagant, overreaching linguistic drunkenness, that *joie d'écrire*. What? You don't? Oh, but you should.

To many of us, Pynchon is little more than our second most famous recluse. The image is false. Unlike J. D. Salinger, for whom "recluse" was a profession having long since supplanted writing and publishing, Pynchon is merely publicity-averse. True, he avoids the press and public occasions, sometimes going to extremes, as when he sent comedian Professor Irwin Corey to accept his share of the 1974 National Book

Award. It was by all accounts an odd scene. The streaker probably didn't help. But he is out in his home communities, which have always been huge cities—Mexico City, Los Angeles, New York—doing ordinary things like delivering his child to school. More importantly, he has remained engaged. There was a long hiatus between *Gravity's Rainbow* and *Vineland* (1990) that made his fans wonder if he had done a Salinger. Even then, however, there were hints that he was still in the game, an essay in 1984 asking, "Is It Okay to Be a Luddite?" or a message, also in the *New York Times Book Review*, for Salman Rushdie in 1989 after the fatwa against him. *Vineland* began a period of regular book publication, with *Mason and Dixon* (1997), *Against the Day* (2006), and *Inherent Vice* (2009) following at surprising speed, given their length and complexity. And each of those novels addresses themes large and small about the self in the world, about entropy of course, this being Pynchon, which is to say about living with the supreme ontological joke of everything from our own lives to the entire universe inexorably winding down toward dissolution, about power and its inevitable abuses, about conspiracies and counterconspiracies, about the lunacy of popular culture or perhaps simply culture, about randomness and pattern-finding, about the divine self in a godless cosmos. For make no mistake about it, the self in Pynchon is no less Beat in all senses of the word than it is in Kerouac.

And like Kerouac, he finds the margins—of the page, of the novel, of society itself. And so does Oedipa. I commented a bit earlier on her great discovery coming about in an odd way. One of the basic elements of Anton Chekhov's plays is that while the characters pursue some entirely trivial entertainment—a dance, a party, a dinner—something very momentous and usually life-shattering if not life-ending is happening elsewhere. The party held by the bankrupt owners in *The Cherry Orchard* coincides with the event they are trying mightily not to think about, namely the sale of their property to Lopahin, the wealthy man whose parents were serfs on the estate. This novel makes use of something like that paradox. The mystery that comes to obsess Oedipa amounts to nothing, really. Does it matter at all if there has been a rogue postal system competing with but hiding in the shadows from the official system, even if it has gone on for centuries? Will the world be better for bringing this truth to light? Or for not doing so? Will she? Not at all. But the Trystero is not the only secret she discovers, and the other one does matter. Oedipa's perambulations take her to all sorts of places she's never been and show her things she's never seen before, never seen because she has never looked. The homeless. The destitute. Hungry children. The disenfranchised. Immigrants. In short, *the other America*, as the title of Michael Harrington's seminal 1962 study of poverty in the wealthiest nation on earth would have it. This other place isn't marked on maps, doesn't show up on her television programs or at her Tupperware parties or on the national news with Chet Huntley and David Brinkley. That doesn't stop it from existing. This shadow America bears roughly the same relationship to the one portrayed in *Ozzie and Harriet* or the advertisements in *Life* or *Look* magazine as the Trystero bears to Thurn und Taxis or the U.S. Postal Service.

She finds it by leaving her other self behind. As so often happens in the mythic quest, the quester must divest himself or herself of the trappings of civilization or home in order to enter the special kingdom. Only then can real understanding and growth take place. Ike McCaslin in Faulkner's "The Bear" must leave behind his watch, compass, and gun in order to see Old Ben, the legendary Bear. So it is with Oedipa, who leaves behind husband, friends, shrink, lover, and even her shiny automobile in order to be vouchsafed this vision of a world beyond her experience. This new realm almost defeats her but does not. She determines to push on, perhaps not even realizing that this larger mystery has subsumed the original one. But it has, as we realize when she comforts the dying old sailor, something she never could have done at the outset of her journey.

Oedipa spends a good deal of time concerned that someone has perpetrated a conspiracy against her. Someone has, but not Pierce Inverarity and not the one she fears. Oh, it is just possible that, dying, he did set up some monstrous practical joke against her. He owned everything that matters to the story: Zapf's bookstore, the Tank Theater that puts on the play, the subdivision, the lake, Beaconsfield, Yoyodyne, virtually all of San Narciso. He had the means and the opportunity, whatever the truth about motive. But even if he did, the results matter little in terms of any story of intrigue involving the mail. Because he also gave her a gift; he lifted the scales from her eyes. The truly appalling conspiracy of which she has been a victim has allowed her to live her entire life to this point and have no awareness of that other America. That knowledge may be Pierce's real legacy:

> What was left to inherit? That America encoded in Inverarity's testament, whose was that? She thought of other, immobilized freight cars where kids sang back, happy as fat, whatever came over their mother's pocket radio; of other squatters who stretched canvas for lean-tos behind smiling billboards along all the highways, or slept in junkyards in the stripped shells of wrecked Plymouths . . . drifters she had listened to . . . and walkers along the roads at night . . .

in other words, the whole litany of the dispossessed, the unsupported, the down-and-out, hidden from view by billboards and automobiles and telephones and the trappings of comfort with which successful America insulates itself from poverty and despair. Not a gift one seeks, perhaps, but valuable nonetheless.

Which is also Pynchon's gift to us, or one among many gifts. His narrative is so busy, so fraught with oddity, that first-time readers may find themselves too busy to notice the things that aren't unusual at all but should be, that should trouble our sleep more than all the revenge tragedies ever written. Want. Hunger. Madness. Loneliness. Those are the horsemen of his apocalypse, and they are always with us. Even in the midst of plenty and more than plenty. What more can a slight book offer?

TWENTY FOUR

RACE. RELATIONS.
Song of Solomon

Amerian literature is one long bildungsroman, one long story of becoming, not for an individual, as is typical of the form, but for a nation. We have built up a narrative of our own growth and development as a vast place with a people diverse in interest, background, aspiration, purpose, place, and race. Sometimes. Racial difference did not receive very full play in the early days of our literature. To be sure, there have always been writers of color. But throughout much of our history, racial minorities had less access to a culture of writing than the great mass of white Americans. The native peoples had strong narrative traditions, but those were oral, not written. Nor was being harried by an influx of settlers conducive to development of written materials. Slaves were largely forbidden to learn to read and write, and in a host of ways those practices lingered long after emancipation. The explosion in writing by persons of African descent would trail that of their European-descended counterparts by about a century. But when it did arrive, it came on like gangbusters.

The English writer Virginia Woolf once famously remarked, by way of explaining the literary phenomenon of modernism, that "On or about December 1910, human nature changed." She was being arch, as her selection of a specific month would indicate; she means only that at some point early in the twentieth century, the way we understood human existence underwent a radical shift. And although she was not talking about writing by folks with African lineage (England just then being somewhat lacking in them), she might as well have been. That date will work as well as any other to indicate the beginning of something very big, but let's move it back just a touch, to the beginning of the century. From James Weldon Johnson to Amiri Baraka, from W. E. B. DuBois to Edwidge Danticat, from Paul Laurence Dunbar to Paule Marshall, things have been busy. And frequently wonderful.

I mean that last word in its original sense, as full of wonders. Black writing has a great deal in common with any other sort of writing, but it also can exude qualities specific to it, that no amount of reading in Hemingway and Fitzgerald and Frost would ever turn up. Those properties are specific to the experience of being black in America, but they are also often made strange, as elements of history and myth come bursting forth in astonishing ways. Nowhere, perhaps, is that tendency as marked as in the novels of the woman who in many regards came to dominate American fiction in the latter part of the century and the beginning of the next, Toni Morrison. And within even her remarkable oeuvre, no novel displays the tendency more vigorously than her third novel, *Song of Solomon* (1977), which did for African American fiction what just a few years earlier Gabriel García Márquez's *One Hundred Years of Solitude* did for Latin American fiction. Neither was first on the scene, but each was so amazing and so unlike anything else that had appeared that it set the standard, if not for writing itself, for the ways we think about writing from their respective communities.

Almost from the first her novel was compared to García Márquez's and the phrase, "magical realism," that attached to his was also applied to hers. Like him, she has sometimes chafed at the term, feeling it in some ways allows works to be dismissed in favor of a label. Indeed, it is difficult to find any practitioners of magical realism who embrace the term. Yet it gets at something essential in Morrison's fiction, that perpetual bursting forth of the miraculous, the horrific, the fantastic within a framework that is strongly realistic. Hers are not alternative realities, except in the ways that fictive realities are always alternatives to the actual.

The plot of *Song of Solomon* is, superficially, quite complicated, but that masks its real story, which is very simple. The busier version involves the movements of a family called Dead from the South to Michigan and the movement back again of one of them, Milkman (Macon III). His father, Macon Dead Jr., and aunt, Pilate, represent different ways of relating to one's identity as a descendent of slaves and a black person in predominantly white America. Macon tries to run as far and as fast from his rural, black past as he can, becoming a slumlord and marrying the daughter, Ruth Foster, of the city's only black doctor. Neither of those things makes him happy. Pilate is also an entrepreneur of sorts, offering the community folk remedies and homemade wine; unlike her brother, she is completely in touch with her community and its history, at least as she knows it.

Macon and Pilate, then, engage in a war for Milkman's soul from before his birth, offering two options between which Milkman must ultimately choose. For his part, Milkman is the worst sort of spoiled child. At thirty-two, he is still living with his parents and acting very much like an adolescent. He is irresponsible, promiscuous, often drunk, shallow, and self-centered. In other words, in the logic of fiction he is primed to have to make important life choices.

In order to make those choices, he will attempt to steal a treasure from his aunt at the behest of his father, go to Pennsylvania and thence to Virginia in further search of first one treasure and then another, shuttle between those places and his unnamed Michigan city, survive attempts on his life first by his lover, Hagar, who as Pilate's granddaughter is also his cousin, and then by his best friend, see Pilate murdered in his stead, and take flight. As I said, busy and not a little convoluted.

The story behind that mass of surface detail, however, is extremely simple. And very old. A young man goes out into the world to seek his fortune. Stories about young men seeking their fortune have been told since, well, young men began seeking fortunes. Morrison has frequently said that she likes going back to the old stories, the clichés, the essential myths of human societies, whether they involve the breaking of taboos (the mother forced by circumstance to kill her child, as in *Beloved*), the pairing of good and evil through two friends (*Sula*), the community closing ranks in ignorance and hatred against outsiders (*Paradise*), or this one. And in some ways no myth is so basic to human experience as the quest. Or so American. The actual goal of the quest never matters. It can be elbow room, greater freedom, a postal mystery, or a white whale. That goal, usually unreached, is but the pretext for a vastly more significant discovery. And for that discovery to really matter, there has to be some important deficiency in the hero. Milkman Dead is a perfect candidate for the job. When the quest begins, his life is so much wasted space. He has a cozy but meaningless job in the family business, for which he is poorly suited and to which he has never made meaningful contribution. His love life is split between empty conquests and a cruel mistreatment of the only woman really devoted to him. Although he has both given name and nickname, he has no identity, no sense of place in the world, nothing to anchor him anywhere. He even has the physical corollary to his ethical and spiritual deficiencies that is the hallmark of the quester: his left leg is noticeably shorter than his right. His adventures align nicely, allowing for some postmodern irony, with the stages of the quest as outlined in Vladimir Propp's *Morphology of the Folktale* (1928). Milkman may not go through all thirty-one stages, or at least not in immediately recognizable ways, but almost no hero does. But he does encounter helping and blocking figures, a clear-cut villain, branding, even receipt of a magical agent, and transfiguration. This last is in some ways the most significant of Milkman's stages, and it happens in multiple ways. Like Ike McCaslin in Faulkner's *Go Down, Moses*, he must divest himself of the trappings of modern, white society—car, suit, even his watch, which a woman with the ironic name of Grace steals as the last item to be discarded—in order to achieve his goal. His quest is very elemental; he enters the dark earth in the form of a cave, enters water twice (once when he splashes through the creek and again when he swims with Sweet, the woman he takes up with in Shalimar, the place of family origin in Virginia), and of course, he rides the air at the end. In other words, he hits about every mark available to the quester.

It should come as no surprise, then, that the fortune Milkman finds is the furthest thing from the one he starts out seeking. More often than not, the stated object of the quest falls away in favor of some greater treasure: self-knowledge or spiritual power or recognition by a society that has earlier rejected the hero or that has been previously unknown by him. When Milkman returns to Shalimar, he is hailed as a returning son of the community. More importantly, he has become a different, better person, able to recognize his faults and accept responsibility for his actions. And, for the first time in his life, he has a home, a place he has come from and to which he has returned. He is, in short, utterly transfigured.

From the first page of the novel, names play a huge role. The street on which the Deads live, as it were, is officially Mains Avenue but universally known by locals as Not Doctor Street, their response to corrections by that branch of officialdom, the post office, to their customary addressing of the street the doctor lived on as Doctor Street. The hospital, Mercy, that does not accept black patients, is rechristened No Mercy Hospital. This bit of naming whimsy suggests much about the control over aspects of their lives exerted by members of a community that has little actual control. And it leads into dozens of other namings, renamings, and misnamings. The main family got its name when a Union soldier drunkenly filled out postslavery papers for the patriarch by putting answers on the wrong lines, so that the city of origin became the given name, the status of parents the surname for the newly christened Macon Dead. Family practice dictates that babies not called Macon be named by random pointing at biblical texts, so Milkman's sisters are First Corinthians and Magdalene, called Lena. His aunt is Pilate, her daughter Reba (for Rebecca) and her granddaughter Hagar. All biblical, if not well-chosen. Few characters are called by their birth names. Milkman's best friend, for instance, is Guitar, so called because as a small child he badly desired one. For his part, his nickname comes about when the family handyman sees him being breastfed long past the age when children are nursed, with his feet almost touching the floor. And the ancestral hometown is called Shalimar, a corruption of Solomon, the family progenitor, just as the song sung by Pilate and her progeny uses another displacement, Sugarman. No name is secure, no identity entirely trustworthy or stable, in such an environment.

One of the great charms of reading Morrison is discovering, again and again, that she's one of the truly great prose stylists. Although she is not fond of the label "poetic novelist," her work bears a highly lyrical imprint:

So the ginger sugar blew unnoticed through the streets, around
the trees, over the roofs, until, thinned out and weakened a little,
it reached Southside. There, where some houses didn't even have
screens, much less air conditioners, the windows were thrown wide
open to whatever the night had to offer. And there the ginger smell
was sharp, sharp enough to distort dreams and make the sleeper be-
lieve the things he hungered for were right at hand.

Even if we have never been in such a night, never experienced such an
aroma, we cannot miss the power it exerts over the sleepers and dreamers. Her writing displays real power, sometimes incantatory, sometimes
driving, sometimes speeding up or slowing to a crawl. Yet Morrison's
style is not an idle showpiece meant to impress the critics. Rather, it is
an essential element in reaching her target audience. As she tells Tom
LeClair, "The language must be careful and must appear effortless. It
must not sweat. It must suggest and be provocative at the same time. It
is the thing that black people love so much—the saying of words, holding
them on the tongue, experimenting with them, playing with them. It's a
love, a passion." Hers is a style that must work on multiple levels for multiple audiences, and in her best books, it does its jobs beautifully.

At its best, her writing soars, which is appropriate for this novel.
From first page to last, flight is a major element of *Song of Solomon*. The
book begins with the insurance agent Robert Smith announcing that
he will use a set of blue wings to "fly across Lake Superior." He does
not succeed. Nearly all the community is present for this advertised
miracle, including Pilate's household and a very pregnant Ruth, along
with her daughters. The excitement of the event pushes her into labor
that brings our protagonist into the world. Throughout his childhood,
Milkman dreams of flying. And of course, the Sugarman/Solomon
song and legend weave their way through the entire narrative. Flight,

of course, is a powerful imaginative draw in almost any human society, but Morrison's meaning is strongly based in her own cultural experience, as she tells LeClair: "If it means Icarus to some readers, fine. But my meaning was specific: it is about black people who could fly. That was always part of the folklore of my life; flying was one of our gifts." Nor is the flight merely physical. When Pilate dies, Milkman realizes that, "Without ever leaving the ground, she could fly." That flight embodies spirit as well as escape from the dross of earthly existence.

One of the most notable issues of the novel is the question of how African Americans relate to their history. Not for nothing does the tale culminate in 1963. One group of characters, the Seven Days, can be seen as following an extreme version of Malcolm X's "by whatever means necessary" approach, although they come closer to the later Black Panthers in embracing violence. The Days always number seven, are always men, and carry out acts of retribution against the white community. Each man is assigned his own day of the week. If a murder of a black person anywhere in the country takes place on, say, a Tuesday, then the Tuesday man is responsible for killing a white person in as nearly the same circumstances as possible: same gender, age, number, mode of death. Their premise is logical-sounding but statistically naïve. If one is in a ten-to-one minority, tit-for-tat assassination can only lead to destruction of the race one defends. Clearly, there must be a better way of protecting their people. However faulty the rationale, though, it is their rationale, and they follow it religiously. In order to carry out this vigilante justice, they must remain "pure"—no alcohol or drugs, no relationships, no distractions. The results, predictably, are disastrous. Robert Smith's "flight" at the beginning of the story is really a cover for his suicide, which seems to him to be the only way out of the Days. The loneliness and isolation has become too much for him. Similarly, when Porter takes up with Milkman's sister First Corinthians, he has to leave the group, and there is some question about whether it is possible to leave and live. Much of the action of the novel is driven by the members of the Seven Days. When Guitar joins, he tries to recruit Milkman, or at least make him see the wisdom of having joined. Later, convinced that Milkman has cheated him out of the gold that would underwrite the Days' activities (his decision is justified in his mind because the desire for treasure isn't selfish), he begins his assassination efforts against his childhood best friend. The message is pretty clear: violence will eventually turn against itself. Even if the mission of the Seven Days, killing whites in reprisal for the deaths of blacks, did make sense, it is virtually inevitable that it turn against their own people. The bookend events of Robert Smith's self-given death at the beginning and Pilate's murder at the end argue strongly against such strategies.

The alternative isn't, as one might suppose, the nonviolent resistance of Martin Luther King Jr., although loving one's neighbors and one's enemies does come into the matter. Rather, the novel suggests, real empowerment comes not from accepting the terms of historical definition, which the Seven Days' ideal clearly does, terms that have been placed on African Americans by whites, but from gaining genuine self-knowledge, understanding acquired through contact with one's own history and not that imposed from without. Yes, one can argue that *everything* having to do with Africans being in America was imposed by someone other than the Africans in question, yet such a view reduces black Americans to the role of passive victims, which role seems not to interest Morrison very much. Instead, her heroes, like Pilate, like Milkman, take matters into their own hands, fashion identities for themselves aside from those the world seeks to hand them. In discovering his own history, Milkman doesn't so much become a better person as find a better person he can become. At the end of *Beloved*, Paul D tells Sethe that she is her own "best thing," a statement that could end this novel as well. Milkman has needed to become his own best thing, not an appendage of some relative or friend or social construct. In her characterization of him, Morrison has said that he "must learn to be a civilized human being." In the language of the novel, such learning makes possible the miracle of flight: "Without wiping away the tears, taking a deep breath, or even bending his knees—he leaped. As fleet and bright as a lodestar he wheeled toward Guitar and it did not matter which one of them gave up his ghost in the killing arms of his brother. For now he knew what Shalimar knew: If you surrendered to the air, you could *ride* it."

You can ride the air, too, if you're Toni Morrison. But not if you imitate her. She may well turn out to be more like Faulkner than Hemingway: the writer from whom a great many writers learned a great deal but whom no one dares emulate. Everyone writes like Hemingway. No one writes like Faulkner—and gets away with it. Yet like Faulkner, too, she's a diagnostician of the problems of America. She examines her patient as he did, even if the sufferers are quite different from one another. What does it mean to be an American of African descent? How does one relate to one's history when so much of it has been lost, stolen, or twisted out of recognition? What are the limits of civilized behavior? How does one live within one's community? These are big questions, important questions, human questions. While many of them are addressed to a specific community, almost all have universal implications. Ours is a society that has issues with history—the history we lack, that goes back a thousand years or two or three, and the history we have, which does not always comport to our desires for what it, or we, should be. In such a society, we deeply need those writers who hold that history up for us to examine, who suggest how we might begin to accept, own, and understand it. Few are the novelists who can do that for us, which makes them all the more essential to our being.

TWENTY-FIVE

HOME, HOME ON THE RES
Love Medicine

For most of my childhood, what I knew about Indians was this: they were warlike, perfidious, dressed in buckskins and eagle feathers, dependent on the buffalo, limited to monosyllabic speech, and extremely susceptible to falling off their horses whenever John Wayne fired his rifle. And extinct. Okay, there was that one trip up the old, two-lane U.S. 27 in the 1950s when I saw a couple of their modern avatars on the village sidewalks of northern Michigan, where they seemed as exotic to a kid from southwest Ohio as the pine trees that filled the landscape. So there was a hint they might exist. But television and the movies kept telling me otherwise. And what was I to believe, the wonders of modern media or the evidence of my own seven-year-old eyes? That's what I thought, too. Besides, the only actual Native American I knew to live and breathe was Jay Silverheels, trapped by Hollywood into colluding in the myth of his own nonexistence, playing the last of his tribe in a long-past time. I'm with Bill Cosby on this one; I always liked Tonto better. He was my hero; I just didn't think the man who played him was quite real. After all, in my corner of heaven we had reduced the native presence to some school mascots and a scattering of place names from the Great Miami River to Tippecanoe to Chillicothe.

Then I went to a college that had been founded to educate the Indians a couple of hundred years before I got there and which, about the time I arrived, had acquired religion on getting back to its roots. So there were card-carrying tribal members walking around campus, and I got to know about them. And one of those figures, although I did not know her, would grow up to be a writer. A serious writer. A seriously funny writer. It has been my good fortune to grow as a reader at the same time she has grown as a writer, and it was her good fortune to come along at a time when the country was ready for what she had to say.

The 1960s and 1970s were a tremendous time in the field of Native American writing, with such luminaries as N. Scott Momaday, Leslie Marmon Silko, and James Welch leading the way with works that were about—and more importantly by—our most invisible minority. In works like Momaday's *House Made of Dawn* (1968) or *The Way to Rainy Mountain* (1969), Silko's *Ceremony* (1974), or Welch's *Winter in the Blood* (1973) we discovered a world of stories that we didn't know were out there, in an America we barely knew existed. Those books were mixes of inherited tribal tales and contemporary situations with a good dash of mainstream literary technique, about which the writers were both knowledgeable and slightly suspicious. Nor were the stories all the same. For one thing, every indigenous people's master narrative—its history, legend, mythology, religion, relation to the land—was different. For another, so was its tale of encounter with the invading and colonizing dominant culture and of decline from a former state of autonomy. Reading these writers, and those of the subsequent generations, was both exhilarating and disquieting: exhilarating in the way new discoveries always are, especially those of new voices and new approaches to a beloved art form; disquieting both in how watching a different world from the outside feels voyeuristic and in the way that, implicitly or explicitly, these texts remind a member of the dominant culture of the damage that culture has done. Native American writing is the closest thing we have, strictly speaking, to a postcolonial literature. No other writers, whatever claims they may have against "America," are indigenous peoples who have been displaced and yet remain, more or less, in their own space. And yet, again speaking strictly, one cannot be sure that it is at all "post" or merely a later phase of "colonial."

However that bit of literary-psychosocial-geopolitical history may play out, there was a next generation of writers, a veritable explosion of Native American novelists and poets and playwrights beginning in the 1980s. And one of them was a young woman from so far north that she was almost Canadian, a part German-Irish member of the Turtle Mountain Chippewa band (yes, "Chippewa" is a contested term, along with "Ojibway" and "Anishinaabe" and every variant spelling of all three, but I've seen her describe herself as Chippewa, so I'll defer to her on this point). She was only thirty years old when *Love Medicine* appeared in 1984, having been rejected by numerous publishers before it found a home, but despite limited publicity and a first-run printing that suggested a short life, the novel sold like crazy and made Louise Erdrich a rising star in American fiction. Not hyphenated American. American. Very few novelists hit the big time with their first book. Here's how it's done. Write a very good book (whatever constitutes "good" in your chosen field). Make it appeal to readers, so that they proselytize for it with other readers. Get a few good notices. Sell something close to half a million copies almost entirely on the strength of word of mouth. It makes you hard to ignore. Or so it made her. She has gone on to write a host of novels and poetry collections: among them

The Beet Queen (1986), *Tracks* (1988), *The Bingo Palace* (1994), *Tales of Burning Love* (1997). In later years her titles have become more fanciful, with such items as *The Master Butchers' Singing Club* (2003), *The Plague of Doves* (2009), and my favorite, *Last Report on the Miracles at Little No Horse* (2001). Some, although by no means all, of these novels are set on and around a reservation near the Canadian border.

The narrative strategy of *Love Medicine* owes much to Faulkner. My students often suggest a similarity to *As I Lay Dying*, and indeed there is the element of the community or family sharing the responsibility for the creation of the story, although in Erdrich's case those individual narratives, while also first-person, are more self-aware than in the stream of consciousness of Faulkner's short parable. I would argue that this book is more like the one we have already discussed, *Go Down, Moses*. Both are composed of loosely connected short stories in a structure that is sometimes called linked short stories or a short-story composite or a packet novel. I'm willing these days to simply call it a novel, since she does (as did Faulkner). Neither example of the species can be accused of being heavily plotted. But we might do as well to compare it to Eudora Welty's *Losing Battles* or Boccaccio's *Decameron*, both of which have lots of narrators telling lots of stories and loose structures, which pairing comes very close to redundancy.

In the present instance, the story setup runs something like this: a death occurs in an extended family, providing both the framing device for a series of narratives by and about the members of this and another family *and* the spur to a new series of events that culminate in the restoration of at least one set of family connections. In the midst of an Easter blizzard, June Kashpaw freezes to death while drunkenly attempting to walk home across the prairie. She is a member of the clan by birth, as the niece of the family matriarch, Marie, and by an early, failed marriage to Marie's son, Gordie.

A victim of rough circumstances and her own hard living, she has been on a binge when, in an effort to escape from an ill-advised tryst in a pickup truck, she ignores the deep snow: "June walked over it like water and came home." There are enough cultural references and symbolic possibilities in that sentence alone to drive a smallish dissertation. From this incident grow any number of tensions and events. Grief and remorse are present, of course, along with recrimination and exploration of the past and inheritance.

This is the saga of two families whose lives intersect at various points. At the center of these two clans are women, Marie Kashpaw and Lulu Nanapush, each representing a very different way of living in the fallen world of the reservation. Before we get to that, however, we should note the two things they have in common. One is their stature as clan matriarchs. Each represents the stability and strength of families in which certainty can be in short supply. There is no ongoing male presence in Lulu's household. Her children are the products of liaisons with various men—husbands Henry and Beverly Lamartine (who are brothers) and an unidentified Morrissey man— and various lovers, beginning with the magical and frightening Old Man (Moses) Pillager, who is her cousin. While Marie's home does have a continuing male presence, and considerably less intrigue in the matter of paternity, his accomplishments are largely a product of her efforts at controlling and directing him, which efforts are only partially successful. Which brings us to the other thing the two women have in common: Nector Kashpaw. He is Marie's husband of almost fifty years but was courting Lulu before he fell into his relationship with Marie. Not only that, but some twenty years into his marriage he has a lengthy relationship with Lulu that produces a son, Lyman Lamartine, whom he never acknowledges. Indeed, it is not entirely clear that he knows Lyman is his son. We discover in the next novel in the cycle, *Tracks* (1988), that he is also Lulu's uncle, his older brother Eli being her father.

This tangled involvement provides a great deal of the plot interest. Nector manages, for instance, to accidentally burn down Lulu's house while trying to make a break from his marriage and join her. Lulu and Marie have ongoing nasty things to say about one another, although after his death they become a formidable team. But it is the differences that signify in this novel. Marie represents the spirit of accommodation with the white power structure. She is proud that her husband has testified before Congress, proud that he's tribal chairman or more particularly that she has been able to engineer that success. And Nector himself is a product of such accommodation. He is the son who was given over to the government schools, who spent time in Hollywood getting shot off horses, who has played the game by the white man's rules. His brother Eli "stayed wild" in his terms, living on and from the land, always keeping his distance from organized society.

The difference is even more striking between the two clans. The Kashpaws are respected as the traditional tribal leaders, but they led their people to accept government allotments of land, a recognition of United States sovereignty over the tribe. Their leadership has not led the tribe to success or even stability. Lulu is descended from the Pillagers, the family of medicine men and women "who had been the holdouts, the ones who wouldn't sign the treaties, keepers of the birch-bark scroll and practitioners of medicine so dark and helpful that the more devout Catholic Indians crossed their breasts when a Pillager happened to look straight at them." Lulu and her children live on the fringe of the reservation on tribal rather than allotment land. Her oldest son, Gerry, is sentenced to life in federal prison for killing a state trooper in a reservation standoff that recalls the one at Pine Ridge in 1973. Henry

Lamartine Jr. is destroyed by his service in Vietnam. Only Lyman becomes co-opted by the system, opening a factory under instructions of the Bureau of Indian Affairs, but we should remember that Lyman is Nector Kashpaw's son as well as Lulu's. That neither clan has prospered is less an evaluation of the different poles they represent than a diagnosis of the real problem: their weakness and dissolution stems from division, from the internecine battles that tear them down and apart. Unity is strength, but here there is no unity.

The novel operates on a structure highly representative of its time. Indeed, I have often had difficulty getting some students to acknowledge that it is a novel at all. Like *Go Down, Moses*, it is a short-story composite, a series of stories unified by place, family, history, theme. Of all contemporary novelists, Erdrich is perhaps the truest inheritor of the Faulknerian mantle. Even so, her novel is more problematic than Faulkner's, due largely to her profusion of narrators. As with *As I Lay Dying*, many story-chapters are narrated by individual characters—Nector, Marie, Lulu, Lyman, Albertine Johnson, Lipsha Morrissey—but there are also several in which a third-person narrator takes the reins, and that shift, rather than any between characters, seems often to trouble readers' sense of unity. Yet that disunity, as it is sometimes seen, makes a major thematic point, that this community is fractured and at odds with itself; while no overarching view is possible, neither can the inhabitants, individually or collectively, take in the whole scene. If the profusion of voices sometimes comes close to cacophony, we do well to remember that discord is an important concept.

And what a musical discord those disparate voices make! These are some of the funniest and saddest narrators ever created. They can be very warm one moment, wildly caustic the next. Sometimes, as with Nector, there is a dissociation of action in which he cannot quite get his head around his own agency:

> *This is, in fact, how the terrible thing happens.*
>
> *I am so eager to smoke the next cigarette that I do not notice that I have thrown down my half-smoked one still lit on the end. I throw it right into the ball of Lulu's letter. The letter smokes. I do not notice right off what is happening, and then the paper flares.*
>
> *Curious and dazed, I watch the letter burn.*
>
> *I swear that I do nothing to help the fire along.*

Well, I'm sure we all feel better about that. The resulting fire destroys a house, nearly kills his illegitimate son, and burns off all of Lulu's hair. Permanently. Other than that, no problem. He didn't really *do* the thing he just described himself doing. Contrast that to Marie's handling of the note he had written her earlier announcing that he was leaving her:

> *I folded the letter up, exactly as it had been found, and I put it beneath the salt can. I did this for a reason. I would never talk about this letter but instead let him wonder. Sometimes he'd look at me, and I'd smile, and he'd think to himself: salt or sugar? But he would never be sure.*

Nector had, of course, left the letter under the sugar canister, so Marie's moving it is an act of control, something she values as a person who came from a situation she could not control. Her smugness is undercut, however, by her waxing herself into a corner while she thinks about the note. In fact, the narrations reveal the qualities most evident in the characters who utter them. The narrative choices are more than mere exercises in point-of-view: as individual as the persons telling them, they are revelations of character as the driver of plot and theme.

To return to Marie's subversive act, by which she takes control of her marriage, it emphasizes the matriarchal nature of the society of this novel. It is *Marie's* family even if it has Nector's family name. Similarly, the Nanapush-Lamartine clan is *Lulu's* family, that fact being clearer for the absence of a strong adult male in the household. Where this social structure matters most is in the missing family. Early on in the novel, Lipsha gives his unknown father a pass, not feeling too bad about never having been acknowledged by someone who might not even know of his existence (of course, when he is acknowledged at the end of the novel, that's a different matter). But he expresses nothing but contempt for the mother who walked out on him. He wants nothing to do with her, doesn't even wish to know who she is or why she made the choice she did. In a world where mothers are everything, being a child of no mother steals a large portion of one's identity. Again, when he does discover who gave him up and what his life would have been like with her, he can see his being given to Marie as an act of love and even maternal protection. He can also see how much better off he is than King, the son June did acknowledge and fail. Ultimately, Lipsha comes to understand belonging to a parent as more than ownership or proximity. Love can come in many forms.

That notion of belonging assumes major proportions in the novel. What does it mean to belong to a parent, to a family, to a tribe, to a nation? What are the consequences of exclusion and of inclusion? The costs of not knowing are high: throughout the novel we follow a trail of unhappiness and despair, of madness and mayhem, of self-destructive acts and self-given deaths, and sometimes of incredible generosity. The damage that June, the lost child, and confused, tormented Gordie visit upon themselves, each other, and the child they create is inestimable. So too the damage to Lipsha, June's child with Gerry. The thread of connection is broken, owing partly to failures of the parental generation, who seem never quite to know their place in the world. That confusion passes along as outright loss to the younger generation.

But there is also another broken connection that informs all the action of the novel—the connection to the tribal past. Over and over again, some character makes a statement to the effect that "the old people knew how to do that, but no more." In this regard, Lipsha's "substitution" of frozen turkey hearts for wild goose hearts is diagnostic. Even though he knows the proper love medicine, he tries a shortcut to get results, ostensibly because of a modern need for quicker, easier results. With each passing generation a little more knowledge is lost, so that the youngest—King Kashpaw, Lipsha, Albertine Johnson, even Lyman Lamartine, although he's technically one step earlier on family trees—are almost wholly unaware of much wisdom and ritual. The generation just offscreen, the parents of Nector, Marie, and Lulu, were still tightly connected to the old ways; Fleur Pillager and the original Nanapushes, Kashpaw and Rushes Bear, still possess the old knowledge. Fleur, in fact, possessed powerful medicine, as we know from later books in the cycle. The distinction is drawn in the novel's first tier by the division of fates of Nector and his brother Eli. Eli, the one who "stayed wild," may be a bit bewildered, but he seems genuinely content, whereas Nector can never quite find the fulfillment of all his early promise and consequently feels permanently lost, unsure of identity. The rupture with tradition, Erdrich suggests, has devastating and ongoing impact in native cultures.

Like the poetry of Langston Hughes, this novel and the ones that follow it form an ongoing dialogue with the dominant literary narrative. Indeed, one hallmark of Native American writing has been the engagement with that dominant tradition and the formation of a counternarrative. Many novelists and poets of the movement—writers as various in other ways as Leslie Marmon Silko, James Welch, N. Scott

Momaday, Michael Dorris, and Gerald Vizenor—if movement it can be called, attended major academic institutions and studied the Anglo-American canon before creating their own. Silko's exchange of letters with poet James Wright forms one of the great correspondences in American literature. Inevitably, then, that writing will form a continuing conversation with preceding American literature. Earlier writing, whether white or black, had interests separate from this great flowering of Native American novelists and poets. Small wonder, then, that we often get glimpses, distorted though they be, of writers we already know. In Erdrich's case, one of the major voices in her personal dialogue is, as we saw earlier, Faulkner. It goes beyond influence, however. Her novel expands the range of the possible in American fiction. We had never seen anything quite like it before *Love Medicine*. Before Silko's *Ceremony* (1977), Momaday's *House Made of Dawn* (1968), Welch's *Winter in the Blood* (1974), and certainly before Vizenor's *Bearheart: The Heirship Chronicles* (1978/1990), for which nothing this side of Kafka can quite prepare us. Yet that newness seems to be just what the doctor ordered. These writers were embraced by readers and reviewers almost instantly in many cases, demonstrating the need for continual renewal of the American canon. And Erdrich has been front and center in that renewal, telling us things we didn't know about people we may not have known existed, and about ourselves, our society large and small, and our communities in the process. We must have been waiting for her and her coevals to come along. And not even known it.

CONCLUSION

FIFTEEN MORE AND THE G.A.N.

I have insisted from the start that this is not a list of *the* twenty-five books that will tell you the whole story. Decency commands that I offer a few of the overlooked items. Feel free to add or substitute a thousand others:

- Hector St. John de Crèvecoeur, *Letters from an American Farmer* (1782). I only sort of violate my precept about Americanness here. Yes, he was French. Many of our best observers and biggest fans have been. Yes, he was born and he died somewhere else. But he came, he stayed for a while, he actually did have a connection to the land and made wonderful observations about the country and its people. He observed how quick we were to take things to court (his favorite word in connection with us is "litigious")—in 1782! Another early addition, his celebration of the ideal America and the corrupted version we were creating. There it is, the whole discussion, right at the beginning.

- Harriet Beecher Stowe, *Uncle Tom's Cabin* (1852). The long novel by "the little lady who started this big war," as President Lincoln said. Talk about writing with a message! Very earnest tearjerker, even if it doesn't travel well. Books have been written on the change of meaning from Uncle Tom to "Uncle Tom" over the course of its first century or so.

- Henry James, "Daisy Miller" (1878). All right, all right, it's not a book. But it's the clearest distillation of all those big novels—*The Ambassadors, The Americans, The Wings of the Dove*— where clashes between Old World and New lead to misunderstanding and a bad end for some near-innocent. He's also one of the very few novelists who focus on the privileged classes.

- William Dean Howells, *The Rise of Silas Lapham* (1885). He has another novel called *A Hazard of New Fortunes*, which could be the title of most of his work. Lapham is a self-made man whose clumsiness in social situations leads to his fall, so he has to go back to the bottom and start again. You figured the title was ironic, right?

- Stephen Crane, *The Red Badge of Courage* (1895). Crane is a great observer of the American scene, even if he was born too late to observe the Civil War about which he writes so convincingly. Although it isn't a book per se, "Maggie: A Girl of the Streets," about a daughter of immigrants whose poverty pushes her downward toward eventual prostitution and early death, deserves our attention.

- L. Frank Baum, *The Wonderful Wizard of Oz* (1900). Here's something not every quest tale has: a yellow-brick road. Yes, there is a book. It was wildly popular, which is why there is the film, plays, and more than a dozen sequels, many by Baum himself. It is more charming and innocent than the 1939

Technicolor marvel, and it has even more wonderful creatures than Dorothy's comrades, the witches from four compass points, and the flying monkeys. Clever, inventive, funny, touching—everything children, or adults for that matter, might want in a novel.

- Sherwood Anderson, *Winesburg, Ohio* (1919). At the other end of the social spectrum, small-town life in an American burg, filled with grotesques, dreamers, and failures. I think I grew up there. I think most of us did. It's also an innovative marvel, a series of linked short stories that add up to something like a novel. They're like popcorn: you read one and are inevitably drawn to the next. You can also read them out of order with little loss to the sense of the whole. They are related more by proximity and locale than by sequence.

- Edith Wharton, *The Age of Innocence*. (1920). Privileged classes? Here's the other writer who covers them. Tempering her criticisms in *The House of Mirth*, this one again focuses on the upper class in New York City, the clash of social convention and personal freedom, and the virtual impossibility of happiness in a world where a mere look can lead to scandal. She is the great chronicler of that milieu.

- Sinclair Lewis, *Babbitt* (1922). Hard to argue with a book that gives us an eponymous noun, Babbittry. It is a comic novel about a hustler—it pretty much invented the stereotype of the real estate salesman as a bad actor—and social climber and self-promoter who comes to question his core values. Or the absence thereof.

- Anita Loos, *Gentlemen Prefer Blondes* (1925). You think I'm kidding, don't you? It's a better expression of Jazz Age proclivities than any novel I can think of; and yes, I can think of

Fitzgerald. It gave rise to a sequel, a Marilyn Monroe film, and every girls-gone-wild tale from *Valley of the Dolls* to *Sex and the City* and even crossed the Pond to offer license for *Bridget Jones's Diary*.

- Hart Crane, *The Bridge* (1930). A technological marvel! An aesthetic miracle! A symbol ready at hand! "Choiring strings!" Twinkling lights! A source of ecstasy and inspiration! And that's just the poem. Crane turns the Brooklyn Bridge and the river it spans into symbols for the whole of American history and geography, each of them dividing something but connecting something else. The East River becomes the Hudson and then the Ohio and then the Mississippi, the Bridge every lesser bridge, ford, ferry, and crossing. Some overwrought moments but a great poem nonetheless.

- Richard Wright, *Native Son* (1940). The classic novel about racial misunderstanding and the violence embedded in the history of race in the United States. Tremendously powerful, sad, poetic, the African American *Crime and Punishment*.

- J. D. Salinger, *The Catcher in the Rye* (1951). Can you say disaffected youth? The favorite of teenagers and their English teachers alike has much to say about the state of postwar America, the breakdown of families, breakdowns, cigarettes, envy, alienation, and self-medicating. It has a lot going on besides being a favorite of book-banners.

- William Carlos Williams, *Paterson* (1957). The personification of place. Paterson, New Jersey, is a city, a history, a mythic being, and a way of understanding the country. In modernism, the local is the key to the universal, and Williams's epic poem in five books takes that thinking about as far as it will go in free verse, news clippings, letters, overheard conversations, and other found materials. So ambitious it is bound to fail on some levels, *Paterson* is nevertheless one of the great achievements of American writing. His descriptions of the Passaic River and its falls alone are worth the price of admission.

• Sandra Cisneros, *The House on Mango Street* (1984). It's a novel. A book of short stories. A collection of prose poems. Cisneros has written a genre-shifting little gem that is very hard to categorize but that goes to the essence of being Hispanic and female and poor in an American city. Sometimes shocking to staid readers and a real eye-opener for much of mainstream society.

And before someone asks, let me tell you right now where I stand on the Great American Novel. I mentioned this in discussing Fitzgerald, but it warrants a fuller examination by way of wrapping things up. You'll notice I didn't pick a candidate or two for the distinction. I have my reasons.

• I don't know what it means. Seriously. This is not a question the French ask. Or the English. I suppose people who talk about it are thinking of the Russian or Spanish model and that *War and Peace* and *Don Quixote* are so patently the national novels of their respective countries that everyone needs one. I'm not sure that's true, and the belief in the precept probably does more harm than good. Is this what drove Thomas Wolfe to such extremes of length and complexity? Or caused Faulkner to try to get the whole world between "one Cap and one period"? Or created Pynchon's magna-novels? Must the G.A.N. be a doorstop?

- We wouldn't know it if it came. Are you sure you haven't already read it? Or walked by it in the bookstore? Or maybe not read it because it hasn't been published. Editors have blind spots too, you know.

- That's just like us to want an easy answer, a one-book-and-pass-the-quiz-and-you-know-all-about-America novel. Ain't gonna happen. We're too big, too various, too obstreperous, too litigious, to use Crèvecoeur's word. We would never agree that the great one was the Great One. This isn't hockey, you know, where statistics tell us who the Great One was, is, and ever shall be.

- You've been reading it all your life. It's not a book, brothers and sisters; it's a process. One novel talks to another, which talks to another, which talks back to the first two and forward to the next, and so one, one generation of narrative succeeding another till the end of time. The effects of literature, and the effects of reading, are cumulative. There is no end in this dialogic process; it's a conversation with no end and, really, with no winner. Literature isn't like science, where what came before is supplanted by a superior understanding embodied in what comes later. What seems like progress where writing is concerned is usually simply a matter of newer work conforming more to our own tastes and our own habits of language and thought. Is *Beloved* really better than *Moby-Dick*? Different, certainly, but not better or worse. At least, not better or worse because more "modern," whatever that may mean. An era, moreover, is not a school of thought. If it were, then how could the panoramic extravaganzas of Pynchon or Don DeLillo coexist with the tight-lipped minimalism of Raymond Carver or Ann Beattie? No, we're not moving closer and closer to—or ever further from—the great book that captures everything about us. We are moving toward an ever fuller picture, but that's accretion, not progress.

- Or maybe it is a book (see above). Are you sure the Great American Novel isn't a slim volume about false dreams and disillusionment during Prohibition? Or a book about a terrible murder of a child by her own mother, as in Morrison's *Beloved*? Or something like *Absalom, Absalom!* that we would all recognize for its brilliance if only we were smart enough to catch up with it? Or a novel that talks back to an earlier great novel, as Jon Clinch's *Finn* does to Mark Twain's more famous Finn book? Or maybe it's a new book by an Irish immigrant, a story of a single day in a single city where lives are tied together by the shared experience of a man walking a tightrope high above the streets, as in Colum McCann's *Let the Great World Spin*. Or by an Indian immigrant writing about the immigrant experience, as in Jhumpa Lahiri's *The Namesake*. Or . . . you get the idea. The great American novel (and only one word gets capitalized) is all around you all the time. Also plenty of not-so-great ones, but that's okay. Even if ninety or ninety-five or even ninety-nine percent of everything is dross, that still leaves a great deal that might be gold.

Find that gold. Go mine it, pan for it, seek it out. Embrace what you find. Listen to what it tells you. Learn its lessons. Set your own standard for excellence and greatness. Don't take someone else's word for it. Not even mine. Me? I'll leave you to it. I've got a book to read.

BOOKS BY **THOMAS C. FOSTER**

TWENTY-FIVE BOOKS THAT SHAPED AMERICA
How White Whales, Green Lights, and Restless Spirits Forged Our National Identity
ISBN 978-0-06-183440-0 (paperback)

In his latest book, Thomas C. Foster applies his combination of know-how, inimitable wit, and analysis to look at the great masterworks of American literature and how each of them has shaped our very existence as readers, students, teachers, and Americans.

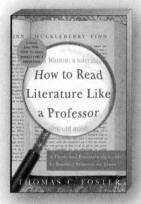

HOW TO READ LITERATURE LIKE A PROFESSOR
A Lively and Entertaining Guide to Reading Between the Lines
ISBN 978-0-06-000942-7 (paperback)

"A smart, accessible, and thoroughly satisfying examination of what it means to read a work of literature. Guess what? It isn't all that hard, not when you have a knowledgeable guide to show the way. Dante had his Virgil; for everyone else, there is Thomas Foster."
—Nicholas A. Basbanes, author of *A Gentle Madness*

HOW TO READ NOVELS LIKE A PROFESSOR
A Jaunty Exploration of the World's Favorite Literary Form

ISBN 978-0-06-134040-6 (paperback)

Out of all literary forms, the novel is arguably the most discussed—and the most fretted over. In *How to Read Novels Like a Professor*, Thomas C. Foster leads readers through the special "literary language" of the novel, helping them get more—more insight, more understanding, more pleasure—from their reading.

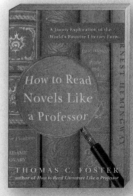